Vision Changing Charity

Vision Changing Charity

RNIB in Socio-Political Context, 1970-2010

Ian Bruce

The Lutterworth Press

THE LUTTERWORTH PRESS

P.O. Box 60
Cambridge
CB1 2NT
United Kingdom

www.lutterworth.com
publishing@lutterworth.com

Paperback ISBN: 978 0 7188 9604 9
PDF ISBN: 978 0 7188 9642 3
ePub ISBN: 978 0 7188 9641 6
Audio Book ISBN: 978 0 7188 97239

A Braille version of this book is available from RNIB

British Library Cataloguing in Publication Data
A record is available from the British Library

First published by The Lutterworth Press, 2023

To my family, particularly Tina who supported and inspired me; to all those blind and partially sighted people who included me; to staff colleagues and trustees, especially my RNIB chairs, who guided me sensitively.

Contents

Part II. Forty-year Trends in the Charity in Socio-Political Context

Contents

List of Illustrations

Unless otherwise stated, all images are reproduced by permission of RNIB

Foreword

As the current RNIB chief executive officer (CEO) with a history degree under my belt from 30 years ago, I was delighted when I learned that Ian Bruce was completing a history of RNIB from 1970 to 2010. We can learn a lot from the past and, if there ever was a time we needed to, it is now. The world is changing fast with real challenges within societal and economic shifts. Climate change needs to be addressed, technology informs our lives, culture wars abound and there are very recent geopolitical challenges to the established liberal world order. Understanding where we have come from is always useful to work out where we should go, and how we should navigate the challenges and opportunities that result from change.

As Ian Bruce draws out, charities have a significant role to play in combatting this turmoil. Their rights and responsibilities have grown dramatically over the end of the twentieth and the start of the twenty-first centuries. Charities, of which RNIB is one, are organisations which are used to working against the odds and winning, eventually. RNIB is a charity which has been tenacious since 1868 in fighting for the rights of blind and partially sighted people and developing and delivering much needed services. As this book makes clear, we have an enviable track record, maintained to this day, to deliver focussed services, based on the needs and wishes of our beneficiaries.

This history describes the evolving organisational techniques we have used to achieve this through applying socio-educational professionalisms combined with organisational methods such as strategic planning, marketing and HR policies. Mostly, we have been successful and sometimes we have failed but always we have learned.

Indeed, RNIB will learn from this history and I believe others can too as we are in many ways a typical large British charity which Ian Bruce has placed in an evolving socio-political setting. Those 'others' to my mind include other charities, students of politics and sociology, people who work for charities and non-profit organisations who want to learn from our successes and mistakes, especially students on charity management courses and, of course, historians of the voluntary sector.

As a major charity RNIB has involved and employed many thousands of staff and volunteers over this history, making it a team effort. I commend Ian for naming so many of them, inevitably a tiny fraction, but showing the co-operative nature of our enterprise.

Matt Stringer,
RNIB Chief Executive

Introduction

To begin with a practical message, those readers who are primarily interested in the history of the Royal National Institute of Blind People (RNIB) and visual impairment might want to start with Part I. Those who are more interested in broader charity history, social welfare policy, charity management and organisation might like to start with Part II.

RNIB is one of Britain's largest charities. It was founded in 1868 in an inspirational way that would still be impressive today. Dr Thomas Rhodes Armitage was a surgeon who went blind. With four blind friends he founded the British and Foreign Society for Improving Embossed Literature for the Blind with the primary objects of the education and employment of blind people and the provision of embossed literature which included braille.

The society's foundation was inspirational in several ways: blind people came together to help each other and others in the same situation – an example of mutual aid; instead of using sighted experts, they conducted their own research to find the best methods and tools to help blind people to be independent; the organisation was led by a blind person, Armitage, and for the first nineteen years of its existence all board members had to be blind; and the Board tried to be as objective as possible in its conclusions and actions. Take the example of embossed writing. In the nineteenth century there were over a dozen different forms of embossed writing for blind people. The group tried them all out and chose, not one of the several English systems, but the one of a Frenchman,

Louis Braille. It was Armitage and his blind colleagues who guaranteed the dominance of braille across the world.

This exciting start and the activities which followed were recorded in the history of RNIB by Mary Thomas who covered the first 88 years to 1956 (Thomas 1957). June Rose in her history included the period up to the late 1960s (Rose 1970). My contribution starts there and ends in 2010.

I hope you will not judge this history on terminology. Our use of language changes regularly, especially terms associated with groups discriminated against, in general, and disability, in particular. Over this 40-year period (1970-2010) we have had 'the blind' (e.g. as in the National Federation of the Blind of the UK); we have had 'visually handicapped', 'visually impaired', 'sight loss' and so on. There are supporters even now for each of these terms. I have used the full panoply, often choosing a particular term according to preference of the decade. Personally, I have always preferred 'blind and partially sighted people', except it takes so long to type!

I should declare an interest – I was chief executive of RNIB for 20 of these 40 years from late 1983 to the end of 2003. I am not an historian. However, even historians come with points of view, while seeking to balance the dual contributions of evidence and interpretation. Clearly, I am favourably disposed towards RNIB and cannot claim to be neutral but, as an academic, I have tried to be as objective as possible in presenting evidence. The advantage I have is that, having been actively involved as chief executive or vice president for approaching 30 of the 40 years, I have much more inside knowledge than an external historian could collect, both about RNIB and the voluntary and community sector of which it is a part. The role of what I see as 'activist observation' needs more attention in the fields of history and memory studies, especially where participant memories are triangulated with records and interviews as I have done (Keightley and Pickering, 2013; Fivush, 2013; Brown and Reavey, 2013). For this study I am grateful to RNIB for unfettered access to records and the official archive, to the dozen RNIB staff and trustees who have read and commented on drafts and to the hundred or more people to whom I have spoken to check facts, recollections and interpretations.

To make fuller sense, a history of RNIB has to be set in the context of the changing role of charities and disabled people in society. Here are my observations (Bruce 2018) on the changes which have taken place in and to charities in general over the 40 years, 1970 to 2010, into which the history of RNIB nestles (I draw on other views, facts and figures later):

- The growth of the sector – both money and people – has enabled a major scaling up of sector roles such as service delivery, policy promotion, innovation and co-ordination.
- Changing support/popularity of causes: environment and arts – up; disabled and old people – down; children, animals and social welfare – unchanged.
- Skills developed: in finance, human resources (HR), marketing, market research, fundraising (F/R), governance, communications (especially social media) and strategy.
- Policy developments embraced: lobbying, campaigning, public education, use by government of our (and the commercial) sector to test controversial initiatives or ideas, charities' statements of recommended practice, diversity, governance and social media.
- Policy changes forced on us: marketisation, commissioning, statutory transfers (of services and assets), the entry of more and more powerful commercial providers into our markets (e.g. Serco, Capita).
- Policy implementations regarded with ambivalence: mainstreaming versus specialisation, mergers, beneficiary rights, European Union (EU) impact, co-operation with professional associations and employment law.

For those interested in an overview of how RNIB responded over 40 years to these various impacts, Part II might be a good place to start reading.

In Part I, recognising the inspirational first two nineteenth-century decades of RNIB's history when blind people ran the charity, what better subject to start with in this book than the heady time between the late 1960s and the first half of the 1970s. This was when representative blind people effectively wrested control of RNIB back to themselves. This start-time also resonates with the finishing decade of this history when in 2001/02 RNIB changed from being an organisation 'for' the blind into one 'of' the blind by becoming a membership organisation with a legal requirement for the majority of its trustees to be blind or partially sighted.

I should like to thank all those who have commented on early drafts including Lesley-Anne Alexander, Tony Aston, Carol Bird, Fazilet Hadi, Stephen King, Lord Colin Low, David Mann, Bill Poole, Jeff Shear, John Wall, Duncan Watson, John Wall and, above all, Professor Fred Reid who as an academic historian helped me greatly with his advice and comments. I am grateful for the active support of the current chief executive of RNIB, Matt Stringer, Sophie Castell, Amelia Billington, Jessica Eaton, Alison Long, David Wilson and especially Jane Backlog, internal project leader, as well as Richard Orme, a valued former colleague from RNIB; and those who have guided me through the publication process: Adrian Brink, Samuel Fitzgerald and Ana Alemida at The Lutterworth Press, and Dorothy Luckurst for her copy-editing. As is normal any mistakes are down to me as author.

To the extent that RNIB has been successful, this has been achieved by thousands of people over the 40 years. I have tried to mention some but clearly most are omitted. If you are one such, or feel under-recognised and are prepared to share experiences, please do contact me.

Lastly, I want to acknowledge my three chairs: Sir Duncan Watson, Sir John Wall and Lord Colin Low who all gave me such great encouragement and support, so vital if a chief executive is to stand a chance of being successful. Our relationship endured long after I stepped down from my role of director general – I dare to call them my friends.

Ian Bruce, April 2022

Ian Bruce CBE
Vice President
RNIB Headquarters

email i.bruce1@btinternet.com or via RNIB

Part I

Four Decades of Change

Chapter 1a

1970-80: How Blind People Took Back Control of RNIB

In the late 1960s an extraordinary and radical notion was growing on the periphery of RNIB which would result in the transfer of governance from the hands of the sighted to blind people. To start at the end: in 1975 the Executive Council (EC), the body legally responsible for governing RNIB, transformed its composition to contain 30 blind representatives of organisations of blind people in addition to 14 individual blind council members out of a total of 111 sitting members. By the time I arrived in 1983 it was a whipped group of 30 voting as a block, with the regular support of many of the individual blind council members. It effectively controlled the trustee council on the majority of issues. It even met the evening before council to decide the line to be taken on major issues, which usually carried the day.

Viewed many years later this transformation may not look radical, but at the time it was for two main reasons, one external and one internal. First, none of the other major disability service charities, such as Royal National Institute for the Deaf, Scope (then the Spastics Society), Mencap, Leonard Cheshire and Guide Dogs for the Blind Association (GDBA) were near to giving the controlling influence in governance to their beneficiaries, and certainly not to formal

representatives of their beneficiaries. Their related beneficiary membership organisations (organisations 'of' where the
majority of trustees are relatedly disabled) were kept at a safe
distance. As late as 2011, some in the above charities still did
not have governance in the hands of formal representatives
of their beneficiaries.

The internal reason that this was a radical change for RNIB
was the conservative character of RNIB – not for RNIB the
radical campaigning advertising of the then Spastics Society.

How did this progressive change come about, against the
external norm and in such an internal conservative setting?
Researching this part of RNIB's history involved discussion
with over 30 people who were active at the time, both staff
and trustees, blind and sighted, conservative and radical; and
reading the minutes of all the Executive Council, committee
and formal one-off meetings. The story, as is often the case,
is about able and committed people being in the right place
at the right time. How they became so able, and who put or
allowed them into the right place, is also significant, as is
RNIB's historical tradition of democratic and accountable
governance.

What Happened?

On the outside, demanding greater power and authority in
RNIB were the organisations 'of' blind people, predominantly
the United Kingdom National Federation of the Blind (NFB
or the Federation) and the National League of the Blind and
Disabled (NLBD or the League). Also included were around
20 or so other special interest groups of blind people such as
the Braille Chess Association, the Association of Blind Piano
Tuners (APBT), Circle of Guide Dog Owners (COGDO) and,
in particular, the newly formed Association of Blind and Partially Sighted Teachers and Students (ABAPSTAS) whose
leaders were particularly active. The late 1960s and early
1970s was a period of renaissance and birth of organisations of blind people creating a vibrant, confident atmosphere

despite some tension between the League and the Federation. In terms of leadership, key players included: from the NFB, Martin Milligan (formerly of the NLBD), Fred Reid, Colin Low, Stan Lovell and Barbara Bussey; and from the NLBD, Tom Parker and Dan West. All these people were blind.

On the inside of the Royal National Institute 'for' the Blind, while decisions were ultimately taken by the full Executive Council of over 100 people, the lead was always given by what was in effect the executive committee called the Policy and Selection Committee. The key players included: John Colligan (sighted) who was director general until 1972 and Eric Boulter who succeeded him as the first blind director general; Lord Head (sighted), chairman until 1975; Duncan Watson, vice chairman until 1975 (blind), and then chairman; the three chairs of the standing committees (two sighted) which included another future chair, John Wall (blind); and in the background the deputy director general, Eddie Venn (sighted).

Timeline of Events

1969

Resolution No 16 passed at the 1969 Annual Delegate Conference of the National Federation of the Blind of the UK demanded that 50 per cent of the representatives on the governing boards of all charities whose 'sole purpose is to serve blind people' were to be blind 'representatives elected by, and answerable to, blind people'.

Contrast that call for 50 per cent with the eight per cent at the time and one can begin to understand, first, how far apart the two sides were, second, how radical, verging on foolhardy, the demand was and, third, how unreasonable, verging on outrageous, the demand must have seemed to the RNIB establishment. Add in the supremely confident air of RNIB, one of the top charities in the country in terms of size and popular affection, and I doubt that the RNIB Goliath even recognised it was looking at David, in the form of the organisations of blind people. They were puny in comparison, with only the League having, for example, any paid staff.

1971

The NFB's campaign and the rising interest from organisations of the blind wishing to become members of RNIB's Executive Council was such that the powerful RNIB Policy and Selection Committee at its 1 April 1971 meeting agreed to set up a sub-committee: 'to consider the applications for vacancies in Group D [organisations 'of' the blind] and to look into the question of participation of the blind generally with regard to the rules laid down in the Royal Charter; and to submit a report at the next meeting'.

While the NFB was a tightly directed and focussed group of players pressing the demands of Resolution No. 16 from its national conference, there was a much wider troupe playing than just NFB and the NLBD. At the beginning of 1971 ABAP-STAS (teachers) and COGDO (Guide Dog owners) were both pressing formally for membership of RNIB's Executive Council and this also helped to force the pace.

Critical to decision making in RNIB was, and is, the committee system. Discussions and decisions are formally recorded, signed off by the relevant chairs (then appositely called chairmen) and subsequently agreed as an accurate record by the full committee as minutes of the meeting, providing detailed records of the period in question. The following texts within quotation marks are taken straight from these formal records unless otherwise stated.

So, by April 1971, progress was being made and RNIB Goliath probably thought it was putting out substantial peace offerings to David, namely, the sub-committee set up on 1 April and the agreement to fill four dormant places reserved for representatives on Executive Council. This raised the formal numbers from eight to twelve. However, this was the moment when the first of David's sling shots hit home.

RNIB has traditionally been nervous of adverse national publicity (as opposed to professional and technical criticism). The next phase of the campaign was launched in

May 1971 with an NFB pamphlet entitled *An Equal Say in Our Own Affairs* (1971). This argued for blind representation on mainstream, as well as specialist, organisations impacting on blind people's lives, including local government and organisations for the blind, of which the RNIB was the largest and the primary focus. This short, 2,000-word document was covered in the then pre-Murdoch bastion of the Establishment, *The Times*, on the Saturday of the 1971 Annual Delegate Conference in May, triggered by a press release. The next day, it was covered by the *News of the World* and the *Observer.* What is more, the *Observer* article praising the pamphlet's demands was written by none other than Des Wilson, arch campaigner, founding director of Shelter and soon to lead a successful crusade against all the odds to get lead taken out of petrol.

RNIB must have been reeling with shock. Everyone went home on Friday night and by Monday the attack by the blind people's lobby was national news – the campaign was now on a publicity roll. *The World at One*, one of the most influential national BBC radio programmes, picked it up, interviewing John Colligan, then director general, and Colin Low from the Federation as equals. If RNIB ever thought they could ignore the issue, it was now impossible. Nevertheless, Colin Low reports (in a personal communication) that the interviewer briefed them beforehand in terms which asked for a 'responsible discussion' because 'there is a lot of money at stake' – meaning potential loss of donations to the RNIB caused by adverse publicity. It is unlikely that the rugged approach of the producer of *The World at One* would have naturally thought about that. It is more likely that this concern was fed to the producer from RNIB. This suggests the level of its concern, and the need to try to spike the Federation's guns as an increasingly dangerous opponent.

However, RNIB must have withstood this national attack and regained its confidence because when the sub-committee reviewing formal representation met a month later on 24 June 1971 it concluded that: 'they [RNIB] had done everything in their power in respect of ensuring a major participation of the blind in the two groups [D and E] over which RNIB could exercise any control' (taken from the minutes of the meeting).

By way of background, the RNIB Executive Council (the then trustee body) contained five blocks of membership:

- local societies for the blind – Group A
- local authorities (which served visually impaired [VI] people) – Group B
- other national organisations for the blind (with the exception of the Guide Dogs for the Blind Association who were initially not interested and later declined an invitation to join) – Group C
- organisations of the blind – Group D (this was the group which the campaign wished to expand to make it 50 per cent of the trustee total and take the number from eight to 55 out of 110)
- individuals with a particular contribution, one third of whom had to be blind – Group E.

So, what had RNIB done which was 'everything in their power'? First, it filled four dormant vacant seats in Group D from eight up to the Royal Charter limit of twelve by accepting the applications of ABPT (piano tuners), ABAPSTAS (teachers and students), COGDO (guide dog owners) and the British Computer Association of the Blind (BCAB); second, it rejected a request from NFB for two more places on the grounds that it was inequitable for the Federation to have more places than the larger National League of the Blind and Disabled; third, it appointed a blind person to fill one of the three vacancies in Group E; fourth, it decided not to increase the proportion of seats in Group E allocated to blind people; and, fifth, it set up a further sub-committee to look at 'what improvements could be made in public relations with the blind' (in the discussion of the latter it is recorded that 'the Institute's publicity department was continually feeding information to the press but very little appeared in print' – much in contrast to the NFB's successes).

1972

So far, the evidence suggests that the Federation was acting largely alone or even in some tension with the League and perhaps other organisations of blind people. For example, it is unlikely that the NFB's request in the first half of 1971 for two extra seats on Group D would have gone down well with the NLBD because, if granted, it would have given the smaller Federation double the seats of the larger League. However, at his report to the NFB Executive Council in January 1972, Colin Low, on behalf of the Federation's Participation Campaign Committee (PCC), proposed that it 'should take some initiative "in bringing the organisations 'of' on RNIB Executive Council together", in advance of meetings, to "co-ordinate strategy and tactics on a number of issues of common interest"' (*Viewpoint* [March/May 1972], p. 20). Given the relative lack of success to date in achieving its goal of 50 per cent blind representation, this would be a logical tactical adjustment for the NFB, that is, to change from a solo campaign to a coalition one with its concomitant advantages and disadvantages (Bruce 2011, p. 160).

The second proposal presented by Low on behalf of the PCC was for the demand to RNIB to be modified by asking for an increase in the total number of RNIB EC members from 110 to 120 to allow an increase in the number of Group D places, without such a harsh reduction in the numbers in other categories. Once again, this is a logical tactical move to reduce opposition from other council interest groups.

The formal request for council expansion was submitted and considered specifically by the RNIB Policy and Selection Committee on 6 July 1972 but it decided to defer consideration of this suggestion until local government reorganisation had a clearer impact on the composition of Group B (representatives from local government) – clarity being anticipated in early 1973.

Any thought that the major differences on participation meant a total stand-off between RNIB and organisations of blind people or even between NFB and RNIB would be wrong. For example, on 28 October 1973 Barbara Bussey reported to the NFB Executive Council 'that she and Mr Lovell had been making progress on Federation Resolutions not only with Mr Boulter [RNIB's blind, new director general, who succeeded John Colligan] but also with other officials and committees'. This is partial evidence of a fairly widely held view among people I spoke to and who were there at the time that Eric Boulter's arrival coincided with a thawing of some of the more icy relations, and a start of a more sympathetic hearing of the concerns and suggestions of the organisations of blind people.

Evidence of increasing co-operation between NFB and NLBD on the campaign shows in the Federation's Executive Council report of 27 January 1973 in the March/May 1973 *Viewpoint* in which it was reported that the NFB president, Ken Whitton, had agreed with Tom Parker, the NLBD's general secretary, that NFB would support the League's proposal for a Consumers Committee in RNIB. Stan Lovell also reported that NFB representatives felt 'they had made an impact' at the December 1972 meeting of RNIB EC and, in light of this, they agreed that: 'the Federation should not push for more co-opted places on institute's council and committees so long as other organisations did not do so'.

Eric Boulter (L), Director General RNIB, and Duncan Watson, Vice Chairman, during the last 3 years of talks, 1972-5.

1973

Meanwhile, there were other attempts at dialogue and bridge building with RNIB such that, on 5 April 1973, Duncan Watson was able to report to RNIB's Policy and Selection Committee on:

a very useful discussion with three members of the group [i.e. Group D, blind representatives], who had been elected to present verbal evidence on behalf of Group D …

the possible creation of a new committee composed of blind users of RNIB equipment and services [the NLBD demand] … .

The Policy and Selection Committee supported this progress and 'hoped that all necessary action for amendment of the byelaws … would be completed by spring 1974'.

This shows an important shift in RNIB's position since summer 1971. There was now an assumption that the byelaws would have to be amended to allow the numbers in the groups to be changed; and thus a more substantial increase in Group D would be feasible. The other detail hidden in this minute is that Martin Milligan, as one of the 'three members of the group' (the other two being Stan Lovell, also from NFB, and Tom Parker from NLBD) had been drawn into the direct negotiations for the first time. Martin Milligan was one of the main drivers of NFB's Resolution No 16 in 1969, along with Fred Reid and Colin Low. He was chair of the Federation's Participation Campaign Committee and a force to be reckoned with.

Another sign in 1973 of the bridge building was the decision to circulate the minutes of the top RNIB committee, Policy and Selection, to all 100 plus members of RNIB Council (reported by the NFB representative, Barbara Bussey in *Viewpoint* [September/November 1973]). As the organisations of blind people (Group D) had no representation at that stage on this top committee, this access to the minutes gave them the detail of the committee's deliberations which the traditional oral report to Council would not have done. It may also have had the effect of muting RNIB opposition on the committee to the participation campaign because views expressed might well be minuted and thus become public – whereas before they would have remained private.

In the latter half of 1973 a more public debate on participation was triggered by an article in the September issue of

New Beacon (the *Journal of Blind Welfare*, published by RNIB and edited by Donald Bell and Ann Lee, assistant editor, later editor). The journal published a paper given by Jane Finnis (*New Beacon* 57, no. 678 [October 1973], pp. 254-58) at a conference organised jointly by the Library Association and the National Association for the Education of the Partially Sighted on 5 June. In it Finnis covered a wide variety of topics but one remark was to set off a vigorous debate through the correspondence columns of the journal during late 1973 and 1974.

She said, referring to sighted people who 'work with and for the blind and partially sighted', that their attitude was one of: 'Let the visually handicapped get good jobs, they say, and integrate into society and be independent – just as long as they don't want to run the show. We the sighted, who know best, will run it, and make the decisions for them.'

She continued: 'We have a right and a duty to make decisions for ourselves, in those matters which concern us. ... We don't want decisions made for us by sighted people however well-intentioned and however dedicated.'

Given Finnis' comments, there were and are very few charities who would have published such a challenging paper in what was effectively the house journal.

The paper was the catalyst for a lively, letters debate mainly from the pro participation lobby with contributions from NFB's new public relations officer, Bill Poole (two letters), Fred Reid, Hans Cohn and Stan Bell. John Wall wrote three letters in all and John Busbridge, one.

On 13 December RNIB Executive Council heard that: 'Group D members wished to submit their views and arrangements were being made for this additional evidence to be fully considered.'

1974

The drama now moved into its final act. Discussions, virtually negotiations, must have been going on during the first three months of 1974 because a significantly changed set of proposals were presented on 4 April to RNIB's Policy and Selection Committee by Duncan Watson, chair of the RNIB ad hoc committee and vice chair of RNIB. He was in a difficult position. On the one hand, he had the organisations of the blind wanting 50 per cent of the places. On the other, he had four other groups on RNIB Executive Council which could only lose seats to help this happen. He was clearly sympathetic to the demands, being blind himself and a former president of NFB. However, were he to recommend too large an increase in seats, supporters in the committee of the other groups would baulk and oppose the proposals. These other groups, in combination, had the power to vote them down in council.

The minutes show a thoughtful game, reporting him as saying that, following discussions with all the groups, Groups A, B and C had agreed to accept a slight reduction in representation (turkeys voting for Christmas) but: 'although Group D members had requested voting parity by 1980 ... the increase in the Group's representation should be of a limited character'.

So, Duncan Watson's committee recommended sticking with 110 places on the Executive Council, redistributed away from the other largely sighted groups to allow Group D (representatives of blind people) to rise from twelve to 20. In addition, he recommended that Groups A and C should be urged to include more blind people in their representation, that Group E's composition with current provision for one third blind people should be changed to 'at least one third', that a Consumers Committee be established and that (blind) members' loss of earnings should be reimbursed in full when they attended meetings. This latter proposal was radical among charities, in general, then and remained so for the rest of the twentieth century.

This package was endorsed by RNIB's Policy and Selection Committee but not without some disquiet from more conservative committee members.

The Climax of Negotiations

Duncan Watson had probably pushed the Policy and Selection Committee as far as he could. Would their grudging support and the enthusiastic support of the chair, Lord Head be enough to persuade the full Executive Council to back the proposals – especially when several of them would lose their seats? Also, how would Group D (organisations of the blind) on council react – would the proposals go far enough for them?

The minutes of the Executive Council of 25 April 1974 are very full on the matter: Group D spoke with one critical voice demanding that the 'whole membership of Group D should meet with the Policy and Selection Committee to further discuss the proposals'.

In opposition to Group D there were a number of statements paying 'tribute ... to the extremely valuable service rendered to the Institute by sighted members and by those blind people who serve in an individual capacity ...' – in effect a fightback from those sighted members who thought Group D were being too demanding.

Clearly the exchanges became heated and one sighted council member referred to the 'mediocrity' of members of organisations of the blind. The outcome was that the interim report was neither agreed nor rejected – it was 'received' – but it was agreed that 'a meeting should be arranged between Group D and Policy and Selection Committee at an early date for further consideration of the proposals'.

The critical meeting took place on 13 June 1974 between RNIB's Policy and Selection Committee and Group D from which a comprehensive and revealing note exists.

On the RNIB side were Lord Head and Messrs de Silva, Dunlop, Garrow, McFarlane, Vigers and Watson. From Group D the representatives were Messrs Bower, French, Jeans, Kinder, Milligan, Parker, Perham, Price, Mrs Murkin (formerly Bussey) and Mrs Watson (no relation to Duncan). Boulter, RNIB director general, and Venn, his deputy, with Morgan (minutes) were in attendance.

The note reveals fundamental undercurrents, e.g.:

> the view was expressed by some members of the Committee that the claim for parity [of representation]

appeared to indicate an intention by Group D to take over the operation of the Institute …

reference was made to a 'rumour' that a protest demonstration might be organised unless an acceptable formula was devised by the committee. Mr Dunlop and other members of Policy and Selection Committee urged moderation.

There is no doubt a demonstration was planned, as attested to me by Tom Parker (personal communication, 1984), in 1974 general secretary of NLBD, and separately by Alf Morris MP (personal communication, 2005). In 1974 Alf had just been appointed as the world's first Minister for the Disabled in the Harold Wilson Labour government (1974-79) and he had been invited to speak at the RNIB Annual General Meeting (AGM) being held on 24 July immediately after the next critical Executive Council meeting. He told me that the League had asked him to offer support for the fight for 50 per cent representation and, in particular, to show solidarity towards the demonstration which was due to take place outside the RNIB during the Executive Council and the AGM. He said to me: 'I agreed to stop and talk to them [the demonstrators] in front of the cameras but I wouldn't agree to speak on air but the effect would have been similar.' (Personal communication, 2005)

Alf Morris (R) Government Minister and speaker at the critical 24 July 1974 RNIB AGM, with Lord Head, RNIB Chairman.

So, this was the background threat to the meeting on 13 June where failure would trigger a large demonstration of blind people outside the upcoming RNIB AGM on 24 July, implicitly supported by the government's minister for the disabled.

On the size of Council and the number of seats the note says: 'Following considerable discussion, members of Group D suggested that the size of Executive Council should be increased from 110 to 120 seats and that the 10 additional seats should be allocated to Group D in addition to the 20 seats [previously] recommended.'

At 25 per cent this was a significant retreat from the 50 per cent demand. Colin Low has an additional recollection. Before the critical 13 June meeting another meeting was held between the NFB, NLBD and the RNIB director general, Eric Boulter, who made it clear that 50 per cent would never be conceded. He asked what figure the protagonists would consider. A figure of one third was floated and Boulter said he would consult with his colleagues. After conferring, presumably with Lord Head and Duncan Watson (chair and vice chair, respectively) and perhaps others, he came back to the table and asked whether 30 places (25 per cent) would be acceptable. From Colin Low's recollection, it was Tom Parker (general secretary of the NLBD) who stepped in quickly to say 'Yes' – to the private consternation of NFB who felt that more might have been achieved. Fred Reid told me: 'The demand for "one third" is clearly in my mind as the demand I (still) tried finally and unsuccessfully (as president of the NFB) to push on Eric Boulter just before the date of the demonstration.' (See later.) Nevertheless, the figure of 30 was accepted by both sides and the most critical issue had been settled.

The 13 June meeting was the crunch point, but the agreed package had to be put to the Policy and Selection Committee who would decide the shape of the final package going for ratification to the Executive Council and AGM on 25 July. Policy and Selection discussed 'very fully … the outcomes of the 13 June joint meeting' and agreed to recommend to July RNIB Executive Council that:

- EC numbers should be raised to 120 (the maximum number under the existing byelaws) from 110, comprising 30 from Group D

- the new places in Group D should be allocated by a joint meeting of the Policy and Selection Committee and existing members of Group D
- EC reconfirm its April decisions regarding a consumer committee, loss of earnings and at least one third of Group E comprising blind people
- there was no commitment in principle to 50 per cent representation.

The Outcome

On 25 July RNIB Executive Council ratified the recommendations with these decisions being 'welcomed' by Group D. There was no demonstration outside the meeting.

The next stage was to apportion the allocation of the additional seats. On 16 October a joint meeting of Policy and Selection Committee and Group D decided as below. Present from the committee were Lord Head, de Silva, Hill, Spreadbury, Wall and Watson. For Group D were Bower, French, Kinder, Lovell, Parker, Price, West and Mrs Watson.

The seat allocation agreed was:

8 – National League of the Blind and Disabled
6 – National Federation of the Blind of the UK
2 – Association of Blind Chartered
   Physiotherapists (ABCP)
2 – Association of Blind Piano Tuners
2 – Association of Blind and Partially Sighted
   Teachers and Students
2 – British Computer Association of the Blind
1 – Worcester College Old Boys' Association
1 – Chorleywood College Old Girls' Association
1 – Royal National College for the Blind (RNC)
1 – Circle of Guide Dog Owners
4 – others from the above or new organisations as
   the EC might determine

30 TOTAL

This account gives the impression of a fairly well-ordered process. However, the threat of a demonstration and other evidence I have been given suggests that there was a great deal of anger, doubt and nervousness on both sides which left the likelihood of an agreement in real doubt until the last minute of the July RNIB Executive Council meeting. For example, Fred Reid (then president of the Federation) has told me how he and Eric Boulter had a very tense discussion over the phone; there were telephone calls to honorary officers while they were away on holiday to see whether they would be prepared to agree the package as modified; there were disagreements between the League and the Federation as to whether to call off the demonstration, with the Federation refusing to cancel until the last minute, 'even if only three of us turned up' (Fred Reid, personal communication).

Even after 25 July there was a lot of noise in the system. The 'victory of the campaign' as seen from the perspective of the leadership of NFB and NLBD was not universally recognised by their members. The London branch of NFB recorded its formal opposition to the settlement and the influence of the critics was such that the Fred Reid had to give a robust defence in *Viewpoint* (September/November 1974). Responding to the criticism that the negotiators called off the demonstration (and campaign), despite the fact that the campaign demands had not been met, he said:

> This criticism is, in my view, both correct and undeserved. It is correct because it keeps fresh our ultimate objective. It is undeserved because it minimises the importance of the victory won. ... We still intend to achieve 50 per cent representation for organisations of the blind. Our judgement was simply that we could not get it this time round. ... By indicating our readiness to draw back from confrontation [the demonstration], provided the Institute came a significant distance towards us, we gained more seats than the Institute wanted to concede and proved the effectiveness of our political muscle.

The facts remain impressive. At the start of the campaign in 1968/69, 20 members of RNIB's Executive Council were blind; of those 20 only eight were formal representatives of blind people via organisations of blind people. At the end of the campaign in 1975 the 20 had risen to 44 (40 per cent of the occupied places) of whom 30 (up from eight) formally represented organisations of the blind.

The campaigners would have to wait until 2001/02 before 'parity' was achieved, when RNIB's constitution was changed to require 50 per cent of its trustees to be blind or partially sighted – when the same Colin Low of 1974 (who was made Lord Low in 2006) was RNIB chair and I was director general. Even in 2001/02 this was a radical achievement, far ahead of any other service organisation for disabled people.

Societal Influences for Change

While the narrative above emphasises rightly the importance of individuals in the radical change, there were also favourable social and institutional developments which were relevant.

The 1960s and early 1970s were periods of apparent progressive social change. There was an optimistic, 'anything is possible' atmosphere in the 1960s. Blind people were as much a part of that as anyone else.

In particular, there were the beginnings of the radicalisation of the disability movement, for example, the founding of the Disability Income Group in 1965, Alf Morris' Chronically Sick and Disabled Persons Act 1970, pressed by disabled people, the founding of the Association of Disabled People in 1971 and of the Union of Physically Impaired Against Segregation (UPIAS) in 1972.

Internal Influences for Change

Healthy Traditions of Participation

Despite initially being strongly resistant to change, there were many characteristics of RNIB which helped the protagonists of change:

- RNIB had strong early traditions of the involvement of blind people (for the first 19 years, 1869-87, an Executive Council member had to be blind to be appointed [Thomas 1957, p. 13]).
- It had a tradition and established principle of blind representation. (Group D, organisations of blind people, was established as early as 1937.)
- It had a democratic and fair set of rules controlling its decision making.
- It had an accessible, semi-independent house magazine, *New Beacon*, which carried both sides of the debate.
- It had as one of its top three leaders (Duncan Watson, RNIB vice chairman) and two of its top eight leaders (Duncan and John Wall, both blind) who had crossed over previously from the demanding Group D to the group of RNIB corporate leaders. These two contributed a bridging/interpretive capacity, showing the target institution, through their own actions and competences, that the blind demanding change could produce 'responsible' and able leaders and team players.

There was a changed attitudinal climate during 1972 and 1974 which was more sympathetic to the demands of the organisations of the blind. There was the sighted John Colligan's departure and Eric Boulter's arrival as the first blind director general of RNIB in a long time.

The Presence of Able Blind Leaders

If there were historical traditions and institutional capacities to be exploited, there still had to be able blind people to do this. RNIB was one of the largest educational providers, producing a blind elite who knew each other (mainly from RNIB's two residential grammar schools), were highly competent and very literate – just the force of people needed to press for, and take up, governance positions.

There were two powerful organisations of the blind: NFB with its institutional power base among the professions; and NLBD with its power base among skilled and unskilled workers and its links with the trade union movement. Each of these organisations was training a cadre of blind people well versed in team working, and competent and comfortable with negotiation, committee work, standing orders and committee rules.

In addition, these organisations 'of' had several outstanding strategists and tacticians, and astute strategies:

- Martin Milligan, a Marxist academic with astute skills of political analysis who enlisted the substantial contributions of Fred Reid and Colin Low;
- Tom Parker, an experienced trade unionist, well versed in negotiation and not frightened by confrontation; and
- a strategy which 'gave everyone something', for example, the demanded extra places were not all kept for the Federation and the League but shared out to other organisations of blind people, thus widening the support base.

Pressure from RNIB's Blind Consumers

Initially, drawing on organisational minutes and resolutions, I had seen the pressure for increased representation as driven almost exclusively by the participation principle. However, discussion with some of the protagonists has given me an additional set of practical reasons – in essence the need to improve the quality of RNIB activities through the lived experience of blind people. These underpinned the participation principle and provided enthusiastic support from the blind rank and file for the leaders and negotiators. These reasons also help to explain the importance accorded to the establishment of the RNIB Consumer Committee as part of the campaign – indeed it was Tom Parker's passion, as he made clear to me when I arrived in 1983.

Fred Reid said (personal communication, 4 May 2012):

> blind people at large supported the 'participation' campaign because they were very dissatisfied with some important aspects of RNIB services. The term 'consumer committee' gives the clue to one aspect of this. It had to be set up because of the heavy volume of dissatisfaction about the narrow range of assistive equipment offered by RNIB as compared to its counterparts in the USA and Germany. Tom Parker's international work revealed to him how much more in the way of watches, braille writers, etc. was available in these countries, but it was very difficult for individuals to source them, because of customs duties, methods of currency transaction, legislative restrictions on charitable bodies, etc. The solution was for RNIB to import and stock these goods along with their own products. For some reason this was resisted. So there was a practical link. Increase participation and you give a voice to the blind consumer. Another very touchy issue was the refusal of RNIB to admit guide dogs to any of its residential premises, hence COGDO's interest in the campaign and their representative, Wally Kinder's prominence in the lobbying. You can add to that the earlier resistance of RNIB to the long cane until the late 1960s. Finally, ABAPSTAS was very critical of the very small supply of scholarly texts and teaching literature, both in braille and on audio-tape. We knew of the huge supply of the latter by Recordings for the Blind in the USA and we wanted RNIB to adopt their production methods. Again this was resisted.

History is all about through whose eye you look, and I am sure the RNIB's leaders of the time would not have analysed the situation in this way. However, before joining RNIB in 1983, I spoke with several of the BBC Radio 4 *In Touch* team, including Thena Heshell (producer) and Peter White (presenter) and they painted a similar view of RNIB at that time.

Chapter 1b

Progress in the Face of a Dominant Welfare State

A strong feature of the 1970s was expansion and renewal of RNIB services despite a view that charities were becoming increasingly irrelevant. Charities were seen by many as old fashioned and in decline. At best RNIB was described as 'venerable' (Nightingale 1973, p. 327). RNIB's progress and renewal in the 1970s was against that background.

In 1968, the RNIB centenary year, the director general presaged the 1970s approach with the words (Colligan 1968):

> We shall grasp the opportunity which our centenary affords to renew our pledge to extend a helping hand to all Britain's blind in the years ahead. We shall place particular emphasis on the improvement of residential facilities for additionally handicapped children, on more specialised care for the very elderly and infirm blind and, lastly, on the expansion of employment opportunities in keeping with this technological age.

The last of the three policy intentions happened to an extent – no mean feat when there was no supporting legislative framework for non-discrimination. New technology, initially inaccessible, was bursting onto the scene in professions such as telephony and physiotherapy which were traditional strongholds of opportunity for blind people.

With regard to the first policy intention, at this stage the RNIB had two residential schools for additionally handicapped children: Rushton Hall in Northamptonshire – a junior school (founded 1957); and a senior school – Condover Hall (founded 1948). During the 1970s both these schools expanded to a combined maximum of 150 pupils. The six Sunshine House schools as early as 1970 had 84 per cent of their 105 pupils with additional handicaps. By the end of the decade these had reduced to four schools with fewer pupils. What was also apparent to those involved over the decade was the increase in the extremity and complexity of the pupils' needs. During this period the two academic residential schools of Chorleywood and Worcester flourished with combined numbers in excess of 160 and the majority going on to university – breaking ground by doing degrees in such subjects as botany and computer studies. Perhaps the most forward-looking initiative was the foundation in 1972 of the Education Advisory Service led by Heather Jones, comprising at its height twelve highly skilled, early years professionals

A bedtime story at Rushton Hall School.

who would advise and support the families of newly diagnosed children (mainly under five years) in their own homes.
This service was pioneering in several respects, primarily
through reaching out into people's homes and through
utilising and adapting mainstream early childhood education theory for application with young blind and partially
sighted children.

Specialist services for elderly infirm people continued
through the upgrading of the six residential homes for older
people, particularly the deaf-blind. However, in some senses
the trend was away from the infirm towards the fitter, with
three convalescent/holiday homes being translated into
hotel provision for the fitter older person. Two were closed,
Alma Court was upgraded to hotel status, and three hotels
were added: the Century in Blackpool in 1968, the Howard
in Llandudno in 1970 and the Palm Court in Eastbourne in
1971. By the end of the 1970s these hotels were providing
6,000 holidays a year. It is likely that the hotel expansion was
catalysed in part by the growing influence within RNIB over
the decade of the organisations 'of' which comprised mainly
active blind members of working age and those newly retired.

Impressive Services Development

In the last year of the decade (Annual Report 1979/80) the
annual output of easily quantified services was:

- over half a million braille periodicals
- 181 new braille titles
- 64 new braille music titles
- 56,000 Moon books, pamphlets and periodicals
- 54,000 Talking Book Service members (an increase
  from 26,000 in 1969/70)
- 35,000 sales orders for assistive equipment (then
  called 'aids') and publications
- 411 children in RNIB schools and assessment
  centres
- 35 students at RNIB's school of physiotherapy

- 25 orientation and mobility instructors trained
- 200 students supported in higher education
- 400 people attended RNIB rehabilitation centres
- 259 blind people helped to find jobs
- 147 self-employed people supported in home-workers' schemes
- 131 in RNIB residential homes
- 6,000 holidays taken at RNIB hotels.

Campaigning – the RNIB Giant Stirs

Yet, the decade did not simply see greater service provision; the early reawakening of RNIB's pressure group and campaigning role began in that decade.

RNIB was active during the final stages of the drafting of Alf Morris' private member's bill which became the Chronically Sick and Disabled Persons Act 1970. Also, RNIB joined with NFB and the NLBD in pressing government for a 'blindness allowance' to cover the extra costs of blindness. While this failed (the Mobility Allowance of the mid 1970s effectively excluded blindness as a criterion), the campaign helped to bring the three organisations closer and to galvanise a blindness movement of both the organisations 'of the blind' and 'for the blind'. The decade finished with a petition for a blindness allowance which would cover the extra costs which blindness brings (for example, the need for taxis, assistive equipment, readers etc.). This came jointly from RNIB, NLBD and NFB and was presented to Parliament in 1980 by James Wellbeloved MP. The petition contained 461,716 signatures, a major logistical feat given they were all on paper.

Resources – Growth

To achieve all this required significant capital which peaked in the last three years of the decade. In 1977 some £11 million in 1977 prices (150 per cent of 1976/77 annual expenditure) was set aside for capital investment in just four projects: the new braille printing centre in Goswell Road, London (1979);

Table 1b.1. RNIB Income and Expenditure 1969/70-1979/80

Income (£ millions)	1969/70	1979/80
Fees for services	1.16	4.7
Voluntary income	1.61	6.25
Investment income	0.16	0.73
Other	0.13	0
Total	3.04	11.68
TOTAL at constant 2004 prices[1]	31.7	35.1
Percentage growth, real terms		+11%
TOTAL Constant 2004 prices to base 100	100	111

Expenditure (£ millions)	1969/70	1979/80
Services	2.13	9.07
Central administration	0.02	0.16
Net expenditure on fixed assets	0.14	0.90
Cost of appeals	0.67	0.92
Total	2.96	11.05
TOTAL at constant 2004 prices[1]	30.9	33.2
Percentage growth, real terms		+7%
TOTAL Constant 2004 prices to base 100	100	107

[1] UK RPI via the Cleave Calculator

Garrow House, the new hostel for blind people seeking work, in Westbourne Park in London (1978); the new school and student residence for physiotherapy in north London (1978); and the computerisation of the distribution processes of the Talking Books Service (1980).

This investment and overall service expansion was fuelled by large revenue surpluses throughout the decade. These were as high as 40 per cent of income in the early 1970s and were never less than fifteen per cent except in the last year when the £11 million investment programme was in full swing. Indeed, the whole decade was one of income affluence, made up typically of 50-55 per cent voluntary income (mainly legacies), 33-35 per cent service or fee income and 5-10 per cent investment income. Legacy income was hugely important, constituting around one third of total income and nearly two thirds of voluntary income. Table 1b.1 gives the figures for the beginning and end of the decade and the totals in constant 2004 prices.

These figures show relatively modest real growth in income (eleven per cent) and expenditure (seven per cent) – 1970s inflation was high (e.g. thirteen per cent in 1975). They show that, as early as the 1970s and before, RNIB had a very substantial fee income from services provided (38 per cent of total income in 1969/70). RNIB also had a heavy dependency on legacies, one of the least understood and hardest to manage areas of fundraising. Building up non-legacy income became a growing priority over the next two decades. Furthermore, the table shows the very high-cost ratio of RNIB's non-legacy fundraising, around 40 per cent – one of the issues which assumed increasing importance and, eventually, in the 1990s, led to the radical and painful overhaul of field/community fundraising, where paid fundraisers, many of them blind, raised money in their local geographic areas.

People – New Leaders

In short, RNIB enjoyed modest growth and renewal in the 1970s. So, who were the people behind this successful decade?

Most of RNIB's leaders of the early 1970s were present in the 1960s but retirements, promotions and elections led to dramatic changes in the very top leadership positions, and in their authority and style.

The place to start is the effective duo of Chairman Lord Head (retired to the presidency in 1975) and Director General John Colligan (1951-72). This was the old order.

John Colligan had started as a fundraiser, coming from the commercial world of Fyffes in Liverpool to become secretary of the Liverpool fundraising branch in 1940 and then on to RNIB assistant general secretary. He was clearly a gifted leader. In his time RNIB grew enormously in size and influence. He worked closely with a small team, of which the pre-eminent was John Godfrey, chief accountant and then finance secretary (director) for 24 years (1947-71). After lunch in the senior staff dining room Colligan and Godfrey would often go for a walk in Regents Park, nearby 224 Great Portland Street (formerly, RNIB headquarters), to discuss matters of life and work – to be joined occasionally by other key top staff such as Eddie Venn, Percy Ratcliffe, Don Bell, Cedric Garland and Michael Colborne Brown – and to 'thrash out' key work issues (personal communication from Colligan). Such a business method may ring now of a bygone era lacking in transparency but it was, and still is, highly effective in building the top team and consensus.

Another management and leadership method he used to great effect, and seldom seen now, was 'management through trustee committees'.

John Colligan had a very flat management structure with between fifteen and 20 people directly accountable to him at any one time, namely, the ten fundraising branch directors and the heads of service departments. At first glance this is an impossible structure but Colligan had a very neat 'local authority' way of handling it. He 'managed' many people and decisions through his attendance and interventions at committee meetings. He was immensely knowledgeable about the RNIB and was eloquent and persuasive. In addition, he had the facts of each matter before him and the committee via the committee papers. If he agreed with his manager's recommendations to committee, he backed him/her. If he disagreed, he steered a 'no' decision through. This would be regarded as, at least, unusual nowadays and, at worst, as bad managerial practice but, done well, it was highly effective. It was quite a common managerial method in local government throughout the twentieth century.

What of Colligan the man, and how he was regarded? As might be expected, it depends to whom you talk. His closest colleagues regarded him with great affection and respect. His more distant colleagues had great respect but also a degree of nervousness, verging on fear, of him. He was a formidable opponent and used informal networking methods as well as formal ones to achieve the decisions he felt necessary. There is no doubt about his commitment to blind people and he often spoke of the partnership between the blind and sighted. This standpoint was confirmed in John Godfrey's appreciation of him in the Annual Report 1971/72 (p. 21):

> [Colligan has] two guiding principles – firstly the importance of maximum co-operation between the blind and sighted in the planning and conduct of the Institute's work, and secondly the importance of strengthening the partnership between all the organisations concerned with the welfare of the blind both voluntary and statutory, local and national.

However, perhaps there is some significance in Godfrey's use of the word 'maximum', as in 'maximum possible'. The majority of blind people to whom I have talked and who knew him are not so fulsome in their judgement of this partnership. Like so many of us, one senses that there was a difference between his commitment to principle and his practice. Certainly, in the climate of the organisations of the blind campaigning to increase their trustee representation (described earlier), there was a widespread view among the 'ofs' that they had to deal with the covert and at times overt opposition of John Colligan. They did not feel he reached out to them. He warned me on my appointment in 1983 to be wary of the organisations of the blind.

While I met John Colligan a dozen times or so and interviewed him at length on tape, I never met the other half of the 'duo' – Lord Head, his last chairman. However, from my interviews with those who did, I sense a man whose moderating and bridge-building qualities were critical in the period 1970-75 when so many changes of senior staff and trustees were happening and the crucial governance changes were taking place. He was an urbane man of some style and good substance. He could sense the best way forward and quietly steered or went with RNIB in that direction. One of the decisions that he would have had a large hand in was the appointment of Eric Boulter, first as deputy director general, then director general in summer 1972. While RNIB had had many blind chairs, Eric Boulter was the first blind chief executive since the founder Rhodes Armitage in the last quarter of the nineteenth century. The decision was way ahead of its time in that the majority of the disability charities only appointed disabled staff to senior executive positions some 20 years later.

Eric Boulter, although British, had previously been associate director of the American Foundation for the Overseas Blind and had held senior posts in the World Council for the Welfare of the Blind (WCWB). John Colligan knew him well having been for many years the treasurer of WCWB and several people told me he had been a keen supporter of Boulter's candidature. Eric was a quiet, unassuming man whom I did not meet as often as I did John. He was chief executive from 1972 until 1980 and was known for his tact, diplomacy and negotiating skills and for really understanding blindness from the inside. These attributes were revealed in an anecdote related to me by Fred Reid who had presented a paper very critical of the underemployment of blind people to a government committee on which Eric was sitting: 'As usual for the time some on the committee dismissed it as "far too dark a picture".' Eric had also only just joined the committee. Very tactfully, Eric said he agreed that Fred's description was rather too dark, but the scene was indeed 'a very dark shade of grey'! There is no doubt that Boulter's succession eased the path of greater representation of blind people on council. The appreciation of him in the Annual Report 1979/80, on his retirement, acknowledges his instrumental role in this progressive move, so far ahead of its time in other disability charities. He also presided over a decade of some expansion and, in particular, a massive capital development programme between 1977 and 1980. He had a tremendous dedication to detail and to getting things right. It may have been these factors that contributed to him taking an extended period of leave on medical advice because of exhaustion in 1972 and 1973 and to him taking early retirement in 1980.

Someone who was important to Colligan but vital to Boulter was Eddie Venn, who became deputy director general in 1972 and who had been regarded as a strong contender for the director general post after Colligan's retirement. He was vital to Eric Boulter because he brought immense project management expertise. He got things done, and done well. He knew the operational field intimately and had been head of services within RNIB for many years, experience which is elaborated on in the next chapter.

Eric Boulter's initial trustee partner was the chairman Lord Head but for much of his term, from 1975 onwards, it was Duncan Watson. He was a young government Treasury solicitor. Blind from an early age, he came from a mining family. His father had a passion for education and Duncan left his school in the northeast to go to the residential Worcester College for the Blind and on to Oxford University. He became active in the National Federation of the Blind of the UK becoming its president (equivalent to the chair). He joined RNIB's Executive Council in 1964 some two years after his good friend and contemporary, John Wall. They were to make a hugely successful honorary officer partnership between 1975 and 1990, with Watson as chair and Wall as vice chair. John Wall took over from Watson in 1990 and we shall hear more on him later. Initially it was Wall who was elected to trustee office as chair of a major standing committee in 1967 but in 1968, with the particular backing of Head, Watson was elected deputy vice chair and then vice chair of the whole of RNIB. As we saw above, he played a crucial role in the negotiations to increase the number of representative blind people on Council and, as such, was a natural choice to succeed Head in 1975 as the newly elected blind representatives took their places in 1975. Duncan Watson (or Tubby to his friends from school) was a man with gravitas and charm, reasonable and patient until exasperated, and very progressive beneath an establishment air. He steered RNIB from being a somewhat old-fashioned organisation into a twentieth-century charity. These trustee leaders were supported over this time and into the next decade by (usually) a two-person team of treasurers including J.H. Bevan, H.D. McFarlane, D.L. Murison, A.F. Morton, H.D. de Wolf and J.D. Dunn.

On the staff side, there were so many who made the RNIB and its services a success. Michael Colborne-Brown, as head of education, led the introduction of the innovative Education Advisory Service for parents, headed by Heather Jones. He backed the dynamic head of physiotherapy, David Teager, in a relaunch of blind physiotherapy training at the purpose-built North London School of Physiotherapy, and he acknowledged the ground-breaking three decades contributed by Oscar Myers' education services for multi-handicapped blind young people (Myers 1975). Richard Fletcher as head of Worcester College played an important role. On the services side, Tom Drake was reaching the end of his major career contribution to the residential rehabilitation of newly blinded people. The 1970s was also a decade of strong fundraising directors in the regions, all accountable to the director general such was the importance with which they were viewed – Maggie Murphy, Allan Murray, Malcolm Parsons, George Sheppard, Trevor Tatchell, Ken Tidmarsh and Peter Walsh, as well as Elisabeth Ormiston heading up the Sunshine Fund.

What is remarkable and instructive was the relative professional freedom given to RNIB's heads of services outside London in the schools, rehabilitation centres, colleges, hotels and homes. The heads had to be entrepreneurial, professionally competent and, importantly, able to manage within a budget. The arguable consequential weakness was the lack of a unifying philosophy and coherence of the combined service effort. This was one of the reasons why Duncan Watson, in his introduction to the Annual Report 1979/80 (p. 4), announced that: 'In the autumn of 1980 we plan to conduct a comprehensive review of all RNIB services to blind people to identify the needs and priorities for the next decade.'

This clarion call for a new way forward chimed well with the feelings of several senior staff. It has been put to me by some of them that there was a growing air of frustration among senior staff and trustees who wanted a more holistic, policy base for RNIB's development. Apart from the lead from the chair just quoted, this was to show itself in more concrete form at what was to become known as the Sunningdale Conference of 1980, the first year of the new decade.

Conclusion – External Pressures Build

This pressure for change was not just an internal reaction to internal events, it was also driven by the external environment. With the benefit of hindsight, despite the overt success of the decade, the outside world was beginning to change in adverse ways for RNIB. The RNIB/blindness world's traditional assumptions of blind people being the most deserving disabled people requiring blindness-specific solutions, with partially sighted people and those with other disabilities being subordinate in needs, of RNIB being relatively aloof from/not much known by the rest of the voluntary sector, were being challenged. These challenges came from various sources:

- the Chronically Sick and Disabled Persons Act 1970 which addressed all disabled people, not separate impairment sectors
- the Seebohm Report on social work and the subsequent Local Authority Social Services Act 1970, which promoted a generic approach to social work and either abolished or undermined social workers for the blind
- the beginnings of the integration debate (whether blind people should be incorporated into mainstream service provision)
- the growth of other disability organisations such as Scope (then the Spastics Society), Mencap, Guide

Dogs for the Blind Association, RADAR (Royal Association for Disability and Rehabilitation) and the founding of the Disability Alliance

- the failure of the Blindness Allowance Campaign, defeated in some measure by the opposition of the above disability charity players
- the growth of 'strange' electronic assistive technologies as well as RNIB's heartland of mechanical ones.

So, by the end of the decade pressure for change was mounting.

Chapter 2a

1980-90: Early Adoption of Strategic Planning

During the 1980s implicit planning gave way to explicit strategic planning. As a way of setting a course and evaluating progress, strategic planning was well established in the commercial and statutory sectors by the second half of the 1970s. The charity sector was lagging behind in the use of this valuable tool (Medley 1988). RNIB was one of the first major charities to adopt a formal strategic planning methodology in 1983, including middle management involvement via a residential conference of 80 managers in 1985. Arguably, the process started at the Sunningdale Conference in 1980. This process would lead to RNIB's first public strategic plan in 1987.

This move towards strategic planning needs context. While RNIB had opened itself up more to the blindness movement in the 1970s, it was still quite isolationist within the wider charity sector. For example, over the previous ten years I had been, first, assistant chief executive of Age Concern England and, then, chief executive of the Volunteer Centre England and active in many cross-sector initiatives, but I had never previously met a senior RNIB leader until an National Council for Voluntary Organisations (NCVO) reception, convened by

Nicholas Hinton in 1980 as he successfully rebuilt NCVO's pre-eminent role in the sector. RNIB was focussed on the blindness cause and remained suspicious and threatened by what it saw as the increasing popularity and legitimacy of other impairments. A new front was growing and policy makers were increasingly talking about 'disabled people' rather than 'blind' or 'deaf' or 'physically disabled' people. As late as summer 1981, the International Year of Disabled People, the introduction to the RNIB Annual Report, while acknowledging the increasing recognition given to 'new types of disability', admitted: 'Blind people are beginning to feel that they are losing out to other categories of handicapped people' (Annual Report 1980/81, p. 4).

With Eddie Venn's appointment as director general in 1980 and that of Lucille Hall as public relations officer, the RNIB's profile and campaigning increased and became more public. The Annual Report 1982/83 – for the first time – had a major section titled 'Campaigns'.

As RNIB started to develop a new way forward in the early 1980s, it had favourable finances, regularly achieving a ten per cent surplus each year. Also, there was a growing perception inside and outside the organisation that RNIB had been rather narrow and insular in the impact we were having on the outside world. There had been relatively few new services introduced for some while. Nearly all services were direct to blind and partially sighted children and adults (and were often in older inappropriate buildings), with very few indirect services. Lobbying and campaigning was modest except on the blindness allowance. As an incoming chief executive in 1983, I was encouraged by leading trustees to be strongly developmental and to reach out into the external world.

Threats to Single Impairment Causes

By the time we reach into the new decade of the 1980s, several new trends were discernible in the external environment relevant to RNIB. In summary, these were:

- As mentioned above, policy and law makers were talking in terms of 'disabled people' collectively rather than 'blind' or 'deaf' or 'physically handicapped' (*vide*, Chronically Sick and Disabled Persons Act 1970).
- Professionals working with these groups were being required to be increasingly generic in their skills, for example, not a blind person's resettlement officer (BPRO) but a disablement rehabilitation officer (DRO), not a social worker for the blind but a generic social worker.
- There was a growing expectation that professional workers with these groups would be trained and validated not by cause-related charitable bodies but higher and further education establishments, for example, not by RNIB's National Mobility Centre but by a mainstream higher education college.
- Overlaying the two previous points was a new policy of 'integrating' blind people, in particular, and disabled people, in general, into mainstream services, for example, not schools for the blind but blind people being educated in mainstream 'ordinary' schools.

Why were these trends resisted by RNIB in the 1970s? Compared to other disability groups, blind people were relatively advantaged. Thus, it was reasoned that broadening the beneficiary groups to all disabled people and further integrating them into mainstream, would dilute blind people's 'privileged' position. The RNIB argument was that other groups should be levelled up. The majority RNIB view at that time was that moves to genericism and integration (later called inclusion) would also dilute and eventually dissipate the specialist educational and rehabilitation skills developed for a unique impairment such as blindness (or deafness, learning disability etc.). It was argued that this was already showing itself in Scandinavia where integration had taken place earlier and specialist unique impairment knowledge had declined.

With the benefit of hindsight, it is possible to see that in the early 1980s RNIB was at a fork in the road. One choice would mean carrying on as before, long successful, in treating blind people as pre-eminently unique; the other route, accepting the new reality of lost pre-eminence and lost superior resource allocation, was to accept the positive advantages of blind and partially-sighted people's integration/inclusion into mainstream activities. At the time the choice was not that obvious. The weight of opinion inside RNIB and among most of the organisations 'of' the blind was in favour of shoring up, or even better re-establishing, the pre-eminent, separate position of blind people (RNIB Annual Report 1980/81). Just looking at the names of the powerful lobby organisations inside RNIB gives a feel of this climate – the Association of Blind Piano Tuners, the Braille Chess Association, the Association of Blind Telephonists etc. Even the National League of the Blind and Disabled was predominantly a 'blind' organisation which drew its membership base from the old 'workshops for the blind'.

So how did things change? The trustee leadership was important in edging RNIB in a new direction. Many of the blind trustees who led the changes in governance in the 1970s – Duncan Watson (civil servant), Fred Reid (academic), Colin Low (academic), John Wall (lawyer), Bill Poole (antiquarian book seller) etc. – despite having been separately educated at Worcester College for the Blind, were living embodiments of integration in their work and private lives. They were comfortable with adult integration/inclusion and would have it no other way. The director general of the first two and half years of the 1980s, Eddie Venn, was a thoughtful pragmatist, and he was more than cognisant of these changes too. Evidence of the start of this shift in view was an RNIB report of 1981 recommending that the RNIB Commercial Training College should be moved into a mainstream further education college. The fact that in 1983 the RNIB trustee selection committee, comprising a majority of blind people, chose me to be Eddie's successor, rather than George Willson, the powerful internal candidate, shows that they wanted change.

Willson (partially sighted) was the deputy director general who represented the traditional RNIB way of thinking and had the strong support of Tom Parker, still then the leader of the NLBD. Parker told me later that he thought I would only use RNIB as a stepping-stone in my career and would be gone in five years. (Not the 20 I served!)

I made it clear in my interview that, as far as the wider charity sector was concerned, RNIB was a sleeping giant which had largely kept itself to itself, but that it could rouse itself and become a much more major player on behalf of blind people in the outside world. This position carried the day.

The main weakness which I had to try to address was that I had little knowledge or experience of sight loss. One obvious way was to visit all RNIB services and establishments across the United Kingdom – over 60 in all, which took me over a year. Another was to accept the invitation from Fred and Etta Reid, both totally blind, to stay with them and their three sighted children for a few days. This had a profound impact. A third way was to attend our Rehabilitation Centre in Torquay and sample the services under blindfold. This also had a profound effect but not entirely to my credit. My first blunder was to talk too much. Simulating a newly blind person, I experienced the panic of not knowing how I was connecting with people around me and made the classic mistake of talking too much to try and force people to stay with me. One day before lunch I could not understand why no one was responding to me so I lifted my blindfold to discover I was standing completely on my own. The sighted tutors who had left me, repeated what so many sighted people do when talking to a blind person, they did not tell me they were leaving. My second blunder was to be too cocky after a cooking lesson. I had successfully baked my scones under blindfold and was feeling rather full of myself. When the staff asked whether I would like to be guided back from the kitchen block to the main building, I politely declined and said I could manage on my own. I tapped my white cane across the floor to the door to leave but just could not seemed to manage the door handles. I began to get flustered, imagining everyone watching, even glorying in, the director general struggling. The handles seemed to have changed since I entered a few hours ago. Finally, I managed to pull the door open and walked straight into an industrial size fridge which was adjacent to the door out of the building!

Another induction activity was a three-day (freezing) residential introductory course on educating blind and partially sighted children, run by the redoubtable Elizabeth Chapman, a practical academic. I hope I learned more but one striking memory is the importance of ensuring that children with partial sight clean their glasses every day, thus significantly increasing what they can see. This brought home a wider principle – there are wonderful technical aids around, but to work they have to be used optimally.

All these inductions contributed heavily to my contributions to RNIB strategic planning.

First Thoughts on Changes Needed

Looking at this planning system progress in more detail, as already noted, the change was heralded in the Annual Report 1979/80, when the then chairman Duncan Watson announced that the RNIB planned to conduct a comprehensive review of all its services to blind people to identify needs and priorities for the next decade.

This was a significant cultural shift in approach towards planning, implementation and review which was to characterise RNIB for many years to come. The actual and symbolic start to this process was the Sunningdale Conference in autumn 1980, held at the civil service college over a residential weekend. Such a residential weekend was unprecedented and included representative members of the Executive Council (many of them blind), senior staff and other invited specialists – an opening up of planning methods. The weekend was followed by a series of detailed position papers which were considered by committees during 1981: 'reconsidering many aspects of the services we provide … a most stimulating and challenging exercise [to] produce an agreed plan of action' (Annual Report 1980/81, p. 4).

A year later in summer 1982 Chairman Watson announced in the Annual Report 1981/82:

> plans (over the next 10 years or so) to give blind people a better future which include:
>
> 1. establishing a new commercial training college (out of the existing one),
>
> 2. modernising our employment rehabilitation centre at Torquay and, as longer-term projects,
>
> 3. to modernise the Talking Book Service [and]
>
> 4. to merge our two grammar schools (Worcester and Chorleywood).

Second Thoughts – More Radical

By the time of my arrival as director general in autumn 1983, there was a fair head of steam to 'get on with these four projects'. However, closer examination in early 1984 suggested to me that the plans were primarily aimed at upgrading existing services and were not necessarily addressing key external forces of change. I argued, against some resistance from trustees, that more time was needed to review RNIB and its activities in the setting of the new world of disability in the 1980s and of needs not being met. We needed a broader strategic approach.

RNIB's traditional strengths were and still are as a major direct service provider. It concentrated direct services on blind people's education, employment and access to written material. It ran schools and colleges, helped people find and retain work, and transcribed masses of written material into accessible forms, for example, braille, audio etc. This was RNIB's heartland which we were committed to strengthening. However, this effective focus highlighted further challenges. There were many other areas of life crucial to blind people for which RNIB was not providing services, such as finance, health, social services, the arts, housing and sport.

This reasoning led to a raft of some 35 reviews exploring RNIB's potential role in such disparate areas as health, housing, parliament and relationships with local societies for the blind. As a new arrival I spent a lot of time in the first year visiting the contiguous world outside, including critics such as the team at the BBC Radio 4 programme, *In Touch*. From this absorption exercise, I drafted some policy guidelines to steer RNIB development more strategically than merely upgrading existing services. These were debated among committees and staff, amended and published in *New Beacon* magazine (Bruce 1985). The 'guidelines' (slightly amended for contemporary clarity) were:

- more encouragement of local service provision (1)
- RNIB (interest) should span the whole range of concerns of visually impaired people (2)
- the distribution of expenditure/subsidy should be related to the spread of our visually impaired population (for example, by demography, severity of sight loss etc.) (3)
- in particular, we should examine how useful different services are to blind versus those with residual vision. (4)

The consumer is queen (or king) – a marketing approach:

- need for consumer research on existing and proposed services (5)
- always keeping the image of the consumer centrally in mind (6)
- more promotion/publicising of our services. (7)

Linkages/relationships:

- need to make RNIB services more complementary to those provided to blind and partially sighted people by the statutory, commercial, voluntary and informal (family friends and neighbours) sectors (8)
- RNIB activities need to act more as a catalyst to others (9)
- more outreach to organisations locally (10)
- more active in national campaigns and in parliament (11)
- more studies into the effectiveness of other organisation services to our customers. (12)

In order to do the above, there was a need:

- for RNIB to address the needs of the whole person (12)
- to do more for the majority who lose vision in older age (13)
- to serve partially sighted as well as blind people (14)
- to become more customer- and less production-focussed (15)
- to recognise that many other institutions (for example, supermarkets, NHS) are more important to our consumers than RNIB and we need to influence these (through indirect services) rather than simply providing our own direct services (16)
- to become much more of a campaigning/pressure group. (17)

In 1985 there was the first residential senior managers' conference (see Appendix) held at the RNIB hotel in Eastbourne (attended by head teachers, hotel managers, regional fundraisers, librarians etc. – some 80 people in all), creating a real sense of excitement and enthusiasm for change. As a result of views at the conference three more guidelines were added:

- RNIB services should promote integration of visually impaired people into the wider community (18)
- RNIB should continue to be pioneering and innovative (19)
- RNIB projects should be designed to improve the co-ordination of services to blind people. (20)

Many of the above caused initial surprise, even alarm, among many trustees (e.g. the marketing approach and guidelines 3, 4, 8, 13, 14, 15, 16, 18) but, as I was still in my honeymoon period as the new director general, I was given the benefit of the doubt. Indeed, the reaction to all this planning activity and amended direction was generally very positive. A very small minority of senior managers retired early, not always in opposition but sometimes through exhaustion at the increased pace! The following anecdote perhaps gives a sense of the excitement, energy and sheer hard work generated by the whole process and how not everyone found it easy. I know that Donald Bell would not have minded me relating this story. He was a man of immense ability who had been identified by the then director general in the late 1940s as a high-flyer and now was approaching retirement. He had run the publishing arm of RNIB for many years. He came to me at the time and said, 'If we had been doing all this even ten years ago, I would have entered into this [development period] with enthusiastic commitment, but it has come too late for me.'

Market research played a vital role. As early as 1982 RNIB commissioned a customer survey, *Who are Britain's Blind People?* (Hall 1983), among RNIB Talking Book members. Lucille Hall, RNIB's forward-looking public relations officer, was both commissioner and author. Then, in 1985, we completed an *Initial Demographic Study* (Shankland Cox 1985), which reviewed all the demographic data available and concluded that no one really knew how many blind people there were in Britain but that the official registers of blind and partially sighted people maintained by the DHSS underestimated the totals. This led us to start in 1986 the first RNIB needs survey (Bruce, McKennell and Walker 1991), which was fundamental in helping us to understand the number, needs and wishes of blind and partially sighted people. This research project drove much of the service expansion between 1987 and 2000 and on into the 2000s. It remains one of the most cited RNIB publications, along with its partner survey of children (Walker, Tobin and McKennell 1992). The latter was followed up in 1999 by Clunies-Ross, Franklin and Keil.

The early research revelation of very large numbers of unserved people, which would remain a problem even if the RNIB were ten times larger, gave hard evidence of the guideline (16) that we needed a major investment in 'indirect' services. In other words, RNIB needed to persuade different parts of the state, commercial and voluntary sectors to take more account of the needs and wishes of blind and partially sighted people. These RNIB indirect services ranged from pressure group functions, such as establishing a parliamentary office to try to ensure blind-friendly legislation, through to an integration service to help mainstream schools and their staff teach blind children effectively in ordinary classrooms.

For RNIB the policy change towards supporting integration/inclusion was a particularly contentious area in education. The majority of trustees, including blind ones were against educational integration. In addition, there was an understandable institutional bias towards separate provision because that was the RNIB's core business. In those days, this amounted to 20 residential establishments (ten schools and colleges, as well as ten rehabilitation centres, hotels and homes) all aimed exclusively at blind and partially sighted people. The first tentative step towards change built on the strategy guideline to continue to be innovative (19) which emerged from the managers' conference in 1985. Another more dramatic driver was the election of Colin Low as chair of the powerful RNIB education committee – dramatic because Low was a known long-standing supporter of integrated education (i.e. visually impaired children being educated in more local mainstream schools not national residential ones run by RNIB). It was also dramatic because he was elected by only one vote, the casting vote of the RNIB chair Duncan Watson who came specially for the vote. The informal lobbying had been intense.

Implementation of this integration policy came through the establishment of a unit to support young people in mainstream schools, grants for assistive technology to help mainstream schools provide access equipment, training days for mainstream educational staff and vacation schemes for students in mainstream so they could meet others in similar situations and form peer support. Although this policy had my full support, there is no doubt in my mind that this would either never have happened, or happened much later, if Colin Low had not been elected and then forcefully steered the integration activities through.

So how did these intentions get translated into a strategy? Many people think of strategy in a mechanistic way – create the plan and then carry it out. However, in reality, strategic planning is more organic, not regarding the organisation (in this case, RNIB) as a machine, but an organism (Hatch 1997). In the machine analogy, the driver presses the accelerator and steers where s/he wants the organisation to go. Nevertheless, everyone knows (except sometimes the bosses) that organisational life is not like that. All the controls are very spongy and the machine is unresponsive. In the organism analogy the periphery is as important as the centre, because it is the periphery which is most in touch with the real world of the external environment. So, although I took some decisive steps in the first few months of my tenure (for example, the policy guidelines listed above), it took two more years to develop the first public strategy (RNIB 1987). This gave us time to gain wider contribution, involvement and buy-in from staff and from trustees – a process greatly aided by an external consultant, Liam Walsh. Bob Empson of Whitemaple was another external consultant who greatly helped us with marketing advice.

So, the core of the strategy was the group of policy guidelines which were transmuted through debate and consultation into policy directives in a strategy (RNIB 1987) and used fairly rigorously to steer investment of time and money into existing and new activities of RNIB between 1985 and 1993.

The First Strategy (RNIB 1987)

The key points of *Meeting the Needs of Visually Handicapped People: The RNIB Strategy* included the following ones below. The original text is quoted despite the language occasionally appearing arcane to today's reader.

What and How?

There were three aims:

- To achieve significant improvement in the self-determination and quality of life of visually handicapped people.
- To combat discrimination and help visually handicapped people integrate into society on equal terms with sighted people.
- To work towards preventing blindness.

The difference in emphasis of the above in comparison to what had preceded it was a greater focus on rights and self-determination.

There were three methods:

- Services
- Campaigns
- Prevention.

Here there was a significantly increased focus on campaigning complementing the rights approach. More campaigning activity was welcomed among the top trustee leadership but was initially less welcome among the wider NFB and NLBD. They had long subscribed to a model of the RNIB as the service provider with the two of them as the (sole) representatives of blind people lobbying and campaigning for change.

Even more specific changes in approach were signalled under nine policy directives in the strategy which were a distillation of the guidelines mentioned earlier.

Policy Directives – How Should We Develop and Change?

1. To be centred even more closely around the needs of visually handicapped people. This will be achieved by consumer research and representation, by a clearer definition of consumer groups, and by more effective promotion of RNIB products and services – a social marketing approach.

(RNIB had a long tradition of blind people's leadership in policy creation through governance. Implementation and delivery of services mostly did not feel like that. There was a well-established feeling of 'as professionals, we know best' – a pervasive view at the time in the social welfare charity sector. With the full backing of senior trustees, and, to a lesser extent, senior managers, this policy directive was the new chief executive putting a marker down about how he wanted 'things done around here'. A marketing philosophy – start with consumers not producers – and the use of marketing tools became widespread inside RNIB but it took much longer to achieve than I realised it would. The conclusion I would draw here in terms of strategic planning is that fundamental cultural change – in this context putting people with sight loss at the centre of things – is easy to announce, quite hard to put in place in procedural terms, and enormously difficult to gain genuine ownership of. Strange as it may now seem, back then most charities did not say or do this, such an approach did not become widespread till the late 1990s.)

2. To reach more and a wider range of visually handi-capped people, in particular, older as well as younger,

multi-handicapped as well as single handicapped, ethnic minorities as well as the majority, and those with low vision as well as those who are totally blind.

(These target groups were ones that we had identified as being significantly under-represented in our customer profile. The most contentious of the above was the 'extension' into partial sight/low vision. The dominant perceived typical customer in RNIB service delivery and fundraising was someone who was totally blind. Partially sighted people were seen as having far fewer needs, a common-sense assumption which was proved wrong by subsequent research, quite apart from the fact that the majority of registered blind people have some residual vision.)

3. To meet a wider range of identified needs by maintaining our traditional interests but also adding new areas such as health, leisure, electronic technology, welfare benefits and exerting influence on those who draw up and implement policies affecting visually handicapped people.

(This paragraph in the strategy listed key areas that needed to be invested in to take advantage of external change and signalled greater emphasis on lobbying.)

4. To promote properly resourced and supported integration of visually handicapped people into the wider community on the basis of rights, responsibilities and equality of citizenship through combating stereotypes, promoting positive images and supporting mutual aid.

(This was a crucial development of philosophy. What was then called integration and later called inclusion had always been accepted for adult blind people, but RNIB was split on this issue in relation to education of younger people, with the internal majority view preferring separate specialist education.

This guideline needed a lot of negotiation but proved to be fundamentally influential not least because it was becoming the widespread view externally. Strong leadership had to be exerted by a small but powerful group of trustees led by Colin Low. It formed the basis of our developing vision and mission.)

5. To continue to offer effective direct services to visually handicapped people but to respond to changing customer needs ...

(This was a reassurance to the majority of staff that traditional direct services would continue but with a warning that they had to evolve.)

6. To increase the number and scale of our indirect services so as to improve support to visually handicapped people through the statutory, voluntary and commercial sectors and via the informal sector – family, neighbours and friends.

(This was another major statement of intent of a move into indirect service provision which became a major driver of action.)

7. To give more encouragement and support to local initiatives.

(RNIB had a long tradition of joint fundraising with local societies for the blind – through the unification agreement whereby funds raised locally by RNIB were shared between ourselves and the local society – but support and co-operation regarding local service delivery was less in evidence.)

8. To take an even more positive lead in innovation, pioneering and co-ordination work.
9. To increase our work in helping to prevent visual handicap.

(RNIB's contribution on prevention had been primarily through modest funding of medical research into the prevention of blindness. This policy directive paved the way for substantial public education campaigns advising people on how they could reduce the risks of sight loss. It also became the start of our eventual move into not only low vision aids but also optometry.)

Resource Directives – to Help Us Change

Although under-recognised in the literature, implementation of strategy is key to strategy success or failure. We developed five resource directives to give us the organisational strength to change.

To carry out the policy directives listed above and so better meet the needs of visually handicapped people, it would be necessary to achieve significant growth within RNIB during the decade to 1995:

1. For growth to be successful it must be planned with care and founded on a secure financial base. It is therefore imperative to seek ways of raising more statutory and voluntary income.
2. RNIB's key resource – people – will require training and new opportunities for personal development. RNIB will rely on the professionalism and adaptability of committee members (trustees and staff. …
3. Within RNIB, suitable organisation and committee structures are essential to support our new directives. …
4. Both internal and external channels of communication will need review and development … achieving a major increase in public awareness.
5. Divisional and service objectives will require review in the light of the policy directives, while associated qualitative and quantitative targets will be set to aid service evaluation and monitor progress.

The first resource directive was important because RNIB then had a fear of over-extending itself financially and so some caution about growth.

Previously, it was less obvious that RNIB needed to invest in staff and staff development to achieve success, hence, directive number two. Fortunately, we recruited profession-als (such as Jill Rosenheim, Ken Lavey, Alison Beesley, Viv Oxley, Jenny Collis, Carole Buckton, Deborah Jack and others) whose professional human resources practices convinced sympathetic senior managers and trustees. As chief execu-tive, I was keen that all key managers should have marketing training. That keenness expanded into full management training in 1989 with an externally validated, in-house, taught Certificate in Management Studies (CMS) rolled out widely across RNIB. To my knowledge, RNIB was one of the first charities to do this.

It was not only staff we invested in but also organisational capacity, hence, the third resource directive. Support of trustee committees was crucial through: the committee secretariat led so ably by Margaret Alexander and, before her, Mary Bell and, later, by James Rogers and supported by long-standing committee secretaries such as Pat Aylott, Christine Parker, Shirley Gadsden, Helen Mackenzie and Rob Powell; and the secretarial support unit, headed by Dany Luchmun with colleagues such as Jane Peek, Dorinne Mudlamootoo-Facey, Kalpna Shah, Kawal Kaur, Erica Brothers, Vicky Luchmun. Other departments which acted as unsung heroes of the development programmes were estates with Paul Hunt and Robin Mann, finance with Paul Clark and Tony Fazakerley and auditor Ian Andrew, and administration under Pat MacDonald functioning alongside with Ken Lavey and his human resources team mentioned above.

What Action Resulted –
Strategy Implementation

So, what were the practical expansion activities and how did we facilitate the implementation of the strategy?

Examples of the strategic expansion into new direct services:

- Information Technology Unit (1983)
- Benefits Rights Office (1985)
- Braille, large print and audio bank statement service (1986)
- Community Education Unit (1987)
- Support scheme and vacation course scheme for visually impaired children in mainstream education (1989)
- Northern Ireland Service Bureau (1985).

Examples of the strategic expansion into new indirect services:

- Parliamentary Office (1984)
- Integration Advice Service (1984)
- Social Services Consultancy Unit (1985)
- Health Services Development Unit (1985)
- Support Unit for local societies for the blind (1985)
- Ethnic Minorities Officer (1987)
- Arts and Museums Officer (1987)
- Sports Officer (1988)
- Accommodation Officer (1989)
- Integrated Education Service (1989)
- European Office (1990).

Examples of expansion arising from the resource directives are:

- A marketing advisory unit
- Development of the personnel/human resources function
- Expansion of the press office for awareness and campaigns
- A major survey of the numbers, needs and wishes of blind and partially sighted people.

Moreover, while the number and range of the new services rightly seems large, there were an equal number of projects to rejuvenate and invest in existing services, particularly the rebuilding, relocation and refurbishment of long-standing direct services. These were not just 'more of the same', they were imaginative leaps, for example: RNIB New College became co-educational, in mixed cross-age family houses

Chorleywood school for girls.

At co-ed New College, family homes with houseparents replaced dormitories.

rather than single sex dormitories; the fulfilment of Fred Reid's concept of the commercial college rebuilt and integrated into a mainstream college in Loughborough, 100 miles north of its previous London location. There was also a commitment to shift services out of London and the southeast towards the north, including Scotland.

The largest projects (in 1988 prices) were:

- The rebuild of Worcester College (boys – principal, Bob Manthorp) site for merger with Chorleywood College (girls – principal, Peggy Markes); the project started in 1987 and was completed in 1989; the school was renamed RNIB New College – £5 million (13 per cent of annual expenditure at the time)
- The move of the Commercial College (principal, Stan Bell) in London to the newly built college in Loughborough linked innovatively to, and on the campus of, a mainstream college; started 1987, completed 1988 – £5 million
- The relocation of braille and other production and distribution from London to Peterborough (leaders, Maurice Wright and Chris Day); started 1987, completed 1990 – £6 million
- The purchase of a site and complete rebuild of Hethersett to form RNIB Redhill College, completed 1991 (principal, Dr Mike Rowe) – £5 million
- Rehabilitation Centre, Torquay (heads, Brian Hewitt and Don Jackson) – £2 million
- RNIB Sunshine House School at Northwood (heads Kay Dunford and Maureen Walker [now Manthorp]) – £1 million
- Scottish Multi-handicapped Visually Impaired Centre, Glasgow (pioneered by Frances Miller) – £1 million
- Garrow House, accommodation for job seekers (headed by Jon Barrick) – £1 million

- A new block for deaf-blind young people opened at Condover School, Shropshire (principal, Tony Jarvis); completed 1989
- Other projects including: the service centre established in Stirling in Scotland in 1987 (led by Allan Murray) and in Belfast in Northern Ireland in 1989 (Mike McIlwrath); recording studios for Student Tape Library opened in six different regional sites across the United Kingdom between 1986 and 1989 (Dr Chris Smith).

Implementing this massive development programme between 1987 and 1992 (totalling £40 million or 100 per cent of then annual expenditure) was a major challenge and several structural and procedural changes were put in place:

- A development programme co-ordinator post (accountable to the director general), wholly dedicated to facilitating programme implementation, was created and ably filled by Elizabeth Twining. Twining, the director of finance (Barry Gifford, a vitally important figure in the strategy) and I met frequently to monitor and encourage implementation and to identify issues. The management committee, chaired by me as director general and consisting of all five staff directors, met weekly on a Monday morning. It was the management focal point for all corporate issues and major single issues and had regular discussions of the strategy to recognise progress and suggest solutions to problems. For most of the strategy (1987 to 1994) this committee consisted

A deafblind student at Redhill College learns recipes – language through touch.

of: Tony Aston, director of vocational and social services; Tony Lenney (followed by Paul Ennals), director of education and leisure; Maurice Wright (followed by Stephen King), director of technical consumer services; Mike Lancaster, director of external relations; Barry Gifford, director of finance and administration; and Margaret Alexander, head of committee secretariat.

- The Policy and Resources Committee (of trustees – a strengthened committee combining several responsibilities including those of Policy and Selection Committee featured in Chapter 1a) also regularly reviewed progress and was fundamental in the original development of the strategy (it comprised the RNIB chair, Sir Duncan Watson, and his fellow chairs of RNIB standing committees, as well as representatives of organisations of blind people).
- Some 80 to 120 RNIB managers were involved in strategy creation, implementation and evaluation, including through biennial residential conferences in 1985, 1987, 1989 and 1991.
- There were comprehensive reviews of successes and failures in 1988 and 1993 (RNIB 1988 and RNIB 1993).

This degree of professionalism will seem normal to readers now but in those days in the charity sector it was not. I brought the idea of strategic planning across from local government and we recruited a strategy consultant (Liam Walsh) who helped us particularly in the later stages. When Elizabeth Twining left, she was succeeded by Steve Cooper, who set up a strategic planning unit that proved critical to our future successes.

However, at the end of the day, the plans were implemented because of enthusiastic and capable front-line managers and workers getting the work done.

Factors For and Against Success

There were a number of factors working in favour of successful implementation:

- RNIB had uncommitted revenue and capital monies it could put into the programme.
- The majority of managers were either open minded or positively wanting a new way forward because of what were perceived to be quite a few previous years of modest development.
- As the incoming chief executive, I was given a very free hand by the honorary officers and trustees.
- Many of these proposed changes were bringing us into line with changes in the external social welfare environment and/or areas of the external environment very relevant to us which had not been exploited before (e.g. health services).
- There was also widespread senior and middle management and trustee involvement and a lot of communication activity – certainly more than in the past.
- Many of the buildings housing services were patently out of date and unfit for purpose especially our schools and colleges.
- The poor condition of our buildings, often in constrained positions (tightly packed London sites) favoured moving to new, rather than refurbishing old. This allowed us to move some services out of London and the south-east where we were over-represented to other parts of the UK (for example, Peterborough, Loughborough, Worcester, Glasgow, Belfast etc.). In the five years, 1989 to 1994, the percentage of spend and staff in the London region dropped from around 30 per cent to fifteen per cent.

Factors working against the new strategic approach were:

- Some trustees and a minority of staff were very much opposed to change.
- From other trustees there was quite a head of steam to 'get on with things and stop all this discussion and research' and 'we brought this new director general in from the outside to move things fast and all he wants is to debate'. If we had moved too quickly, the development programme would have inevitably favoured the improvement of existing activity (to the detriment of new directions).
- There inevitably was similar frustration among some staff for the eighteen-month delay that research, feasibility studies and staff involvement required.
- When the new development programme was finalised, financial investment was not always wholly congruent with the strategy because in any quasi-democratic, participative organisation different vested interests and passions play an important part. (For example, there were many reasons favouring our two single sex grammar schools merging on the Worcester site rather than the Chorleywood site just north of London. However, the presence of so many more old boys from the Worcester school on the trustee board than old girls from Chorleywood made the difficult decision easier to achieve but left the excellent and pioneering head of Chorleywood feeling under-represented).
- Traditional financial strategy favoured one-off capital investment (e.g. in buildings) which had fewer long-term revenue burdens, whereas we needed to shift towards revenue-dependent indirect services (e.g. training mainstream teachers how to educate blind children appropriately). Barry Gifford as

director of finance came up with a helpful bridging formula of drawing down sizeable pots of money from reserves to be spent as revenue over longer periods of years, typically three.

- There was very little identification of quantitative targets. All the directives were essentially directional and so, when we came to the first review of progress in 1988, it was a matter of qualitative judgement as to whether we felt we had succeeded or not. We corrected this in the next strategy.

Implementing strategy is always much harder than developing the plan. In the main, implementation went well but there were challenges. For example, the loss of so many staff experienced in Braille production in the move from London to Peterborough had a devastating effect on braille output for the first six months or more. One of my regular, more uncomfortable, moments was trying to explain to RNIB Executive Council why the weekly Braille Radio Times was late yet again! However, as the staff gained experience output rapidly doubled from London levels under the leadership of Maurice Wright, Chris Day and John Godber.

This points up sacrifices which were imposed. The geographic relocations (for example, Chorleywood School to Worcester, Commercial College London to Loughborough, Braille House Islington to Peterborough) meant we lost many skilled and experienced staff who did not want to/ could not move. In the case of Braille House in Islington, the losses included a significant proportion of blind workers – and this was despite us negotiating some good social housing agreements with Peterborough Council. However, the geographic disbursement made us less London-centric (as mentioned above, halving London staff numbers from 30 per cent to 15 per cent of a total staff of just over 3,000), as well as reaching out more across England, Scotland, Wales and Northern Ireland.

New presses installed at Peterborough in 1989 printed a world-leading 40,000 braille pages per hour.

Reviewing Our Implementation – Crucial for 'Buy-in'

Did the plans stay on paper? Our first review entitled *RNIB Growth and Development: Corporate Strategy Review 1988* was over 400 pages long. The length partly answers the question, 'How do you get those on the front line of delivery to own this fundamentally new strategy?' – by asking them to write their own mini review of their unit's contribution to the strategy (which is then moderated). Including their own reviews in the overall document gives them recognition for their work. In my experience getting the front line to own a strategy is a far bigger challenge than the superficial solutions offered by the textbooks would suggest. In this case the review gave us the following:

- We now had lots of hard data for analysis which led to actions that would not have happened otherwise.

- It helped us to be more quantitative in our subsequent targeting for the remaining five years of this strategy – that is, we could extrapolate and change gear where necessary.
- It helped us to identify additional areas for investment if the strategy was to be achieved (for example, voluntary fundraising) – that is, the review identified omissions in the strategy.
- For the first time we were able to include other player (competitor) analysis in a review which put us in a more realistic context than simply judging against ourselves.

Strategy reviews are crucial for wider staff engagement (staff see their work recognised), sometimes more so than involvement in strategy creation.

Conclusion – Major, Planned Change Implemented

RNIB was one of the first large charities to adopt a strategic planning process. We started our journey in 1984 with the service reviews (arguably with the Sunningdale residential conference in 1980), policy guidelines in 1985, policy directives in 1986 and the published strategy in 1987 – *Meeting the Needs of Visually Handicapped People: The RNIB Strategy.* Although I made some early attempts at strategy at the Volunteer Centre England in the 1970s (later called Volunteering England, now absorbed into NCVO), RNIB was my first opportunity in a large service delivery charity to use some of the ideas I had been inducted into in Unilever and local government. Nevertheless, the pioneering nature of what we were doing in the charity world was only brought home to me in 1988 when we were visited by George Medley, chief executive of World Wildlife Fund (WWF). Medley had been a keen strategic planner in the business world of agrichemicals and he had been active in the Strategic Planning Society for some years. On joining WWF, he had searched extensively for other charities using this approach but told me we were the only one he had come across apart from WWF. Certainly, the approach was pretty alien inside RNIB in those days and many were sceptical, not unreasonably, given the damage which mechanistic planning can inflict on a passionate organisation (which thankfully we managed to avoid).

The end result was that the 1980s was a decade of fundamental change for RNIB. Butler and Wilson (1990) in an influential, in-depth study of charity management in 31 of the largest 200 charities, describe these changes in RNIB as: 'radical responses to pressures on the organisation from both within and from the immediate external environment' (p. 151).

They described Christian Aid and RNIB (two of the 31 charities studied) as follows: 'these organisations were effectively shaken by the scruffs of their necks and catapulted into new strategic directions alongside the adoption of their new structures' (pp. 151-52).

During the decade three services were closed (two Sunshine House Schools, Leamington and East Grinstead, and the social rehabilitation centre at Clifton Spinney). Closures are particularly problematic for charities, because they nearly always hurt vulnerable people in the short term. However:

- Twenty new services were created, approximately one third direct and two thirds indirect.
- Output of direct services increased very substantially and indirect services massively.
- Campaigning changed from being an exceptional activity to a regular one.
- Income over the decade rose substantially from £10 million per year in 1980 to £39 million per year in 1989 (plus 56 per cent in real terms), a rise achieved by equal attention to growth of both voluntary income (e.g. donations) and earned income (e.g. local authorities paying us for services we delivered). This rise increased RNIB's share of

total income in all of the following income markets: the 20 largest British charities; the fifteen largest social welfare charities; the fifteen largest disability charities; and the seven largest blindness charities (RNIB 1993 and Bruce 1987).

- The investment into the strategy was large, over £40 million in 1988 prices or the equivalent of 100 per cent of annual expenditure.
- Most important of all, the numbers of blind and partially people served directly by RNIB doubled to 170,000 (RNIB 1993, Table 8.2b) and the numbers benefitting from RNIB campaigning exploded.

Chapter 2b

Far-reaching Change

Services – Established and New

So, overall, what were the services and their comparative outputs during the 1980s? Figures are not available for the end of the decade, but output for the year ending March 1988 compared to the year ending March 1980 (in parentheses) taken from the relevant annual reports is as follows:

- over 1,000 (181) new braille titles
- 81 (64) new braille music titles
- 39,000 (56,000) Moon books, pamphlets and periodicals
- 67,000 (54,000) Talking Book Service members (1969/70 – 26,000)
- 341 (411) children in RNIB schools and assessment centres
- 32 (35) students at RNIB's school of physiotherapy
- 23 (25) orientation and mobility instructors trained
- 870 (200) students supported in higher education
- 289 (400) people attended RNIB rehabilitation centres
- 170 (259) blind people helped to find jobs
- 88 (147) self-employed people supported in homeworking schemes

- 131 (131) in RNIB residential homes
- 5,196 (6,000) holidays taken at RNIB hotels.

In summary, services which were not provided in an integrated setting or service, declined or at best were static. Services provided in an integrated setting expanded, with the exception of those for homeworkers.

Of the many new services, several took off like rockets – for example, the Benefits Rights Unit (run by Nigel Pegram, Andy Barrick, Laura Jacobs and Howard Lewis), which gave benefits advice which put more money into the pockets of thousands of blind and partially sighted people by the end of the decade. Another success story was the newly formed advisory unit for families and staff serving multi-

The newly built RNIB Vocational College Loughborough, collocated with a mainstream FE college.

handicapped visually impaired (MHVI) adults – the Low Vision Unit which mutated out of the Health Unit. Others struggled, such as the social services and health service consultancies where there were successes but fee-income-led expansion proved difficult to achieve. In those days, health and local authorities did not expect and were not used to paying consultancy fees to outside agencies in the voluntary sector. We anticipated a trend but were a little early. Other notable service developments of the decade included: the opening in 1989 of the RNIB Vocational College, led by Stan Bell; the revitalising of computerised distribution of talking books based at Wembley, led by

Harry Walton; taking on the Express Reading Service (fast turn-around transcription onto tape using teams of volunteer readers for one book), developed independently and very successfully by Wendy Davies who joined us to become a senior manager, supported by Mandy White; the Thomson Auto Braille press; a unit at Rushton pioneered by Robert Orr for visually impaired young people with severe behavioural problems (profound and multiple learning difficulties); regional tape centres and the near doubling of student text titles to over 1,200 per year, led by Chris Smith; publications in Asian languages, championed by Gladwell Msimang and the Talking Book Service; taking on a new employment rehabilitation centre in Scotland; the school of physiotherapy (principal, David Teager) gaining degree accreditation for its physiotherapy course; and more technical aids such as the telescopic white cane and the vibrating alarm (for deaf-blind people).

One major policy development of the middle 1980s was RNIB extension into partial sight. Language and practice up to the 1980s was largely 'blind people'. There was recognition that many people had some residual vision and that someone could have talking books if they could not read N12 (or 12 pt) print. However, the words 'partially sighted' were practically taboo in RNIB. Arising out of policy guideline two (RNIB [interest] should span the whole range of concerns of visually impaired people) came the recognition that we should be serving many partially sighted people. Also, the early results of the needs survey of blind and partially sighted adults in Britain (Bruce *et al.* 1991) revealed the large number and the extent of need amongst this group. So, gradually a view formed that, where we could, we should serve partially sighted people. This view was opposed by one or two senior staff and trustees as being unconstitutional. The situation was

RNIB School of Physiotherapy gains degree accreditation.

difficult. However, as part of a review of the constitution, we found that the RNIB charter allowed us to serve people who were 'partially or intermittently blind' and in 1987 the Executive Council confirmed that the partially sighted were part of our beneficiary group. It enraged the Partially Sighted Society, which felt we were improperly stepping on their patch. However, for years they had struggled to raise money and employ staff and did not have the capacity at that time to deliver any major services. They did involve an active core of partially sighted people and it was a pity that we alienated them. It took many years to build bridges. While the decision was firmly backed by the blind trustee leadership, quite a few of the blind backbenchers on the 100-strong Executive Council were anxious that the decision would suck resources away from services to totally blind people.

Campaigning – Brave Beginnings

RNIB's moves to open itself up in the 1980s are nowhere so apparent as in the campaigning area. There were an increasing number of reports and surveys which were powerful springboards for publicity and lobbying, such as:

- *Who Are Britain's Blind People?* (1982)
- The survey of the needs of visually impaired pupils in mainstream education (1984)
- The joint survey with the Consumers Association on spectacle usage (1985)
- *Visually Handicapped Workers in Local Government* (1985)
- *Out of Isolation: On Multi-handicapped Visually Impaired Adults* (1987)
- *Directory of Accessible Museums* (1987)
- *Sport and Leisure* (1987)
- *Vision in the Classroom* (1987).

There were also the planned campaigns, far more numerous than in the previous decade. Crucial to these were the newly created parliamentary officers, first Hugh Lawrence, then Gill Tishler (later head of public affairs) working with the knowledgeable subject specialists, such as Louise Clunies-Ross, Marcus Weisen, Gill Levy, Penny Shore, Cedric Garland, Chris Attrill, Carolyn Wardrop-White and Gill Whitney. These campaigns were springboards for media coverage and awareness raising, which Lucille Hall, Pat Orr and Nicky Garsten (Garsten and Bruce 2018) and their teams used to great effect, doubling our coverage in the late 1980s/ early 1990s.

One of the most important campaign successes came in 1982 when the government set up the Personal Reader Service, a scheme which they asked RNIB to administer. This is where blind people of working age are given money to pay for people to read important documents to them – a major recognition of, and help towards, the extra the costs of blindness.

The successful campaign to change safety regulations to allow blind people to go to the cinema unaccompanied caught the imagination of the general public as well as blind people. We argued that a blind person would be more skilled than a sighted one in getting out of a pitch dark, smoke-filled auditorium.

The campaign on 'money' vouchers for glasses costs was one of our first steps into the then taboo areas of optometry and ophthalmology, territory where hallowed professionals reigned supreme.

This decade also saw a diminution in the RNIB's 'go it alone' approach. Since 1970 other charities had grown in influence both within the blindness world and the disability world generally. For example, Sense, the National Deafblind and Rubella Association, was initially regarded with annoyance by many in RNIB as an upstart organisation. However, by 1983 RNIB had come round and was prepared to join the National Rubella Campaign as a co-founder.

Another example of RNIB reaching an accommodation was on financial benefits. The single-minded blindness financial allowance campaign of RNIB, NFB and NLBD was facing growing hostility from outside. Many within the campaign suspected other disability groups of having 'knifed them in the back' when the Labour Party withdrew its previous public commitment to a blindness allowance. My view after a year or so into the job was that we had to pursue our aims within a pan-disability setting rather than go it alone. In the mid 1980s, Amanda Jordan of Scope (then the Spastics Society) and I started gradually bringing the four income-interested pan-disability groups together – namely, the Disability Alliance, the Disability Income Group (DIG), the British Council of Disabled People (BCODP) and the Royal Association for Disability and Rehabilitation (RADAR). It was a slow exercise – such were the fiery personalities and suspicions – but in 1988 we launched the national Disability Benefits Consortium (DBC) with Richard Wood, a wheelchair user of BCODP, and me as founding co-chairs. RNIB provided the secretariat and the other disability service charities provided help on an as-and-when-needed basis (Mencap, Mind, Action on Hearing Loss/ RNID, Scope and later Leonard Cheshire – Once the latter organisation had settled its differences with BCODP.) This was one of the better RNIB strategic positioning choices of my time and laid the foundation for our winning a *de facto* blindness allowance in the early 1990s in the form of the Disability Living Allowance available to blind people of working age.

All the above work relates to the United Kingdom. What about Europe and the wider world? RNIB work in the European Union started in the mid 1980s through the tenacity of one trustee, Tom Parker, but that story really belongs to the next chapter. However, RNIB's influence in world blind politics had a huge boost in the 1980s through RNIB chair Duncan Watson's committed leadership. As one of the world's largest blindness charities (after those of Spain and Russia), RNIB has always played a key international role. Our previous heyday was the late 1940s/early 1950s when one of my predecessors, John Colligan, took a lead role in founding the World Council for the Welfare of the Blind. However, for well over 20 years that organisation had been challenged by an international organisation 'of' the blind, the International Federation of the Blind (IFB). Quite a few of our mainland European counterparts were members of both bodies and in the early 1980s, although there was much talk of co-operation and even merger, there was little to show.

Then, in August 1984, came a conference run by the European Committee of the World Council 'for' the Welfare of the Blind in Hurdal in Norway which had many of the 'of' leaders present. Arne Husveg of the Norwegian Association of the Blind and Partially Sighted was a skilled chair but there was little enthusiasm for concrete action. Early in the four-day conference, Duncan Watson got into determined mood and rounded up a small team to campaign for a merger decision at the conference. Looking back, it might seem obvious but, for example, at the time it was Tom Parker's view that it was too early and would not be achieved – and Parker was one of our most experienced internationalists and was committed to merger. He had reason for doubt in that organisational mergers are always difficult enough in one country and this involved organisations across Europe. After intense lobbying, and, ultimately, a lot of exhaustion, in the final session there was an overwhelming agreement: first, to dissolve the two European committees of the two competing 'of' and 'for' organisations; and, second, to create the unified European Blind Union. Even more extraordinary, this momentum continued, driven by Duncan Watson and others and two months later the same thing happened at the world level: the World Blind Union (WBU) was created in October 1984 at the World Council for the Welfare of the Blind in Saudi Arabia with Duncan Watson and his RNIB team playing a key role.

The first president of the World Blind Union was Sheikh Abdullah M. Al-Ghanim from Saudi Arabia, and Duncan Watson became the second president some three years later at the triennial conference in Madrid where I was his campaign manager.

People – New Professionals

So, who were the people behind all these developments?

In 1980 the deputy director general, Eddie Venn, was appointed the new director general. He immediately formulated a more planned approach to development for which he had all the right qualifications and experience. As a chartered secretary and administrator, he had local government experience before becoming a reforming general secretary of the Royal Leicester and Rutland Institute for the Blind. During his 25 years at RNIB, he had played lead roles in many initiatives such as: the introduction of computerised braille production and the

Talking Book member, ex PM Rt Hon Harold Macmillan, meets Eddie Venn Director General and a Sunshine House School student in 1982.

move of braille production out of Great Portland Street into Braille House in Islington; introducing computer programming as a career for blind people; helping establish the Midlands Mobility Centre and in getting the long white cane introduced in the United Kingdom. As industrial manager, he had been responsible for various units, Rehabilitation Training and Placement into Employment, Special Aids to Employment, Home Industries, as well as the kiosk managers' scheme and social and welfare advice to blind people. He organised the first *Survey of Blind People in Professional and Technical Employment*, which brought forth a wealth of information on which to help build that strand of the placement service. He initiated a management trainee scheme for young blind people. In his part of RNIB, the majority of service managers and officers were visually impaired, including the heads of rehab centres and training college and placement officers.

The tragedy was that by 1983, just three years into the job, he had to retire through ill health. Nevertheless, during that short time under his leadership RNIB had achieved its ground-breaking Sunningdale Conference and had reached four of its main decisions of the decade, namely, to commit a total of £10 million to build a new commercial training college, to modernise the employment rehabilitation centre in Torquay, to modernise the Talking Book Service and to merge our two residential grammar schools.

Working with Eddie Venn were the trustees, ably led throughout the decade by Duncan Watson as chair with his loyal and mercurial deputy chair, John Wall. While most of the leading trustees remained the same as described in the last chapter, they were joined by a new second treasurer, Jack Dunn, who proved a very safe pair of hands during a period of rapid change.

When Venn became director general, George Willson became his deputy. (This was a wise choice because he commanded the respect of many of the powerful blind trustees.) Barry Gifford as finance secretary was to be the lynchpin over the next 25 years, making money and other resources work for the cause. Tony Aston led on employment and brought his creative vision and drive and personal experience of blindness. Maurice Wright and, latterly, Stephen King on tactile media, tape and technical aids brought immense industrial management wisdom. Neville

PM Margaret Thatcher hears how a pocket tape recorder helps a blind boy study – with Ian Bruce at RNIB Northwood school party.

Lawson, education, contributed a very knowledgeable pair of hands and a literary and oral eloquence which guided schools and their boards of governors forward. Lucille Hall brought press and publicity into the foreground. Later, Tony Lenney, after many years as a young director of education in a local education authority, would bring additional credibility and leadership to the integration of blind and partially sighted children into mainstream education; joined, latterly, by Mike Lancaster, with his commercial experience of running inter-city trains as well as his preparedness to challenge shibboleths. Altogether, they formed a powerful team. It now seems shocking that only one, Lucille Hall, was a woman.

My recruitment as director general in November 1983 reflected the RNIB trustee leadership's desire for change. Having started as an apprentice chemical engineer with Courtaulds, I changed direction at university, studying economics, politics and sociology, joining Unilever as a marketing management trainee on a Unilever Companies Management Development Scheme (UCMDS). After completing this and playing roles in brand management on Comfort fabric conditioner and Knight's Castile soap, I joined the charity sector, relaunching the National Old People's Welfare Council as Age Concern, becoming CEO of Volunteering England. After a spell as assistant chief executive of a London borough, I arrived at RNIB at the age of 38. Two months before my arrival, Duncan Watson wrote about the prospect of the new director general, 'bringing challenging new ideas. It is likely that under his leadership we will move more into the mainstream of the voluntary sector' (Annual Report 1982/83, p. 7).

Certainly, my previous experience in the statutory, voluntary and commercial sectors and my passion for a fundamental needs-led marketing approach was to stand me in good stead in helping RNIB come into that mainstream. The trustees, and, in particular, the leading ones, were very positive. The partnership with Duncan Watson was extremely important to me. He gave me support and scope. Tom Parker, chair of the Vocational and Social Services Committee was initially sceptical of this 'young' appointee who knew nothing about blindness. However, we rapidly became professional partners (and, subsequently, friends) bound in our belief in the importance of RNIB becoming influential in Brussels. Other trustee leaders on whom I lent very heavily in this decade were John Wall, Colin Low, Fred Reid and Bill Poole but virtually all the trustees were unfailingly welcoming of a young (38 was young for RNIB), committed, new CEO – even some of those from the organisations of the blind such as Jill Allen King, Wyn O'Grady, Wally Kinder and Hans Cohn – who prided themselves on keeping RNIB on its toes.

I was very conscious of the case for appointing a blind chief executive but my appointment committee of six (five of whom were blind) had no such qualms. To counter my concern, my request for an executive assistant, where a qualification for the job was to be blind, helped a great deal. First came David Mann, then Roger Firman, Peter Bosher, Anne Gosch and, finally, Martin Milligan. In additional support was Betty Brown my long-time secretary. All of them were comrades and they blind-proofed my activities. They were not afraid to call me out, thankfully, in private.

So, I was fortunate to be surrounded by blind people, my chair, vice chair, executive assistant, secretary and normally two of the six senior management team. I always tried to reach out to any blind and partially sighted people I met. Building links to the National Federation of the Blind and the National League of the Blind and Disabled, as the two premier organisations of the blind, was particularly important. I attended their meetings and sometimes their annual residential conferences. Once, Tina, my wife, and our two young children came with me and Hannah and Tom became the delegates' favourites by taking a stream of guide dogs out at lunchtime for a walk. One of my favourite meet ups was monthly on a Friday evening around nine o'clock when the NFB London branch had finished its meeting in RNIB. I would leave work and gatecrash their get-together afterwards in the Albany pub at the top of Great Portland Street. I not only felt welcome, I learned a lot.

RNIB President, the Duke of Westminster, being shown the Talking Books research and repair workshop.

Presidents can be figureheads or even ciphers but for the first half of the decade as president we had the colourful Duke of Devonshire, who was an active fundraiser through his racing connections. He was followed between 1987 and 2011 by the Duke of Westminster who was not only a good fundraiser and so generous with his time, visiting services across the country, he was also wise and had good judgement on our work.

By the end of the decade staff numbered approximately 3,000 of whom between four and five per cent were blind or partially sighted.

Resources – More Income but More Spend

In comparison to the modest growth of the 1970s, the 1980s was more vigorous. In 1979/80 annual expenditure (to end March 1980) was £35.1 million growing to £54.7 million in 1989/90, both in constant 2004 prices – in other words RNIB grew by 56 per cent in real terms in the decade in comparison to 11 per cent in the 1970s.

It can be seen that the proportional split between voluntary income and fees for services delivered (paid for mainly by the

Table 2b.1. RNIB Income 1969/70-1989/90

Income (£ millions)	1969/70	1979/80	1989/90
Fees for service	1.16	4.7	14.3
Voluntary income	1.61	6.25	19.9
Investment income	0.16	0.73	2.7
Other	0.13	0	0
Total	3.04	11.68	36.9
TOTAL at constant 2004 prices	31.7	35.1	54.7
Percentage growth, real terms		+11%	+56%
TOTAL at constant 2004 prices, base 100[1]	100	111	173

[1] UK RPI via the Cleave Calculator

state but partly by individuals) remained roughly the same as it was in the 1970s. The earned income growth from £4.7 million to £14.3 million at the end of the decade represents a real growth of 50 per cent at constant prices. This was no mean feat during a period of Conservative government when public expenditure was being severely constrained, which made it that much harder to raise our fees from local authorities for Talking Book memberships and attendances at our schools.

The reviews of services in the mid 1980s had put into sharp relief the high subsidies (from voluntary income) which we were putting into many of our essential services which were the state's responsibility to fund, for example, schools and, arguably, talking books (a library service) etc. Many of our donors did not want their donations bailing out the state. Equally as important, every failure to recoup £1 expenditure from fee income was £1 less voluntary income for us to spend on discretionary areas of spend – that is, on non-statutory areas of responsibility. In other words, less to spend, for example, on pressure group work and campaigning which are capable of very high returns of benefit for blind and partially sighted people. So, the policy decision was made to become quite aggressive in achieving and raising fee (earned) income wherever we could, primarily where statutory organisations were paying the fees. One of the biggest success areas was the Talking Books Service. Under Stephen King's pioneering guidance, supported by others, we raised the percentage of our costs recovered by fees paid by local authorities from 40 per cent in 1980 to 71 per cent in 1990. At the same time, our membership grew from 54,000 to 67,000. So, we put the price up and increased the number of customers – a feat equalled by only a very small percentage of commercial businesses. We achieved this by raising the price to cover all direct costs, which meant we could promote the service aggressively and recruit more members. In the past this was impossible because the more members we recruited the more money we 'lost', that is, we had to find the increasing cost from donors.

If that was the position of fee (earned) income, how was it with voluntary income (legacies, local and national fundraising etc.)? The growth over the decade was spectacular, trebling in cash terms. However, that hides several ups and downs within the total. Legacies performed spectacularly and we can only speculate as to why this was. First, RNIB was very well known locally through its local field fundraisers which must have gained us legacies. Also, the doubling of blind and partially sighted people served by RNIB in the decade must have spread the word. We were one of the first charities to be very active in legacy marketing, starting in the early 1980s with Barry Gifford's apocryphal leaflet to encourage leaving a legacy to the RNIB, *What Can We Do with Granny's Old Armchair?* This paved the way for a sophisticated marketing plan commencing in 1986. RNIB has continued to be one of the top legacy-marketing charities.

Nevertheless, non-legacy voluntary income, sometimes called fundraised income, was a real challenge. Our field fundraisers were having to 'sell' old fashioned products and our cost ratios were poor. A brilliant fundraising profitability

'Sooty' collection boxes were popular and profitable.

study, undertaken by Michael Caudrey, a consultant, shone a light onto the problem. Methods we were about to abandon, such as collection boxes in shops, pubs and so on, proved to be our most profitable. However, other methods were just too costly. A major shake-up was judged to be necessary and resulted in 1989/90 being one of the worst for net fundraising (excluding legacies). This was the year which experienced the full impact of Mike Lancaster's radical field fundraising reorganisation, before the benefits could show through. One earlier dramatic change, led by Barry Gifford, was the cessation of our fundraising agreements with local societies for the blind which we judged were holding us and them back. The silver lining to this cessation was the creation of the Voluntary Agencies Link Unit (VALU) to support local societies for the blind, led so well by Chris Croft and aided over the years by long-serving able staff, such as Kathy Cash, Don Jackson, Peter Wild, Denise Smith and Kate Stephens.

We were also beginning to experiment with new forms of fundraising which did not work in the early stages (for example, direct mail). It was a period when there was intense pressure on the director, Mike Lancaster, and his team with heart-breaking consequences for some fundraising staff, including some blind fundraisers who were judged unable to make the transition to more modern fundraising methods. We shall have to wait until the next chapter on the 1990s to see whether it worked.

Two special events raised the gloom over field fundraising because of their success: an Ascot Race Day; and a car journey from John O'Groats to Land's End, sponsored by British Gas, with a blind man at the wheel!

The Ascot Race Day in 1985 was given to us by the racecourse, but it was on a day of the week when low attendance was likely and so the fundraising opportunities looked sparse. Our then president, the Duke of Devonshire, was a racegoer and he agreed to invite a few influential people from the racing fraternity, including the Hon. Jessica White (of the Howard de Walden family), to organise an evening dinner and auction at the end of the race day. The event was organised in RNIB by a highly effective relationship fundraiser, Virginia Fisher. I was sceptical and frankly rather intimidated by these immensely strong and confident (mainly) women on the committee who seemed to know everyone in racing by their first names. As someone experienced in fundraising, I regarded charity auctions then as pretty old fashioned and ineffective. I timidly asked how much the auction might raise and was told 'about £250,000' (1986 prices) from merely four items called nominations. I thought they were mad as this was equivalent to just over ten per cent of annual voluntary income at the time. I had no idea what a nomination was and luckily did not ask. (Apparently, it involves taking your racing mare to the stud stables and being allowed a week for her to be impregnated by a pedigree stallion.) This formidable committee recruited the right kind of auction audience and secured some top-rate stallion nominations as donations in kind. Lo and behold, the evening raised nearly £250,000 in 1985 money including £200,000 from just four nominations auctioned by Peter O'Sullevan.

The other event was equally improbable – a blind man driving the length of Scotland and England, north to south, in 1988. In fact, for safety reasons we had to find a route which was over private land, but the publicity we achieved for the driver, Peter Wood of the RNIB and the sponsors, British Gas, was phenomenal. We exceeded the publicity targets the sponsor set by so much that we ended up with £250,000, approximately £180,000 net. This complicated project was managed by Roger Moon with a calmness I envied.

A blind man drives from John O'Groats to Lands End via country tracks.

While on the subject of blind people raising money for RNIB by undertaking exceptional feats, this history would not be complete without mentioning Gerald Price and Miles Hilton Barber. Price did a tandem parachute jump as well as water skiing over frighteningly high ski jumps. To convince me he could parachute, he came to my office one day, somehow climbed on top of a two-metre-high cupboard in my room and jumped off into a side roll. Miles Hilton Barber very nearly walked all the way to the South Pole and later completed the Marathon des Sables. It is described as the toughest foot race on earth.

Not all our special events were so successful – it takes time to build expertise. As a generalisation, charities are much better at the production side (running a good event) than the consumption side (ensuring there are enough guests/runners/purchasers to bring in the income etc.). The most embarrassing for us was 'Best in Britain'. We arranged a high-ticket price dinner at the Café Royal and easily persuaded 100 stars to turn up, including Vera Lynn, the world ice-skating champions Torvill and Dean and many others. The problem was we failed to persuade the public to buy tickets and come along. In fact, we had more stars than paying diners.

Conclusion – More Activity and Money in a Changing State

This was a decade of change and development coinciding with a plentiful supply of resources – it was a happy coincidence!

Externally the changes were dramatic. The shape of the welfare state and its interaction with the informal, voluntary and private sectors was being redrawn. The tired end to Labour government in 1979 and the arrival of a new ideology and the enthusiasm of the Thatcher Conservative government had impact. Voluntary organisations such as RNIB knew they had to change but they were not sure how. They knew their services were much needed by a government retrenching its offerings, but they did not want to be used as a subservient supplier, and they certainly wanted to resist a fall in state support to beneficiary groups.

So, for RNIB this scenario predicted growing direct service provision but demanding increased statutory fee income to resource the growth. It also predicted a growing pressure group role, at least to defend blind and partially sighted people from cuts in state support. In fact, we achieved some additional benefits for them during the period of turmoil. This is easier to analyse now but for those of us there at the time, it did not seem quite so clear. We feared we might be exploited by a resource-strapped state. (For a more extensive discussion, see Leat 2016 and Jung and Harrow 2016.)

Chapter 3a

1990-2000: RNIB Can't Do It All

Expansion of Indirect Interventions: Advising, Influencing and Campaigning

Chapter 3a describes the new policy of indirect service intervention – the logic being that RNIB was not the most important organisation in the everyday lives of blind and partially sighted people. Common sense, backed up by research, showed that RNIB could never directly fulfil all people's needs with their own services. Blind and partially sighted people are like everyone else, they need to shop, to have somewhere to live, to access the NHS, to catch public transport, to enjoy leisure activities. RNIB alone could never meet all those needs itself but, via indirect services, it could and can:

- advise people with sight problems on the best ways to do it
- advise the commercial and statutory providers on how to adapt their services to be accessible
- and lobby and campaign for regulatory and legislative change to enforce beneficial change for blind and partially sighted people.
- Campaigning is the important hard end of the indirect services continuum, with supportive influencing at

the soft end (e.g. consultancy and training). This softer end methodology was given a boost by the report of the Deakin Commission (1996) with its emphasis on partnership working. The examples which follow are mainly from the softer end of indirect services. The hard-end campaigning examples, also driven by partnership working, are shown later.

Advice to People with Sight Problems

By the end of the 1990s vigorous expansion had been achieved in advice services to individuals to get the most out of the systems – for example, through the launching and expansion of:

- the Benefits Rights Unit (6,000 enquiries per annum by 1999), advising individuals how best to put their case in their applications for social security benefits
- the Housing Service (1,100 enquiries), advising how best to find suitable housing
- the Holiday Information Service (6,200), advising on accessible and welcoming hotels and holiday schemes
- the Small Business Unit, advising on how to be self-employed
- the RNIB Helpline (a massive 38,400 enquiries handled), advising people how to overcome problems in their lives arising from visual impairment (Annual Review 1999/2000).

All of these indirect services were new, with the exception of the Benefits Rights Unit (set up in 1985), and achieved significant scale in the early 1990s. Supporting all the above activities and others, RNIB was one of the first disability organisations to launch a website (in 1996) which was receiving 500,000 visits per year by 1999.

Advice to Statutory and Commercial Organisations

Advising people with sight problems on how to access systems is not enough, especially if the services are not easily accessible by culture or design. So, there was a major launch and expansion of 'consultancy' units to engage with commercial and state providers to encourage them to adjust their services to improve ease of access and use. For example:

- The RNIB Physiotherapy Support Service was established in 1991 to support mainstream courses in physiotherapy to adapt to be able to accept blind and partially sighted students. This was to satisfy the demand from young people who wanted to study in mainstream, not at our specialist 'segregated' college.
- The RNIB Joint Mobility Unit (JMU) (also established in 1991) started its consultancy work on advising state and commercial providers of transport and buildings. By 1999 it had expanded into advice on Disability Discrimination Act 1995 (DDA) compliance and was earning £1 million per year in fees (in 1999 prices) from companies in the transport, architectural and building fields. (This unit alone raised in fee income 1.4 per cent of annual expenditure.)
- The RNIB Eye Health Consultancy grown out of the Health Services Development Unit (set up in 1985) was launched in 1991 to advise the NHS on ophthalmic and optometric service delivery from the standpoint of the consumer.
- The Social Services Consultancy, launched in the late 1980s, also expanded significantly during the decade.
- The Education Support Service provided advice to mainstream education services on how to integrate blind and partially sighted students and

was quickly running over 40 courses per year for mainstream teachers and support staff.
- The Broadcasting Unit provided advice to media providers, primarily television.

The business model for these units, which assumed that earnings would eventually cover expenditure, proved wildly optimistic, except in the case of JMU. While earnings were significant, break-even was never achieved in the units serving the statutory sector. This meant that, while there was appreciable expansion and penetration of quality advice and information into statutory bodies, continuing into the twenty-first century, there was a financial constraint on this expansion.

Ironically, some indirect services later offered a bridgehead to providing new direct services. Two of the consultancies (Social Services and Eye Health) developed arms which bid for direct service contracts. For example, by the end of the 1990s, RNIB had won contracts to provide low vision clinics for the NHS and to provide eye clinic liaison officers in NHS hospitals. Another example was that RNIB was winning contracts with local authorities to provide social rehabilitation.

The indirect service which achieved financial viability was the RNIB Mobility Unit, later the Joint Mobility Unit or JMU, developed initially in partnership with the Guide Dogs for the Blind Association. This financial viability was aided by two factors: first, the commercial transport, architectural and construction clients were used to paying the necessary rates to receive technical advice; second, the unit was headed by an able businessman, Peter Barker, who had lost his sight and who had exceptional marketing and sales acumen. JMU was interesting from a policy perspective as well. It started out delivering only visual impairment advice. However, this was not what our commercial and statutory organisation customers wanted. With the implementation of the disability discrimination legislation in the 1990s, our customers (architects, builders, employers and retailers) wanted advice across all disability areas. In recognition of this demand,

I had persuaded my CEO colleagues at RNID, Scope, Mencap, RADAR and Mind to set up the Disability Charities Consortium (DCC) so that we could provide just such a joint service covering all disability requirements. Suffice it to say that, while the DCC survives as a lobbying body, this attempt to set up a joint DDA advice service failed after some initial success. A critical factor was the RNID decision, under its then CEO James Strachan, to pull out of the pan-disability service and offer its own specialist service exclusively on hearing loss. Strachan was an outstanding role model of what a profoundly deaf person can achieve. He was an able entrepreneur, who felt the needs of deaf people were being submerged by the pan-disability approach.

This cloud had a silver lining because it gave RNIB's JMU a free hand to broaden its scope to provide a pan-disability consultancy. As mentioned above, this enabled us to build up a turnover of £1 million per annum at the end 1990s, giving advice across all disability areas employing consultants with a wide range of disabilities.

Campaigning and Lobbying

In the mid 1980s RNIB had some catching up to do on the campaigning and lobbying front in comparison with many other national charities, including Scope and RADAR in the disability field. By the start of the 1990s, it had done this with a vengeance. For example, in the year 1992/93 alone RNIB had around 30 meetings with ministers on various subjects of interest and concern to people with sight problems (RNIB 1993). Over the full decade RNIB ran over 90 campaigns, some of them vocal, others were quieter using sheer graft in parliamentary committee stages. (As a comparison, I would estimate there were around 20 campaigns in the 1980s and ten or less in the 1970s). Successful examples from the 90 or so campaigns of that decade include:

- Disability Living Allowance (DLA) (introduced in 1992)

- persuading all political parties to produce their manifestos in braille and tape (1992)
- defending the free postal service for blind people (1993)
- ensuring the basic DDA legislation was created to be 'visual impairment friendly' (1992-95)
- Access to Work budget increased by £9 million instead of being cut (1996)
- leading the European campaign which reversed a decision to produce all Euro notes in the same size (1997)
- free eye test for the over sixties (1999)
- DDA Code of Practice on goods, services and facilities has a valuable section on blind and partially sighted people (1999)
- right for alternative voting formats built into law (2000).

A snapshot from the mid-term review of the RNIB's Strategy 2000 gives a graphic picture:

> campaigns over the last three years included the Education Act and subsequent codes, DDA, See It Right, Audetel, the Broadcasting Bill, DLA (Disability Living Allowance), Access to Work, Eye Health, Teleterminals, VAT, Eurocurrency, Postal Services, EU Treaty Revision, saving In Touch, VI Jurors and Judges, Building Society Payments, Housing, Copyright, Libraries and Mobility/Transport. ... arguably, for example, under the Education Act and the Disability Discrimination Act there are in reality several campaigns running (RNIB 1997: 42-43).

An essential lobbying tool was the campaigning report, of which RNIB produced many, especially in the second half of the 1990s. All were carefully researched often using minimum samples of 500 people. Most of the reports below were written or edited by Steve Winyard. What a contributor he proved to be, heading up the campaigning and lobbying side of RNIB for many years. Winyard came originally from a campaigning background and improved what was already an effective lobbying function:

- *Blind in Britain: The Employment Challenge* (1996)
- *Losing Sight of Blindness* (1997)
- *A Question of Risk* (1997)
- *The Eye Examination: A Test of Quality?* (1997)
- *Within Reason: Access to Services for Blind and Partially Sighted People* (1998)
- *Lost Vision: Older Visually Impaired People in the UK* (1998)
- *Ill Informed: The Provision of Accessible Health and Medical Information* (1998)
- *A Right Denied: Access to Voting for Blind and Partially Sighted People* (1998)
- *Rights of Way: Transport and Mobility for Visually Impaired People in the UK* (1999)
- *A Right to Read: The Impact of Copyright Law on Visually Impaired People* (1999)
- *Get the Message: Making Information Accessible for Blind and Partially Sighted People* (1999)
- *The Costs of Blindness* (2000)
- *Disconnected? Are Utility Companies Meeting the Needs of Visually Impaired People?* (2000).

We were sufficiently confident in the quality and quantity of our campaign output that the 1997 review recommended we more than double our targets from 'at least one significant campaign success for each age group (young, working age and older) every three years' to two successes for young and working age and three for older (RNIB 1997, p. 14).

A major recurring issue was financial support needed by blind and partially sighted people. In 1988 RNIB had been a key co-founder of the national Disability Benefits Consortium, of which, at its height, over 500 disability organisations were members. Through its active membership of this consortium,

RNIB won in this decade what was arguably our most important campaign of the twentieth century. We did this through careful backstage negotiations with the government ministers, MPs and the civil service, led by Andy Barrick using crucial evidence from the first RNIB Needs Survey (Bruce, McKennell and Walker 1991) which showed that blind people got out and about less than disabled people in general. This finding led to the inclusion of working-age blind people in the mobility and care elements of the new Disability Living Allowance, putting some £40 million per year (at 1993 prices) into the pockets of blind people. For fifteen years from the 1970s onwards a group of RNIB, NLBD and NFB representatives had been campaigning thus far unsuccessfully for a blindness allowance. In 1992 this was finally achieved through our three organisations, working inside the pan-disability DBC, campaigning for the inclusion of blind people in the new Disability Living Allowance.

Another area of undoubted campaigning growth and success trailed in the last chapter was the European Union. In the late 1980s a leading trustee, Tom Parker, recognised the EU as a potential source of funds. This was realised by grants achieved by RNIB's chief scientist John Gill. In addition, we rapidly gathered, ahead of most other charities, the amazing potential to shape UK legislation and policies by working in Brussels and Strasbourg where EU directives were drafted. By 1990 we had a lobby officer for the EU and by 1992 we had a dedicated team of three – Jane Peters, Sally Kneeshaw and later Barbara McLaughlan – working in partnership with RNIB subject specialists: such as Stephen King, on Euro currency; John Gill and Richard Orme on IT; Robert Meadowcroft on employment; Louise Clunies-Ross, Gordon Dryden, Adam Ockelford, Eamonn Fetton and Neville Lawson on education; Alison Harding, Sue Grindey, Deborah Hamlin, Andy Barrick, Malcolm Wood, Linda Seru and John Robinson on community services. We became the campaigning power house of the European Blind Union (EBU), lobbying at the EU level with a whole string of successes helping the situation of blind people, culminating in two massive wins:

- the design of Euro currency which blind and partially sighted people could use (1992 to 1999) – initial Euro proposals were to copy the US dollar designs, all notes the same size and same colour, a disaster for blind and partially sighted people who use the different note sizes, colours and contrast to distinguish between note values
- the inclusion of disability powers in the 1997 EU Amsterdam Treaty, 1997 (previously the subject of disability was an EU permissive power and any one country could veto an initiative – a growing threat as the number of member countries increased).

Of course, there was major co-operation between RNIB and those other visual impairment and pan-disability organisations across EU countries. Nevertheless, RNIB put more time and money into these efforts than anyone else across Europe.

How, in general, did our campaigning work? The public, publicity-seeking campaign is just the tip of the iceberg of pressure group work. The vast majority of activity is quiet evidence gathering, solution generation and 'selling' these ideas to ministers, backbench MPs, civil servants, parliamentary committee clerks, commercial companies, local authorities, regulators, quangos, professional associations etc. RNIB developed amazing skills and expertise in these methods, characterised by a drip, drip, drip approach, not a waterfall of publicity. Publicity comes primarily with the launch of a campaign, and/or at the end when a campaign is being won or in danger of being lost. This kind of work requires good networking and contacts who know what is happening before it does. Most of those people I cannot name, but I thank you. One I can mention is Kevin Mulhern, a blind freelance TV producer, who seemed to know so much before I did and whom I could phone day or night. There were many media people who listened to what we had to say but, in the press, two who listened to us, however near their deadline, was David Brindle of the *Guardian* and Stephen Cook of Third Sector. On radio, Peter White and *In Touch* were both our scourge and our champion. Media coverage is particularly essential in a public education campaign which is also promoting public awareness (putting RNIB in front of the public in lieu of a large advertising budget) and behaviour change (social marketing, for example, the annual RNIB eye health campaigns persuading the public to look after their eyes and get their eyes tested).

Underpinning many of the campaigns and much service development as well, was the first RNIB needs survey published at the beginning of the decade (Bruce, McKennell and Walker 1991). Coming from a commercial marketing background, I was committed to (market) research amongst consumers. Such an approach built on the tradition, established by RNIB's founder, Rhodes Armitage in 1868, of basing RNIB's position via the views of blind people which provide the evidence base for action. In 1985, given that there were so many blind people among the trustees, it was not straightforward gaining acceptance of a major survey of blind people. 'First generation' blind trustees often thought that as they were blind their experience was sufficient to inform decisions. In my parlance, 'second generation' blind trustees recognised that, by becoming a trustee they were not typical, they were part of the blind elite. These 'second generation' blind trustees welcomed information and views given by the general population of blind and partially sighted people who were hidden (from us) many miles from London and our services. The RNIB needs survey had a fundamental impact on our service designs and our campaigning and it was the most frequently mentioned RNIB achievement cited by respondents in an independent stakeholder analysis carried out in 1993 by Compass Partnership and led by Mike Hudson. Again, RNIB was one of the first charities to undertake independent stakeholder analyses to test how we were regarded by people and organisations who had power and authority to support or thwart our objectives (for example, politicians, civil servants, business leaders, other disability charities and so on).

To return to the RNIB needs survey, one of its major strengths was its sample. This was largely a sub-sample of the government's major disability survey (Martin, Meltzer and

Elliot 1988), a brilliant resource negotiated by my co-research director, Aubrey McKennell. This meant that the sample included blind and partially sighted people previously unknown to service deliverers – a first in visual impairment research.

Face-to-face interviews were conducted by professional interviewers from the Office of National Statistics and questions covered demographics, media reading habits (print, tape, braille, readers), mobility and daily living (including shopping and transport, leisure, employment) and support services (social security, social services, health services, local voluntary organisations). The research produced some surprising major findings as well as masses of detailed data in all the areas listed: for example, that there were at that time approaching a million people who could have been registered blind or partially sighted, over three times as many as were actually registered; for example, that blind people went out less than disabled people in general, the reverse of what successive governments believed, a misperception which had blocked blind people's access to the government mobility allowance (introduced in 1976); for example, that newly blind people and their families were at their most resistant to accept help at the time of sight loss but were much more receptive one to two years later. This RNIB research, with its evidence-based conclusions, was unique among single impairment charities and boosted our campaigning effectiveness. While I put a lot of time into the survey, particularly from the policy perspective and in the drafting, the major credit goes to co-researchers Aubrey McKennell (part-time) and Erroll Walker (full-time) (Bruce, McKennell and Walker 1991).

If I were to nominate the most important campaign successes of the 1990s decade it would be these:

- Winning the DLA for blind people of working age. This campaign (led by Andy Barrick) is described in more detail in *Meeting Need: Successful Charity Marketing* (Bruce 2011, pp. 152-55).

- Influencing the drafting of the Disability Discrimination Bill to ensure blind and partially sighted people's needs and rights were met. We achieved this through our highly effective parliamentary officer, Alun Thomas, leading our membership in Rights Now, the pan-disability lobby working on the drafting of the bill. This was another example of the change in tactics by RNIB, i.e. not going it alone, but joining and disproportionately supporting the broader disability lobby.
- Being one of the leaders of the Europe-wide campaign (the RNIB lead on this was Jane Peters) to include a clause on disability in the EU's Amsterdam Treaty.
- Leading the campaign (headed by the RNIB's Stephen King) to prevent the issue of same-size Euro notes, with an outcome of differential sizes for different denominations and really clear print for partially sighted people. If you cannot handle money, you are disempowered.

Chapter 3b

Expansion and Extension

The first half of the 1990s saw a concentration on reaping the maximum benefit from implementing the rapid and extensive RNIB strategic planning decisions in the previous decade. The expansion of indirect services is discussed above but direct services also expanded rapidly. This expansion was to include many more people, especially older, and those in Northern Ireland, Scotland and Wales – areas previously significantly underserved.

This expansion was not easy because the first half of the 1990s saw financial problems in the UK economy. These impacted on RNIB to the extent that the three middle years of the decade saw RNIB expenditure being reined in, just one of nine factors impacting on RNIB at that time, namely:

- tough economic climate (recession in the early years of the decade)
- downward pressure on public expenditure
- expansion of competitive tendering for government contracts (rather than grants)
- more service provision at local/community level (a challenge for a national organisation)
- growing emphasis on value for money and efficiency (which often threatened reductions in

quality and/or the serving of less challenged/ 'cheaper' clients)
- increased requirement for generic services (for example, disability rather than blindness specific)
- rapidly growing importance of the EU as a source of UK law and regulation (Brussels, not Westminster) (RNIB 1993, pp. 10-12).

In addition, there was the discovery of the presence of approximately one million registrable blind and partially sighted people in the UK by contrast with previous estimates of under half a million (Bruce, McKennell and Walker 1991). This estimate was increased in the late 1990s to two million people with the inclusion of a broader definition of 'uncorrectable sight loss' – those whose sight is not bad enough to be registered as blind or partially sighted, but whose sight cannot be corrected by glasses sufficient to pass the driving test eyesight requirements.

Progress of the First Strategy, 1985-95

RNIB's first corporate strategy 1985-95 (RNIB 1987), outlined in chapter 2a above, was reviewed in 1993 (RNIB 1993, pp. 5-7) and a new one started in 1994:

2.1 An Overview
The first RNIB Strategy called for 'significant growth' to help us achieve the policy directives laid out in the document. In the eight years to March 1992, expenditure per annum has risen by 61 per cent in real terms and staffing has increased by approximately 35 per cent …

2.2 Policy Directives
The first RNIB Strategy ([19]87) identified nine policy directives. Seven of these have been progressed

substantially, and two partially (No. 1 social marketing and No. 9 prevention of blindness).

This review and subsequent strategy work was co-ordinated
by a talented and expert strategist, Steve Cooper, who took
over from Elizabeth Twining. He was an excellent highly
professional foil to my more intuitive approach and I, and the
whole of RNIB, sorely missed him after his early death.

A New Strategy for 1994-2000

With the evidence of the 1993 review we developed a new
strategy which built on the first – concentrating on unfinished
business (RNIB 1994):

Vision
RNIB wants a world in which people with visual
impairments enjoy the same rights, freedoms,
responsibilities and quality of life as people who
are fully sighted.

Mission
Our mission is to challenge blindness by
empowering people with a visual impairment,
removing barriers and helping to prevent blindness.

There were five strategic priorities:

1. Challenging blindness, raising awareness and tackling discrimination
2. Extending services to more blind and partially
   sighted people
3. Increasing the priority given to older blind and
   partially sighted people
4. Improving the quality of services
5. Improving resourcing strategies.

Under these there were 28 objectives which had quantitative targets associated with strands of our work. At the time setting quantitative targets seemed the right way to develop strategy implementation after the experience of the first strategy. Here follows the key extract from the RNIB's second strategy (1994):

Strategic Priority 1: Challenging Blindness, Raising Awareness and Tackling Discrimination

Objectives
1. To raise awareness and understanding of the needs of blind and partially sighted people in order to encourage others to be more positive in their attitudes and actions.
2. To raise awareness of RNIB's crucial role in meeting the needs of blind and partially sighted people.
3. To reduce discrimination through highlighting and campaigning against social, economic and material barriers that handicap blind and partially sighted people.

Strategic Priority 2: Extending Services to More Blind and Partially Sighted People

Objectives
1. To increase the proportion of people reached by RNIB's direct services.
2. To investigate and, if successful, implement a mass membership of blind and partially sighted service users and others such as carers, professionals, donors and other supporters.
3. To measure and increase the impact of RNIB's indirect services, particularly to improve the nature, range and quality of services of other organisations.

Strategic Priority 3: Increasing the Priority Given to Older Blind and Partially Sighted People

Objectives
1. To reduce the incidence of preventable sight problems.
2. To increase take-up of RNIB services for older blind and partially sighted people.
3. To expand high volume lower cost services relevant to older blind and partially sighted people.
4. To expand pressure group work and other indirect services relating to older blind and partially sighted people.
5. To tackle and reduce the barriers faced by older blind and partially sighted people.

Strategic Priority 4: Improving the Quality of Services to Users and Supporters

Objective
1. To improve quality of service to users and supporters.

Strategic Priority 5: Resourcing Strategies

5.1. Efficiency and effectiveness

Objectives
1. To increase the impact and value for money of RNIB services.
2. To deliver services to users with maximum efficiency.
3. To develop further our policies and rational criteria for allocation of RNIB subsidy to service areas and users.

5.2. RNIB people

Objectives
1. To increase investment in professional development and training of staff.
2. By the end of 1999 all managers who have been
   in post for six months or more should meet the
   required level of job specific core competencies
   needed to discharge all the responsibilities of
   their post.
3. To ensure that committees are effective and
   that committee members are aware of their
   responsibilities particularly under the Charities
   Act 1992 and are otherwise supported in their
   role of policy formulation and monitoring.
4. To achieve a target of 10 per cent blind and
   partially sighted staff in RNIB by 1999.

5.3. Structure, infra-structure, processes and planning

Objectives
1. To further develop management information
   systems that give service level, divisional and
   corporate management the information needed
   to manage services effectively from a customer
   viewpoint.
2. To develop and implement an integrated information strategy.
3. To optimise our portfolio of buildings and make
   them suitable for people with sight problems,
   appropriate wherever feasible for people with
   other and additional disabilities, and economic to
   operate.
4. To update organisational structure in 1994 to
   ensure it is appropriate to deliver the strategy,
   and to review it subsequently where necessary.

5. To bring in service planning which puts the customer at the heart of the planning, delivering and monitoring our services, products and ideas.

5.4. Income

Objectives
1. To increase net annual voluntary income by over £5 million pounds in real terms by 1999.
2. To raise £10 million pounds net from new capital/ revenue development appeals by the end of the strategy period.
3. To review the potential of a retailing initiative.
4. To grow service income in real terms by five to 10 per cent per annum for the next five years. [This was revised downwards to three to six per cent in 1997.] (RNIB 1994)

How Successful Was the Second Strategy, 1994/95-2000?

Jumping six years forward, the review of 2001, *Learning from the Past* (RNIB 2001), looked at the degree of success and failure of the strategy in detail covering most of the1990s, via a 114-page report. The following extract gives a succinct summary:

During the last six years RNIB has grown and developed in terms of services provided and our organisational experience. The Corporate Strategy has guided our efforts, harnessed our energies, and given us a strong platform for moving forward. Under an umbrella of five Strategic Priorities, we set ourselves 28 objectives with targets. We have achieved or exceeded target on 22 objectives and missed target on six, in most cases by just a little. (RNIB 2001, p. 4)

The ones that were missed were mass membership, preventable sight problems, maximum efficiency, ten per cent blind staff and service income growth by three to six per cent per annum in real terms.

This report was produced under the leadership of Jane Peters, supported by Karen Allsop. Peters had taken over as head of corporate strategy from Steve Cooper. Having been promoted earlier from her European role, she brought a quiet but superlative competence. She was followed by Nicholas Johnston who cemented RNIB's reputation as a strategy-led organisation and also had the ability to hold steady under the inevitable fire which the person in charge of strategy and evaluation comes under. Other people critical to this strategy were the objective leaders, who besides myself included Lynne Stockbridge, Steve Winyard, Deborah Jack, John Godber, Andy Barrick, Olivia Belle, Ros Oakley, Eamonn Fetton, Shelley Devonshire, Deborah Hamlin, Sue Grindey, Ian Andrew, Ian Vickers, Alison Beesley, Margaret Alexander, Ken Lavey, Patrick MacDonald, Paul Hunt, Mike Lancaster, Hilary Partridge, Gwenn McCreath, Catherine Wardle, Theresa Dauncey, Mike Palfreman, Valerie Morton. All the objectives were nestled under the five strategic priorities led in various combinations by the directors: Mike Lancaster, Stephen King, Tony Aston, Jon Barrick, Paul Ennals, Fazilet Hadi and Barry Gifford.

Jane Peter's conclusion to the strategy read:

> The way in which RNIB Strategy 1994-2000 was implemented resulted in many positive achievements. In particular it led to increased cross-divisional working, and innovative and focussed prioritisation by senior management and senior trustees. It encouraged managers to think corporately as well as divisionally when planning activities (i.e. thinking of our customers holistically).

The complexity of the strategy and of RNIB meant that it was difficult to develop systems and processes that were always effective and suitable for all stakeholders. In this context the implementation process offered opportunities for organisational learning of which we took advantage in our development of the implementation process for our new strategy, *Strategic Directions 2000-2006* (RNIB 2001, p. 237).

Direct Service Growth

Services delivered direct to people with sight problems increased dramatically across the 1990s. This was achieved through expansion of some existing services but, in particular, by introducing new ones.

These included (with the lead person in parentheses):

- 1,600,000 braille and large print bills and bank statements for approximately 40,000 visually impaired customers of banks and building societies in1999/2000 (Dr John Gill)
- the opening of further regional education centres in Cardiff, Leeds, Birmingham and Edinburgh (Eamonn Fetton, Joyce Chatterton)
- the opening of employment centres in the North East and Scotland (Robert Meadowcroft, Kate Storrow)
- the opening of regional tape-recording centres (Chris Smith and Wendy Davies)
- family mutual support weekends (58 families with children in mainstream education) (Eamonn Fetton, Neil Andersen and Louise Clunies-Ross)
- vacation schemes (for 92 blind or partially sighted children in mainstream education, to help them meet other children in the same position and improve specific skills, such as braille) (Eamonn Fetton, Neil Andersen and Louise Clunies-Ross)
- *See for Yourself* explanatory booklets (50,000 per year in 1999/2000) (King, Cuthbert, Harvey, Sismore and Siggery 2003).

**Britain's first large print
newspaper.**

- services to the MHVI (Gill Levy and Mark Gray),
  including a new day centre in Glasgow in 1994
  (Frances Miller)
- Big Print UK's first large-print newspaper for
  partially sighted people
- Audetel – audio description on television (Denise
  Evans)
- a Physiotherapy Support Service to support stu-
  dents in mainstream physio training, based at the
  University of East London (Jane Owen Hutchinson)
- the RNIB website was launched in 1996 (Julie
  Howell).

More long-standing direct services expanded overall but
this masks a differential picture, some of the expansions
were:

- the old Hethersett College moved onto a new
  site and doubled its numbers to become RNIB
  Redhill College (1991) and launched its first two
  community houses in 1994 (Mike Rowe)
- also in 1994 we launched our first 52-week residential provision at Rushton Hall School (Robert
  Orr) (later near Coventry as the Pears' Centre in

recognition of the major support from the Pears family))

- *Understanding Eye Conditions*
pamphlets, produced in co-
operation with the Royal College
of Ophthalmologists, increased
from 26,000 to 185,000 per
year; understanding a condition
and its prognosis helps people's
rehabilitation

- the launch of the RNIB Helpline
in 1997 was a phenomenal success reaching 15,000 calls per
year within two years and due
to expand even more dramatically in the next decade. (Some
of the people crucial in this
were Andy Barrick, Fran
McSweeney, Julie Polzerova, Moira Routledge,
Wayne Chapman, Colin Palgrave, Randolph
Reid, Mary Cox, Paresh Jotangia, Barry Jones,
Judy Cobbett and many others.)

**Roger Smith
running a student
radio show after
studying at Redhill
and the Vocational
College.**

At the same time several direct services closed down,
either through drops in demand, changing policies towards
integration (inclusion) or prohibitive investment requirements. The flagship North London School of Physiotherapy,
led so ably and for so long
by David Teager, shut in
1996 but not before he
became president of World
Physiotherapy, the international body representing
over half a million physiotherapists worldwide – thus,
promoting the practice of
blind people as physiotherapists and raising RNIB's

**Cycle maintenance training
at Redhill.**

profile in another international sphere. The RNIB National Mobility Centre, which trained mobility and orientation officers, transferred to the then University of Central England. The Sunshine House School in East Grinstead closed because of declining numbers and major capital spend required. Other direct services remained static or declined, for example, the numbers of young people in RNIB schools fell to 271, down from 367 at the beginning of the decade, and membership of the Talking Books Service fell to 54,000, down from 67,000 at the start of the decade.

The combined impact of these changes meant that by 1999/2000 RNIB direct services were reaching vastly more people, especially older, newly visually impaired people as required by the strategy – a total served of 462,000 in 1999, up from 181,000 at the beginning of the strategy in 1994 (RNIB 2001).

Another characteristic of the 1990s was more equitable distribution of services across the UK. Internal customer studies had shown a long-standing bias of RNIB activity in the south of England. During the decade, education, employment and recording centres were gradually rolled out across the whole of the UK, not initially in concert, but eventually co-located in some ten regional offices. The multi-handicapped centre was built in Scotland and a separate co-ordination director for Scotland appointed in 1992 – Allan Murray, supported by Liz Kennedy. A consultant, Mike Hudson, recommended in 1999 that directors accountable to the director general be appointed in Northern Ireland, Scotland and Wales to run services in those countries. Allan Murray was appointed in Scotland, later succeeded by Mike Cairns (supported by Billy Watson, Bryn Merchant, Elizabeth Kennedy and Kim Main); Susan Reid in Northern Ireland (supported by Mike McIlwrath, Charlie Mack, Margaret Al-Saigh and Martin Walls); and Joyce Chatterton in Wales (supported by Byron Green, John Sole and Frances Hynes). Chatterton was previously head of education in Wales and a passionate advocate of early childhood education. Thus, RNIB Cymru, RNIB Northern Ireland and RNIB Scotland were created, anticipating trends in devolution, and several years ahead of comparable devolutionary changes in many other UK charities.

A service which evolved significantly during the 1990s was the RNIB Employment Service led for more of the decade by Robert Meadowcroft. It transmuted away from the model of the 1960s-1980s of RNIB employment officers finding, and helping individuals into, jobs – with funding coming from the Department of Employment. From the mid-1980s into the 1990s, RNIB had to start contracting with the government employment services regionally and later locally to provide specified support such as assessment, ICT training and other forms of training. (Bruce 1991). The regional RNIB managers had to become much more adept at bidding for and winning contracts and not simply being expert on employment rehabilitation. In the mid 1990s David Allen, Susanna Hancock, Kate Storrow and Roger Stowell were regional managers of the service. Other successes were the Small Business Unit, led by Beryl Morton, and the introduction of the concept and practice of Disability Leave for newly visually impaired people, developed by Gill Paschkes-Bell.

Campaigning – Example of Accessible Digital Communications

One strand of RNIB campaigning in the decade 1990-2000 was so effective it deserves more detailed description.

Possibly most transformative for the lives of most blind people of working age (and later the over sixties) was the work RNIB led nationally and globally to ensure much of the digital world was usable without sight, for example, mobile phones, computers, televisions and broadcasts and e-books. This all began with the early work of Dr John Gill, RNIB's chief scientist, in the 1980s. He identified the coming risk to inclusion and employment as control of everyday technology shifted from exclusively keyboard control (easy for blind people) to more visually oriented control (mouse and touch screen). RNIB invested strategically in research and development and built key capabilities and global alliances in technologies such as speech synthesis, screen reading and information processing. Under the leadership of Stephen King, we had a strong team including John Gill, Steve Tyler, Richard Orme, Peter Osborne, Denise Evans, Leen Petre, David Mann, Jillian Harvey and many others who put together, and contributed to, global alliances that transformed access to information and everyday culture.

It is a little-known story that RNIB put up the key seed capital to create a programme that would read the screen of then ubiquitous Nokia mobile phones, enabling them to be independently controlled by a blind person and to be used for all sorts of other things, such as navigation. The mobile phone rapidly transformed the lives and independence of thousands of working-age blind people and, later, older people. This fed through to significant global consortia advocacy work with Apple, Google and Microsoft leading to the situation that all mobile phones had and have access services built into them to enable them to be used by people with a whole range of sensory and physical impairments.

Similarly, Kevin Carey (later to become RNIB chair) had identified watching television as a key cultural inclusion. RNIB's focus, until the mid 1980s, had been on reading and radio, the cultural communication norms of the late nineteenth and the first half of the twentieth century. We knew that television was popular but in 1988/89 from early results of the RNIB needs survey (Bruce, McKennell and Walker 1991) we learned that watching television was the most popular pastime. However, people were incredibly frustrated that they had to rely on family and friends to know what was going on in the non-speech sections. Audio description had been well proven in the theatre; but it could not be delivered on television because of limited broadcast bandwidth. In the mid 1990s RNIB spotted the opportunity of television going digital. Through its campaigning and technology development work, it campaigned successfully to ensure that audio description services became a licence requirement for broadcasters.

People – Training, Development and Recognition

This was a decade of heavy investment in developing our people: including a myriad of short courses and an in-house but externally validated Certificate in Management (started in 1989/90). Management competences were developed for staff in categories and annual appraisals were introduced across the organisation linked to professional development. These initiatives were led by Ken Lavey as head of personnel, a rock to be relied upon, and several key developers, including, in particular, Jill Rosenheim, Alison Beesley, Carole Buckton, Deborah Jack, Jenny Collis, Trudy Hindmarsh, Maureen McMahon, Howard Platt and Viv Oxley.

Also, by the end of the decade, some 25 RNIB managers had completed the postgraduate Diploma in Voluntary Sector Management at City University London's Business School (Cass, now Bayes Business School). Trustee support of professional development was such that I was given two hours each working week for external meetings plus weekends to found and develop the diploma (1995) and MSc (1999). I founded the charity management centre (1991/92, initially Volprof, later, the Centre for Charity Effectiveness), with the support of Diana Leat and then Mary Harris, to help the charity sector transition into the more professional but more complicated world of competitive contract culture of the late twentieth century. However, it was also a way of widening my horizons and introducing new ideas into RNIB. Jill Rosenheim had helped me to develop the diploma after she left RNIB to do a masters in adult education. I like to think that being the course director of the diploma and MSc from 1995 through to 2002 kept me fresh and on top of the latest developments in charity management and leadership to the benefit of RNIB during the second decade of my time as director general.

In addition to the above initiatives, the biennial RNIB two-night/three-day residential senior management conferences assumed increasing importance in the 1990s and had around 150-180 attendees – aiding communication, involvement and solidarity.

A major development at trustee level was the retirement in 1990 of Duncan Watson. He had been chair since 1975 and had steered RNIB from being a somewhat old-fashioned organisation into a twentieth-century charity. He was succeeded by another blind leader, John Wall (previously vice chair) who would stay in this post for ten years until 2000. Another successful lawyer, this time from the commercial sphere, John had a remarkable facility with figures which kept us all on our toes, not least Barry Gifford, director of finance and administration. Wall could charm the birds off the trees and had an endless supply of anecdotes which kept whatever company he was in in good spirits. He could advertently and sometimes inadvertently create quite a stir, such as the time when one of his glass eyes popped out and rolled across the floor. The other senior trustees remained the same with Colin Low chairing the Education Committee; Tom Parker, Vocational and Social Services; John Wall, Technical Consumer Services; and Alan Morton (sighted) succeeded by Jack Dunn (sighted) as treasurer and chair of the Finance and Resources Committee.

Remaining on the senior management team from the 1980s were Tony Aston, Barry Gifford and Mike Lancaster. New were: succeeding Tony Lenney as director of education, a young Paul Ennals, who came from Sense, with his immense knowledge of direct service delivery to multi-handicapped blind young people; Stephen King, who came from publishing and retail to lead Technical and Consumer Services (TCS) (braille, tape and technical aids) with great strategic vision and an acute knowledge of trends in information technology (IT); and Fazilet Hadi started in the middle of the decade, a blind lawyer, who came from local government, she headed up a newly created Policy Division to which she applied her acute intelligence and good judgement.

Later, in 1997, Tony Aston retired after a distinguished RNIB career starting in the early 1960s. (and soon became Chair of Guide Dogs). During my early years as director general, he was one of my most progressive allies. He was supported by a whole series of able deputies, including Mavis Sutter, Deborah Hamlin, Robert Meadowcroft, Alison Harding, Andy Barrick, Jon Barrick, Malcolm Wood, Charlie Dixon, Linda Seru and others. Aston was succeeded by Jon Barrick, who had made a major contribution as an RNIB assistant director with the dynamism which would take him to become RNIB director of community services and then on to be the highly successful CEO of the Stroke Association in the mid 2000s. After just over eight highly successful years of building up our education and employment services, Paul Ennals left to become the highly regarded chief executive of the National Children's Bureau, from which position he received his knighthood in 2009. Paul is highly skilled at bringing people with different interests together and forging a team committed to a new, necessary direction of work. He was succeeded at RNIB in 1999 by Eamon Fetton who became RNIB's second blind director of that period. He had proved his worth by expanding the Education and Employment Division particularly in the early childhood section. It was a senior management team of great and many talents – individualistic, entrepreneurial people who were committed (but, as a consequence, sometimes had to be coaxed) to work as a team. Moreover, they all had real depth in their divisional staff which helped to translate strategy into action, a crucial requirement with a staff numbers approaching 3,000 people at the end of the decade.

Two of the directors were blind or partially sighted (fourteen per cent) and we had a target for the whole organisation of ten per cent by 2000. That we had such a high target set across 3,000 staff was partly at my insistence, but we failed. It was approximately four per cent at the beginning of the decade and we reached just over seven per cent by 1997 which encouraged us to go for ten per cent by 2000. However, as blind and partially sighted staff always wanted, we only appointed people if they could do the job. We failed to reach our target partly because we followed that rule and partly because as managers we were not always flexible enough to create the right openings. For example, we broke through seven per cent in 1997 but then suffered a reversal. With the rapid recruitment of temporary staff, particularly fundraisers for the telephone lottery, we did not spend long enough making the posts visual impairment friendly. We finished the decade at six per cent, a significant growth over the decade start of four per cent and with absolute numbers of 122 increasing to 166 – but well short of target. While overall it was six per cent, it was heartening that at managerial levels it was 12.5 per cent.

A feature distinguishing us from most other charities was our 1990s expansion of the people resource we applied to Europe and the EU. Many trustees were involved, Tom Parker, Duncan Watson, John Wall, Fred Reid, Colin Low, Jill Allen-King and more. On the staff side, our RNIB European officers were crucial – all very able and diplomatic. These included Jane Peters, Sally Kneeshaw, Barbara McLaughlin (already mentioned) and later Leen Petre, Kate Seymour, Egon Walesch, Bridget Keam and Jurgen Grotz (as international policy co-ordinator). This team gave us extra access and influence.

There were so many people who made this a glorious decade. From the Community Services Division: Tony Aston, Jon Barrick, Andy Barrick, Deborah Hamlin, Anita Boguslawski, Pete Lucas, Laura Jacobs, Frances Miller, Alison Harding, Chris Croft, Andy Winders, Sue Grindey, Lorraine Waddington, Rose Ashbee, Nigel Caleb, Andrew Gatenby, Barbara Scott, Graham Smith, Sally Wadsworth, Peter Barker, Sherree Westwood, Judy Treseder, Julie Joyce, Wendy Kane, Moira Routledge, Barry Jones, Sheena McBride, Val Slade, Andy Fisher, Richard Cox, Carl Freeman, Marcus Weisen, Denise Evans, Jill Aspey, Stan Bell, Graham Willetts, Simon Labbett, Ann Baxter, Tim Pope, Gill Whitney, Yvonne Howard, Jill Taylor, Denise Smith, Andrew Hodgson, Martin Milligan, Mike McIlwrath, Anne Veart, Kate Stephens, Peter Wild, Don Jackson, Kathy Cash, Clive Philips, Fran McSweeney, Julie Polzerova, Rod Wilson, Alan Suttie, Dennis Davis, Mark Browne, Lynne Nichol, Rebecca Griffiths, Mitchell

Thompson, Linda Seru, Lisa Carter, Malcolm Wood, Maxine Miles, Simon Jones, Caroline Brown, Stuart Hornsby, Sandra Cronin, Fiona Derbyshire, Shelley Devonshire, Stuart Davies, Charlie Callanan, Sharon McCarroll, Deborah Beale and others.

From the Education and Employment Division: Jennifer Makin, Louise Clunies-Ross, Sue Keil, Robert Meadowcroft, Gordon Dryden, Richard Botheras, Herprit Rana, Issy Cole-Hamilton, Matthew Parsonage, Olga Miller, Maria O'Donnell, Paddy O'Rourke, Sue Hitchcock, David Sullivan, Emily Brothers, Susanna Hancock, Seema Dass, Judy Bell, Tony Best, David Hussey, Rita Kirkwood, Helen Williams, Adam Ockelford, Joyce Chatterton, Rory Cobb, Katherine El Dahshan, Neil Todd, Dave Allen, Anne Boylan, Elizabeth Clery, Sharon Da Cunha, Nancy Chambers, Colin Cribb, Ken Bore, Geoff Jackman, Gillian Eldridge, Harry Dicks, Ian Bland, Jill Read, Judy Bell, Kevin Connell, Loraine Stewart, Madeleine Spears, Martin Coleman, Neville Lawson, Nick Ratcliffe, Pat Howarth, Philippa Simkiss, Richard Orme, Rob Dyke, Sue Wright, Tracy de Bernhardt Dunkin, Michael Brothers, Joyce Deare, Brian Hewitt, Stewart Long, John Milligan, Jane Owen-Hutchinson, Craig Stockton, Kate Storrow, Christie Taylor, Olufunmi Adeoye and others.

From Technical Consumer Services: Stephen King, Chris Day, Carol Cotton, Janice Richards, Wendy Davies, John Godber, Dr John Gill, Steve Tyler, Peter Osborne, Angela Fuggle, Tony Gibbs, Jillian Harvey, Paresh Jotangia, Cathy Rundle, Ian Turner, Joyce Bis, Martin O'Keefe-Liddard, John Crayford, Keith Gladstone, Ian Vickers, Dave Pawson, Mandy White, Alison Long, Malcolm Staniland, Linda Brady, Rob Longstaff, Jerry Wyndham, David McKelvie, Pete Cleary, Martin Pugh, John Crampton, John Siggery, Dave Pawson, Susan Cuthbert, Sylvana Berrill, Bernard Quinn, Andrew Douse, Alyson Badnell, Mark Prouse, Paul Porter and Selinah Shah.

From Policy Division: Fazilet Hadi, Margaret Alexander, Jane Peters, Nicholas Johnston, Kishor Patel, Steve Winyard, Alun Thomas, Helen Dearman, Joshua Archer, Linda Mears, Ruth Mountstephen, Egon Walesch, Jurgen Grotz, Christine

Tillsley, Kishor Patel, Dan Vale, Dermot Ryan, Caroline Ellis, Mark Baker, Evelyn Russell, Fiona Mackenzie, James Rogers, Leen Petre, Nigel Charles, Stef Abrar, Stella Smith, Jan Nesbitt, Julie Howell and Julie Howell.

From Finance and Administration: Barry Gifford, Ian Andrew, Tony Fazakerley, Lis Goodwin, Amelia Billington, Ken Lavey, Alison Beesley, Jenny Collis, Maureen McMahon, Viv Oxley, Trudy Hindmarsh, Howard Platt, Paul Hunt, Robin Mann, Barry Goold, Caroline Dalton, Es Parker, Giselle Low, Jackie Weston Davies, Jim Richardson, Kate Stephens, Pat MacDonald, Peri O'Connor, Tim Stone, Brian Law, Jim Mahoney, Mark Steele, Adam Gilbert, Jean Harding, David Mould, David Pacey, Stephen Martin, Lis Goodwin, Eleanor Morgan, Mick Giannotti and Pete Witt.

From the External Relations Division: Mike Lancaster, Ros Oakley, Nicky Garsten, Gwen McCreath, Hilary Partridge, Hilary Todd, Ann Paul, Ann Lee, Bernard Fleming, Margaret Meyer, Joe Korner, Olivia Belle, Liz North, Becca Bryant, Kate Summerside, Fiona McCarthy, Jim Richardson, Howard Lewis, Sue Sharp, Martin McEwan, Paul Tranter, Jane Desborough, Mike Palfreman, Lynne Stockbridge, Paul Marvell, Pauline Lutman, Kath Howard, Phil Robertshaw, Patrick Holmes, Duncan Bell, Ciara Smyth, Demis de Sousa, Fiona Blakemore, Catherine Wardle, Debbie Harrison, Hugh Yexley, Karen Sutter, Katherine Eckstrom, Margaret O'Donnell, Maria Pemberton, Nancy Maguire, Peter Storey, Sharon Wilding, Sioned Clutton, Jaqueline McMullen, Doug Thomson, David Miller, Lisa Dickinson and Chas Gainsford.

Resources – Growing the Brand, Fees and Fundraising

Brand Relaunch

A major resource of any charity is its brand or public identity. Research we undertook suggested that the public and blind and partially sighted people did not know about the successful steps we had taken to modernise and become

RNIB in the
news...

This year we had more coverage in the press, on radio and TV than in any year of our 125-year history. We can't do it justice in two pages - these are merely a few of the highlights.

A major achievement was to enlist the support of the **Prime Minister** to unveil our new corporate identity in September 1993. John Major spoke movingly about his father's loss of sight in later life. To commemorate the occasion, Mr Major was given a bronze miniature of our new logo by six-year-old Nicholas Killen who lost his sight as a result of a rare cancer of the retina.

The launch of our new identity grabbed the headlines in virtually every national paper and many local ones. A piece in *The Times* focused on the reason for our re-launch - to raise awareness of RNIB, the importance of our work and our style - 'At the leading edge', as the paper put it.

A collection of newspaper coverage of RNIB campaigns and events. Public awareness rose significantly through the RNIB relaunch of 1993.

more relevant. People trusted us and thought we did a good job but they saw us as slow and old fashioned. This led Sanchi Heesom (now Murison), our dynamic head of communications, to recommend that we needed a relaunch on the basis of our market research and a strong internal demand for change. As John Wall, chair since 1990 said in the 1992/93 Annual RNIB Report:

> Awareness was lower than we would wish, even among the people we are here to help. People without direct knowledge of us thought of us as cold and remote and old fashioned. None of those words describe us, yet, if people perceive us that way, we have to set about changing that perception.

With the help of public relations agency Gavin Anderson & Co. with their inspirational creative director Juliet Jordan, through Sanchi Heesom and her immediate team, Hilary Todd (now Bradley), Cathy Lee and Rachel Hone, we created a more modern persona in line with RNIB's changing reality. This included a new logo and strapline. In 1993, out went are old-fashioned, vertical 'stick man' logo and in came a much more friendly, dynamic androgynous figure, striding powerfully along showing confidence and competence. The visual logo changes, a concentration on the initials

Logo change 1993 – new (R) compared to the old (L).

RNIB and the new strapline 'Challenging blindness' formed the practical basis of a more modern visual identity. The philosophy we wished to engender was of blind people as confident, competent people, not as stilted objects to be pitied.

Crucial to the successful RNIB relaunch was making a short video for staff, explaining why this was not a waste of money, was really necessary and the best solution. Each director and I separately took the video out to 56 different RNIB locations and answered questions and put ourselves fully behind the change. You could sense strongly how, although initially sceptical, staff changed their minds positively and decisively.

In the year of the relaunch, despite having little money for paid advertising (£276,000 in 1993 prices), spontaneous awareness doubled to reach fourteen per cent and prompted awareness 66 per cent, giving a total public awareness of 80 per cent. Media relations led by Pat Orr with Nicky Garsten and Kevin Johnston were crucial for editorial coverage. We achieved thousands of column inches and dozens of television and newspaper pictures from the launch of the new identity. For me, the high point was a twelve-centimetre-square picture on the front page of *The Times* of the prime minister chatting to a blind boy from one of our schools (with the permission of the child and his parents) who had on a tee shirt sporting the new RNIB logo. In that article and many others, John Major described in moving terms the impact of his own father's sight loss.

Some of the people who drove our awareness raising activity forward at the time and over the coming years included Pat Orr, Sanchi Heesom, Lynne Stockbridge, Rachel Morgan, Fiona McCarthy, Paula Miles, Nicky Garsten, Olivia Belle, Joe Korner, Ciara Smyth, Kate Summerside, Julie Howell, Madeleine Sugden, Julie Robinson, Jean White, Hilary Todd, Iris Steen, Debbie Galvani, Judith Riley, Midge Blake, Josein Williams, Grant Imlach, Paul Gustafson and Richard Lane.

Financial Growth

The 1990s were another boom decade, with a growth of 47 per cent in real terms in income and 51 per cent in expenditure. We remained by far the largest and fastest growing sight loss charity.

The massive growth in earned/fee income (doubling in cash terms and 47 per cent in real terms) was a challenge to achieve and is a huge credit to the fee earning services. The majority of the larger services managed to double income as well as expenditure in cash terms (Condover, Rushton, New College, Redhill and products and services for independent living.) This was a great achievement given that the majority of these services had the national financial policy tide moving against them, under both Major's Conservative government and then the first couple of years under the Blair Labour government, when it stuck to its electoral promise not to exceed planned Conservative budgets. Indeed, that adverse tide rolled back the rehabilitation centres, the homes and the hotels where income declined in real terms. The first half of the decade saw the majority of the growth, while the second half averaged only a few points above inflation.

Fundraising and the Rise of Raffles and Special Events

On the voluntary income side, Mike Lancaster's 1989/91 radical shake up of fundraising proved its worth. Fundraising also doubled in cash terms with equally strong growth in legacy and non-legacy voluntary income. Non-legacy fundraising raised its share of voluntary income from 26 per cent in 1989/90 to 31 per cent, or £12.9 million, in 1999/2000. This turnaround in fundraising represented the fruits of a huge team effort over many years and into the 2000s and involved many people. Some of the many fundraisers who helped make this happen included Kath Howard, Gwen

McCreath, Hilary Partridge, Jane Desborough, Deborah Jack, Marion Forde, Suzie Diamond, Valerie Morton, Anna Purser, Paul Tuohy, Paul Tranter, Ann Paul, Julie Otley, Vinnie Smith, Trevor Griffiths, Mike Palfreman, Cat Barker, John Harvey, Ciara Smyth, Rob Jackson, Theresa Dauncey, Peter Storey, Mike Finlayson, Karen Gold, Karen Sutter, Maria Pemberton, Nancy Maguire and Sharon Wilding. Underpinning this work was the competent pair of hands of Sioned Clutton as head of finance and operational support.

In non-legacy fundraising, the star of the show was the RNIB raffle/lottery scheme. At its height the scheme was raising £7 million a year (1999 prices). We also invested heavily over the 1990s in legacy generation, once again ahead of most of our charity fundraising competitors, and this appeared to pay off, with legacies doubling in cash terms.

The formula for raffles was developed in our northern region by Kath Howard who rolled it out across the country. It consisted of recruiting volunteers over the phone to sell raffle tickets to their friends and neighbours and themselves. By the late 1990s this method was raising seven to ten per cent of total income and a staggering 33-40 per cent of voluntary income, excluding legacies, a position maintained through the 2000s. RNIB was the market developer and market leader.

So how does it work? An RNIB representative rings a person in a selected road and asks, 'Would you be prepared to sell some raffle tickets for RNIB?' It is intrusive, but it proved far more acceptable than asking for money. An impressive one in three people said, 'Yes', and on average sold half the tickets we sent them to neighbours and friends and bought the remaining half themselves – in effect a donation. Throughout the decade and beyond it was an amazing success for RNIB.

The lottery is an example of a fundraising scheme which has the advantage of regularity, allowing lessons to be learned from year to year, incremental improvements to be made and future income to be predicted.

Special events are much more exciting and have great publicity potential. The ideal is to link fundraising and publicity together. One success for us was building a relationship with Stevie Wonder who not only gave us two concerts at the Royal Albert Hall on 22 and 23 May 1995, he participated in a cause related marketing launch of an accessible BT phone card which gained us and BT a great deal of publicity.

RNIB lobbied for a Phone Card useable by blind people. 1995 launch, Stevie Wonder with Ian Bruce.

However, special events do have downsides. Income, especially net income, is difficult to predict. While there are similarities between events, they are primarily one-off and there is only one chance to get it right. Relatively small problems can throw a spanner in the works or unexpected luck can produce success. An example from this decade was a splendid concert, *Hey Mr Producer*, celebrating recent songs from Sir Cameron Mackintosh's repertoire of shows, held in front of the Queen and the Duke of Edinburgh at the Lyceum Theatre. It is impossible to overstate the importance of having the Queen as a charity's patron and we were also graced

At an RNIB event, Sir Cameron Mackintosh introduces the cast of *Hey Mr Producer* to the Queen 8 June 1998.

by having Her Majesty Queen Elizabeth, The Queen Mother as well for much of this history.

For a big event you need a big-name backer, but you need to engage that person, something everyone is trying to do – including other charities. Our target was Sir Cameron Mackintosh. We had at RNIB Redhill College a learning unit for 18 to 25 year-olds with sight loss as well as other profound and multiple learning difficulties. One, Derek Paravacini, was a musical savant (savant – someone with severe learning difficulties who has one or more abilities far above average). Derek is a brilliant musician, primarily on piano and keyboard, even though for him meaningful conversation is restricted. He had been tutored on the piano for many years by one of our senior education staff, Adam Ockelford, who later held the chair of music at the University of Roehampton. Adam and I took Derek to meet Sir Cameron to try to persuade him to back our charity. Our hope was for Derek to play for Sir

Cameron to show how even the most disadvantaged young blind person can be helped. Derek rose to the occasion and played magnificently. In response, Cameron played a piece of music in return. It was likely to be included in an upcoming musical and had only been heard before by three people. Knowing Derek's gift of being able to learn music very quickly, I took a risk and asked Sir Cameron whether he would like Derek to play the new composition back to him. This had not been planned but Adam communicated with Derek and, to Sir Cameron's understandable amazement, Derek replayed the piece by ear and note perfect. Derek was pleased, we were pleased but, most importantly, Sir Cameron was delighted. Then the only question was, how could he help?

The decision finally was that Sir Cameron and his staff would put on a show at the Lyceum Theatre celebrating 25 years of Mackintosh musicals called *Hey Mr Producer'* choosing the most popular songs and selected singers who had performed them. While we had no production costs, hiring the theatre and only having a two-night run meant net profit to RNIB would not be much – the key was television rights, or so we thought. For whatever reason, only Channel 4 was interested and their financial offer was disappointing. We put a brave face on it and went ahead; the show was brilliant and the Queen seemed to enjoy it. However, underneath, from the financial perspective, we were pretty depressed. A few weeks later Sir Cameron's people approached us to ask whether it would be alright for the film of the live performance to be taken by a cruise ship company and, with little hope of reward, we said, 'Yes'. Well! Over the next few years we received payments totalling over £250,000 – a financial transformation!

So, with successful fundraising and earnings, over the decade of the 1990s income rose by 47 per cent in real terms (nearly 100 per cent in cash terms). This growth almost equalled the dazzling income growth of the 1980s (56 per cent in real terms). Could it last into the 2000s?

Table 3b.1. RNIB Income and Expenditure 1969/70-1999/2000

Income (£ million)	1969/70	1979/80	1989/90	1999/2000
Fees for services	1.16	4.7	14.3	28.6
Voluntary income	1.61	6.25	19.9	41.5
Investment income	0.16	0.73	2.7	2.5
Other	0.13	0	0	0.5
Total	3.04	11.68	36.9	73.1
TOTAL at constant 2004 prices	31.7	35.1	54.7	80.2
Percentage growth, real terms		+11%	+56%	+47%
TOTAL at constant 2004 prices to base, where 1969/70 is 100[1]	100	111	173	253
Expenditure (£ millions)	1969/70	1979/80	1989/90	1999/2000
Services	2.13	9.07	32.4	63.5
Central administration	0.02	0.16		1.7
Net expenditure on fixed assets	0.14	0.90		
Cost of appeals	0.67	0.92	4.3	9.5
Total	2.96	11.05	36.7	74.8
TOTAL at constant 2004 prices	30.9	33.2	54.4	82.1
Percentage growth, real terms		+7%	+64%	+51%
TOTAL at constant 2004 prices to base 100[1]	100	107	176	266
Legacies included above in voluntary income	0.838	4.0	14.8	28.8

[1] UK RPI via the Cleave Calculator

Conclusion – Major Growth in Activity and Reach

The 1990s was a decade when expenditure grew from £37 million to £82 million, a 51 per cent growth in real terms; when a large and mighty charity cranked up its outputs. This was to implement a strategy calling for growth: for widening of the customer base into partially sighted and many more, older people; for a widening of the range of subjects covered by services; and for a vastly increased focus on indirect services introducing many new ones, especially campaigning, in order to reach out and benefit the majority of people with sight problems in this country. Services delivered direct to people with sight problems reached many more people across the decade, from around 150,000 to 460,000.

On the resource side we invested heavily to expand fundraising, to enhance the RNIB brand but to some extent we underinvested in trustee development and this was to be a key focus of the next decade.

Chapter 4a

2000-10: Governance and Merger Revolution

The first decade of the 21st century saw major structural and systems change in RNIB. The key drivers for the constitutional and governance changes came from inside and out. From within, there was the momentum from two previous strategies to put blind and partially sighted people in the driving seat and, in particular, the unfinished business on membership and trustee development from the 1994-2000 strategy. From outside, there was: the European Union's views on the dominant legitimacy of organisations of, rather than for, disabled people; changes in the UK Charity Commission's guidance on governance; the declining strength of the National League of the Blind and Disabled and the National Federation of the Blind; and the financial pressures of the economic downturn. However, change was also triggered by new people in the RNIB bringing in fresh ideas – for example, the new chair, Colin Low, in 2000; the new chief executive, Lesley Anne Alexander, in 2004; and a further new chair, Kevin Carey, in 2009. There were also new trustees ushered in through governance changes as well as the return of past active trustees such as Fred Reid.

Historical legitimacy

Until the 1920s RNIB was an organisation 'of' the blind, founded, run and governed by blind people. In 1868 it was founded by a group of blind people and for the first few decades you had to be blind to be a trustee. In the 1920s it changed into an organisation 'for' the blind with a stunning range of representation from across sectors of society (Thomas 1957, p.43).

The trustee body, the Executive Council of 100 or so trustees, was the primary vehicle for cross-sector co-operative governance of RNIB from the 1920s through to 2002. This model proved remarkably robust and reflected the mixed economy of welfare – that is, it incorporated all the main representative actors from the voluntary, statutory and commercial sectors. It contained five blocks of trustees:

- Local societies for the blind – Group A.
- Local authorities (which served visually impaired people) – Group B.
- Other national organisations for the blind (with the exception of Guide Dogs who were initially not interested and later declined an invitation to join) – Group C.
- Organisations of the blind – Group D.
- Individuals with a particular contribution, one third of whom had to be blind – Group E.

This Executive Council was even called a 'parliament of the blind' because all the major players were there. However, the contradiction was that its main legal purpose was as the trustee body of RNIB and, as such, was there to govern RNIB affairs, not the broader shape of inter-agency policy.

Further, it was seen variously as either an unimportant body that existed purely to rubber stamp decisions of the 30 plus committees or a slow-moving bureaucratic

nightmare. It comprised of only a minority of blind and partially sighted people. The tripling in size of RNIB activities
in the late twentieth century led to even greater complexity
of decision making. These factors, together with an increasingly fast-changing external environment and the arrival of
a new chair, Colin Low (later Lord Low), with a determination to lead from the centre, were all strong prompts for
change.

Becoming an 'of' Organisation

There were several reasons why it was important that
over half of trustees should be blind or partially sighted.
First, philosophically, it was seen as morally right for blind
and partially sighted people to be in charge of their own
organisation, sending a clear message of empowerment.
Second, it enshrined and helped effect a crucial RNIB
axiom that decisions should always be based on the needs
and wishes of the people it serves. Third, it was adroit
positioning to defend and increase our significant leverage
and legitimacy within the EU – whence the vast majority
of UK law then emanated. The EU had for many years
favoured lobbying from organisations 'of' disabled people
rather than ones 'for' and I judged that our significant EU
lobbying capacity was in danger of being undermined by
our 'for' label (Bruce, paper to Policy and Resources Committee 2000).

In some ways this was an easy move to achieve because
visually impaired people had for some years hovered around
the 40 per cent level on the trustee body. Also, it was the
culmination of the inspirational 1970s demands of the NFB
and the NLBD. It would have been wonderful if Martin Milligan,
who drafted the original 1968 NFB motion demanding 50
per cent plus had lived to see this day. Nevertheless, while
these arguments won people round, it was also apparent
that this move would weaken the NFB and to a lesser extent
the NLBD. So, it was statesmanlike of the two organisations
to give support.

Trustees Reduced from 120 to 24

At the same time as the 'of' debate was going on, there was a parallel one on the role and efficacy of the large trustee body – the Executive Council of 120 trustees – a debate promoted strongly by the new chair, Colin Low. As part of this, a survey of members of the Executive Council revealed widespread dissatisfaction with its composition and role. Recent revised Charity Commission guidelines also recommended that trustee bodies should be smaller. From autumn 2001 through to spring 2002, proposals were considered and implemented by the Executive Council, which created a Board of 24 trustees and turned the Executive Council of 120 into a National Advisory Assembly of 90. Persuading 120 people that they should give up their trustee status took all of Colin Low's considerable persuasion and determination to achieve.

The new Assembly continued to meet three times a year to be consulted but its primary legal function was to provide the electorate for electing Board members.

So, in 2001/02 the trustee body became the Board, with a membership of 24 of whom 50 per cent or more were to be blind or partially sighted. RNIB became the Royal National Institute 'of' the Blind, the first major disability service charity to do this. This was a major source of satisfaction to Colin and me, achieving the spirit of the revolution of the early 1970s. That first 2002 board comprised 24 people, sixteen of whom were blind or partially sighted. It included as honorary officers Colin Low, Kevin Carey and David Gadbury; country representatives James Cook (Scotland), Richard Godfrey (Cymru) and Henry Mayne (Northern Ireland); service experts Alan Suttie, Ian Fell, Fred Reid, Terry Moody, Mike Townsend and Michael Crowther; representatives from organisations of the blind Carol Borowski, Gareth Davies, Brendan Magill and Dr Amir Majid; representatives from organisations for the blind Richard Bignell and Richard Evans; and co-opted Lisa Charlton, Arif Khan, Julie Hollyman, Suzanne McCarthy, Richard Martin and Robert Silberman.

However, the blind trustees' representativeness remained indirect, coming through the electoral college of organisations 'of' and 'for' on the Assembly.

Blind Membership

Thus, the innovation of membership, mainly of blind and partially sighted people, was launched in 2001/02 to increase RNIB legitimacy and effectiveness and by 2011 had grown to just over 10,000, each member paying an annual fee initially of £17 (£15 by direct debit). RNIB membership came with a bi-monthly magazine full of practical advice, campaign news and various discounts aimed at people with sight loss. Importantly, it also gave access to the RNIB election and participation process. Members could vote whom they wanted onto a National Forum.

By the end of the decade, members could attend one of the nine regional members' fora in England or in Northern Ireland, Scotland and Wales which in turn chose four members each to serve on the national UK members' forum. There were three regional meetings per year and some 1,000 members participated, with more giving their views in advance by teleconference to their regional representatives. The meetings were regularly attended by RNIB service delivery staff who gained a lot from this direct interaction with blind and partially sighted members around the country. The three top issues from each forum went up to the National Forum for debate. The Forum was also particularly vital in that it provided the basis of the RNIB AGM, electing people to the RNIB trustee Board, and 'helps identify and shape major strategy, service and policy issues' (Annual Report 2009/10, p. 120).

By the end of the decade, under chair Lord Colin Low and CEO Lesley-Anne Alexander the transition of power and authority was well and truly complete. The Advisory Assembly was abolished and had been replaced by the UK RNIB Members' Forum with the authority and influence outlined above. To carry on the tradition of related external organisation influence, a Third Sector Forum for other organisations 'of' and 'for' the blind was created by Vision 2020 UK.

Executive Systems Changes

The influence of strategic planning on direction and action continued to be a priority in the 2000s and, if anything, grew in importance under the new leadership. The last strategy of my tenure started in 2000, the first of Lesley-Anne's tenure was 2005 and the second in 2009. They were:

- *Strategic Direction 2000-2006: Inclusion, Support and Independence* (RNIB 2000)
- *The Future @ RNIB 2005-2009: Independent Living: Campaigning for Lasting Change for People with Sight Problems* (RNIB 2005)
- *Strategy 2009-2014: Ending the Isolation of Sight Loss* (RNIB 2008) – 'Stopping people lose their sight unnecessarily; supporting independent living; creating an inclusive society'

This next section describes the contrasting implementation methods during the decade 2000-10.

In 2000 there were six priority directional themes:

- to promote social inclusion and challenge discrimination
- to offer timely support and prevention
- to enable independence through accessible information
- to improve customer focus
- to improve our people, culture, governance and structure
- to raise income and awareness.

This was my final strategy and incorporated a significant move away from conventional strategic plan implementation in RNIB and the wider voluntary sector. All activity units in RNIB were given the responsibility to propose how they would significantly raise or amend their activities and outcomes to implement these six priority directional themes. Here the responsibility for implementation (and detailed planning) as well as targets was devolved onto the activity managers, to be signed off subsequently by senior managers and committees. This was a bottom-up approach rather than a top-down with consultation. At the time this method of implementation was seen as radical because it reduced the power of the centre of RNIB to dictate and relied on the front line to lead or propose. I promoted this approach from observation of the most successful aspects of previous strategies and bolstered by the work of Mary Jo Hatch (1997). The assumption was that the periphery or edge of an organisation is more in touch with the complex reality of customers – in our case, primarily people with sight problems – than the top or centre. In addition, the approach assumes, as I do, that the majority of managers want to, and will, do their best, especially if openly trusted to do so. While the monitoring showed good progress after the first year, we shall never know whether this approach would have ultimately succeeded. At that moment RNIB was hit by the financial vicissitudes of the early 2000s and the Board, encouraged by the treasurer, judged it was necessary to take back more command and control to reduce expenditure and keep the budgets at break-even. This we achieved and the strategy targets were largely met but without the creativity and sensitivity that we might have had.

In the next strategy (RNIB 2005), the first under Lesley-Anne Alexander's leadership, execution was again devolved but four implementation methods were prioritised – campaigning, in particular:

- Campaigning to improve the lives of people with sight problems
- Leading by example
- Building RNIB's expertise
- Maximising our impact.

These priorities were given additional funds, for example, by 2009 campaigning was attracting an annual uplift of £1.5 million.

The 2005 strategy had a mix of top-down and bottom-up implementation. The top-down aspect was broadly financial, with the Board identifying a pool of development funds to drive forward strategic priorities, whilst simultaneously reviewing and squeezing ongoing funding for those areas of work that contributed less to priorities. A cadre of senior and middle managers were trained up to populate a prioritisation forum, with service managers bidding for funding, setting out how these bids would help to deliver the strategic goals. This process achieved a lot by developing many future leaders and improving financial and business skills in the organisation. However, financial challenges again meant that development funds were scarcer than planned, which impacted on budgets and programme management capacity.

For the 2009 strategy a different approach to implementation was put in place. There were three priorities:

- Stopping people losing their sight unnecessarily
- Supporting independent living
- Creating an inclusive society.

Under each of those headings, specific targets were set and activity units had to say in what way and how much they could contribute towards these targets. In the words of Fazilet Hadi, the director of inclusive society, 'We [the top of the organisation] decided the "what" but left the "how" to the activity units.' Activity units effectively justified their existence against how much they contributed to strategy.

As with previous strategies, each priority was sponsored by an executive director, a programme management capacity was developed, and across-organisation programme managers appointed. These managers came mainly from the cadre of leaders who had emerged from the previous strategy review processes. Each priority also had a non-executive board drawn from trustees and co-opted experts to support the lead director and to provide assurance to the trustee board. The programme managers worked across the organisation and, though budgets were still allocated via departments, programme managers had significant authority within the budgeting process and had to agree to sign off spending. The aim of all this was to help RNIB operate more effectively as a single joined-up organisation to deliver strategic priorities rather than as a collection of complementary but sometimes competing services.

All three strategic plans over the years 2000 to 2010 were serious attempts to form an effective practice link between strategy and implementation – a link so often missing in conventional organisational strategic planning. Each had a different assumption about where the balance of expertise in strategy creation and implementation lay and used organisation learning and capacity building to continuously improve strategic delivery.

RNIB Co-operation with the VI Sector

In the middle 1980s RNIB made the change to ally itself with the broader disability sector. However, this pan-disability approach left a gap in formal co-operation within the visually impaired field. Surprisingly, because it had been over the years more aloof, the first to propose additional intra VI sector co-operation was the Guide Dogs for the Blind Association. In 1989 their chair, Lord Jenkin, proposed the establishment of the Visual Handicap Group (VHG) whose members would be the main national organisations for the blind. RNIB agreed to join, provided the two main organisations of the blind, the NFB and NLBD, were added. This was accepted and RNIB offered to help by providing the secretariat – which also provided a counterbalance to GDBA chairing. VHG operated as a loose co-operative body publishing occasional, sometimes quite influential, reports and holding conferences.

In the late 1990s, discussions between VHG and the UK Committee for the Prevention of Blindness, work on a National Agenda for Action on Visual Impairment and a national consultative conference led to the recommendation for a UK Vision Forum. In 2001 this mutated into Vision 2020 UK under its first chair, Stephen Remington, from Action for Blind People, with Fazilet Hadi leading for RNIB. It had an initial membership of 38 national organisations concerned with sight. By the middle of the decade this had risen to 50 and included a wide range of members, including the Association of British Dispensing Opticians, the RCN's Ophthalmic Nursing Forum, Sight Savers International and all the national charities. To achieve a forum where all the major players participate, co-operate and agree is quite remarkable for a field sometimes characterised as 'not blind welfare but blind warfare'! Due credit should be given to Stephen Remington in his chairing role. Socially gifted, his charm and fairness of treatment helped the group grow and stay together.

Arguably smoothed by the relationships engendered by the above, another cross-sector initiative was gestating. In late 2006 Lesley-Anne Alexander held talks with the CEOs of GDBA and Action for Blind People and proposed what would become known as the UK Vision Strategy. She floated this idea at a conference in York in January 2007 convened to discuss the Department of Health pilots on eye health. It was an ideal setting, attended by all the major statutory and voluntary organisation players. Crucially, RNIB offered to fund the initiative, to the tune of an initial £300,000 per annum which would reduce in time to £220,000 per annum. Three months later, in April 2007 there was a conference at the Design Centre in London to decide in principle what went into the strategy. By June a draft was written and by autumn it was out for consultation. Rewritten between December 2007 and February 2008, it was launched formally in April 2008. Anyone experienced in sector collaboration will acknowledge the speed of this

**Launching the UK Vision Strategy
in April 2008 at the Design Centre.**

initiative and credit goes to all the players. However, from
an RNIB perspective, Lesley-Anne's leadership was crucial, as were the contributions of Fazilet Hadi and Anita
Lightstone on ensuring an open consultative process and
preparing the final document.

The UK Vision Strategy laid out a path to:

* improve the eye health of the people of the UK
* eliminate avoidable sight loss and deliver excellent
  support to those with a sight problem
* enhance the inclusion, participation and independence of blind and partially sighted people.

Over 650 organisations and individuals committed to, and
played a role in, developing the strategy. These included
people with sight loss, users of eye care services, eye health
and social care professionals and all the key statutory and
voluntary organisations. The UK government and the devolved
powers also gave their support to the strategy. It was the first
time that such a breadth of groups had come together to set
the direction for eye health and sight loss services across
the UK – a major achievement. It also showed that RNIB
could be a team player despite being the largest sight loss
organisation by far.

Partnerships through 'Associated Charities' – Major Mergers

While the 1990s had seen several attempts at mergers and take-overs, few were effected. This was about to change.

The first major merger was the absorption into RNIB of Visual Impairment Services SE Scotland (VISSES) in 2003, one of the largest voluntary societies in the UK at around two per cent of RNIB turnover. This merger succeeded for many reasons but two major ones were, first, that VISSES thought it was becoming financially unviable and wanted a merger before the chronic financial problem became acute and, second, because the two executive leaders (Allan Murray – RNIB, and Bryn Merchant – VISSES) were non-flamboyant, sensitive and forward-looking professionals. This gave RNIB Scotland a major service base in Edinburgh and throughout the south east of the country. There were also successful mergers with local societies, Bristol and Stoke, in 2003.

RNIB's new chief executive, Lesley-Anne Alexander, from 2004 onwards, led a new impetus for association with other independent organisations working with visually impaired people. A specific breakthrough was the development by Lesley-Anne of RNIB Group, a new constitutional formula adapted from the housing association movement. This model allowed an external charity to be legally included within RNIB as a wholly-owned subsidiary but, at the same time, allowed the included organisation to retain its board and its name/ brand. This approach removed, or at least reduced, the feeling of 'takeover' which so often unravels charity mergers.

The largest such association occurred in October 2008 when it was announced that from April 2009 Action for Blind People would become part of the RNIB Group as an 'associate charity'. Action was a large charity with a turnover of 20 per cent of that of the RNIB, much larger than any of the previous link ups. Action became a 'delivery agent' for RNIB which withdrew from some services and handed them over to Action, most particularly, RNIB's regional services. So, both charities gained and, more importantly, blind and partially sighted people could receive better co-ordinated services. In addition, competition over fundraising and contracts ceased, and services and management were rationalised. Some might argue the opposite, that blind and partially sighted people's choice had been reduced (one provider to choose from, not two), but that presumes there was previously an excess of supply over demand which was not the case.

The warmer inter-organisational climate and the associate charity formula, combined with the much more adverse UK financial situation of 2008 onwards, created propitious circumstances for other charities associating with RNIB. The benefits seemed clear: better co-ordination and less confusion in the delivery of services to blind and partially sighted people; more effective sharing of back office functions and other activities, such as volunteer development and fundraising – a move welcomed by major funders; and more carefully defined common offerings.

However, mergers do not increase the volume or necessarily the quality of services and activities to people with sight loss. Research literature on mergers (admittedly mainly in the commercial sector) shows the challenges and frequent failures of mergers to add value. Funders, especially from the commercial sector, generally favour charity mergers, arguing that they reduce competition and duplication. However, duplication only becomes a systemic problem if supply exceeds demand – which is hardly ever the case in the charity world. The mergers increased RNIB size but only marginally increased the total volume of service delivered.

Cognisant of cultural tensions that mergers can evoke, in the next few years RNIB worked successfully on making these associated partnerships work, concentrating on linking and unifying cultures.

Conclusion

RNIB ended the first decade of the new century a very different organisation systemically from the one that began it. True, much remained the same but there were major changes. Under Colin Low and my leadership, RNIB:

- became an organisation 'of' blind people rather than 'for', on the basis of 50 per cent of trustees with sight loss
- introduced membership, primarily of blind and partially sighted people, as a source of increased legitimacy, a mechanism for improving support for blind and partially sighted people and a more democratic elective process
- reduced the trustee body from 120 to 24, elected by an advisory council, a proportion of whom were elected by the (largely blind) membership.

Under Colin Low and then Kevin Carey, and Lesley-Anne Alexander's leadership, RNIB:

- developed a successful model of close association with other charities in the sight-loss field (associated charities) to an extent that would have been unthinkable in the twentieth century; in particular, persuading Action for Blind People to join RNIB Group
- took a more active leadership role on VI sector co-operation and, in particular, leading on the UK Vision Strategy
- re-balanced RNIB activity commissioning to be more centrally, strategically driven
- further emphasised the importance of membership as a source of legitimacy and activity proposal building and upgraded the importance of the UK Members' Forum and introduced regional fora
- created a new legal structure in 2005-06 – RNIB Group as a method of incorporating associated charities.

The rate of expansion of RNIB activities as measured by expenditure rose modestly over the decade, by 28 per cent in real terms (taking account of inflation), much less than in the two previous decades. Moreover, this figure included the addition of Action for Blind People's expenditure which stood at approximately 20 per cent of RNIB's. Income growth was even more modest at seventeen per cent in real terms. (See Table 9.2 below.) The absorption of Action for Blind People into the RNIB Group gave a good start to the 2010-20 decade of public expenditure reduction and restraint, and increased localism. The challenges that remained included: decisions over the extent of the associated charities' integration; the creation of a viable brand strategy with Action for Blind People's brand unknown among the public in comparison to RNIB's stronger presence; and poor income growth.

Chapter 4b

Services: Launches, Relaunches and Closures

Renewing Services

In the early part of the noughties there were several important launches and relaunches of existing services.

RNIB Radio

A major success of the decade was the launch and expansion of RNIB Radio, Europe's first radio station for blind and partially sighted people. It started in RNIB Scotland in 2003 with the launch of VIP On Air on the internet, broadcasting four hours a day, five days a week entirely based on volunteers with all the presenters being blind or partially sighted. After three successful years it relaunched in 2007 as RNIB Insight Radio, appearing first on FM, then on Sky and later on Freesat reaching 85,000 listeners and offering:

> everything from your daily newspapers, movie reviews, TV, events and job guides plus lots more ... hints and tips on everything from cookery, DIY, gardening and every day there's an in-depth report on problems faced by the blind and partially sighted

community, be it medical, personal or political. (RNIB website 2010)

Digital Talking Books

A major service relaunch in April 2002 was talking books in digital format, led by Stephen King and his team. The decision on which digital audio platform to change to had been an issue for over ten years. It was a decade which had seen several new digital audio platforms launched in the commercial market by individual companies but nearly all had failed to become the industry standard. We were determined not to repeat the mistake of the 1960s when RNIB chose the (then) revolutionary long-playing tape cassette (12 hours) as its method for recording talking books for blind people. Only two or three years later we were upstaged by the launch of the very much shorter but smaller compact cassette which became the industry standard and dominated the world market for 25 years.

After flirting with several of the new digital delivery methods such as digital audio tape (DAT), RNIB finally decided simply to transfer all our analogue tape masters into a digital database; although it sounded simple, it was not. By April 2002, we had sufficient digital books on CD to launch in the new format – 4,300 titles, including 400 recorded directly onto digital. An even more challenging strand of pre-launch activity was the development of a digital playback machine (or player). Our marketing team worked with the engineers to develop a player which suited the majority of our members. The majority, who are 75 years or over, are often confused by player complexity, not only because of sight loss, but also because of arthritis in their hands and wrists, and hearing problems. Moreover, any company helping us to develop the player could not be allowed to gain exclusive rights of production through patents, for example – a mistake of the 1960s.

By 2002 we had developed a suitable player to launch and by the end of the year 12,000 members had transferred to the new playback machine, 23,000 by 2004. The transfer was complicated and sensitive because so many older members saw the new digital machine as frightening. However, through the patience of our 2,000 volunteer engineers, led for so many years by David Finlay-Maxwell, working in people's homes, progress was rapid. In 2006/07 the introduction of DAISY (the Digital Audio Information System) CDs improved members' ability to navigate and gave a better listener experience. Membership of the digital Talking Book system reached its zenith in 2006/07 at 45,000 lending two million books but the trend declined as local authority budget cuts curtailed membership numbers.

All this cutting-edge development meant that in 2005 RNIB could celebrate the seventieth anniversary of Talking Books with confidence. On the publicity and fundraising side, two key figures were Ciara Smyth and John Harvey, respectively. Through meticulous research in the RNIB archives, Ciara developed a stunning 'audio experience' of the history of Talking Books. This was launched on 8 November at the Arts Club in Mayfair to an audience of literary figures and supporters. Ciara and John persuaded people to come, such as Lord Bragg, Julian Fellowes, P.D. James, Joanna Trollope, Jaqueline Wilson, David Blunkett and George Martin. Both Ciara and John gave exceptional service to RNIB over more than tenyears each. Ciara improved our strategic communications approach and made greater use of what has subsequently been called insight research; John built strong relationships with many of our major donors using his charm and openness to full effect. This Talking Book celebration was also integrated with campaigning via the Right to Read campaign, led by David Mann. Another fundamental player in the history of Talking Books between 1970 and 2010 was Ian Turner, who, over virtually the whole of this period, was either in charge or in the number two position, supported by Janet Sturmey, Peter Parish and Peter Jones. Popular with actor readers, staff and trustees, it would be hard to find a more liked RNIB manager than Ian.

Shopping Online

Another service breakthrough in early 2002 was the launch of shopping online for RNIB products, with 2,300 orders in the first nine months. Helped by online ordering, sales of products from liquid level indicators through to talking computers and phones tripled from £2 million per year to over £6 million by the end of the decade.

A further reason for the expansion was the integration of:

- Customer Services in Peterborough which handled all the sales and distribution of products as well as numerous enquiries
- the RNIB Helpline (originally started in 1997) in London which gave individual advice on a wide range of topics
- and various specialist advice and support services, such as legal advice and counselling (Emotional Support), providing 3,000 counselling sessions a year.

The RNIB Shopping Online launch in early 2002 led to a big increase in stock holding.

The new integrated RNIB Helpline was supported by additional investment of £1 million in 2008. Over the decade the number of enquiries quadrupled to a massive 400,000 in 2009/10, or 2,000 enquiries each working day, a real success story involving many people, with Andy Barrick and Jan Kerr playing key roles.

Talk and Support

The year 2001/02 also saw the start of Talk and Support telephone befriending groups, championed by Jon Barrick, which within a year involved 450 participants representing 22,500 hours of teleconferencing. This used the 'old' and therefore familiar, non-threatening technology of the telephone to facilitate mutual aid and discussion amongst people losing their sight. Getting together to share experiences empowers people. They hear from people who are further through the sight-loss process and who can share their coping methods. Talk and Support simply translates this into the telephone (conferencing) milieu. Although this medium lacks the warmth of face-to-face meetings, it makes it much easier for newly blind people to participate because no travel is involved. During the 2000s the service was headed by Julia Polzerova and by the end of the decade 130 groups were running each week. Here is a quote from one participant which featured in the tenth anniversary newsletter (October 2011): 'In a group where every participant has some degree of sight loss, you soon learn that you are not the only blind person to get things wrong. Because we are all in the same boat, we can learn as well as laugh at our misfortunes together.'

Eye Health

With RNIB's increasing emphasis on eye health since the middle 1980s, it was perhaps inevitable that the step into optometry would come. In the late 1990s Barbara Ryan, a fully qualified optometrist, was recruited to develop our role in that field (later supported by Marek Karas). She set out an inspiring strategy for low vision. By 2000 a low vision services eye clinic was planned for the new RNIB headquarters part-funded by contracts with local health authorities. It was a proud moment when, at the same time as our move into our new HQ in Judd Street in March 2002 we opened the low vision clinic on the ground floor and the flow of patients began. By this stage, Barbara had moved on and our eye health activities were led by another able optometrist, Anita Lightstone, supported by Stuart Hornsby, Low Vision Officer, and others. She extended our low vision service work by delivering contracts with health commissioners in Camden, Islington, Kensington and Chelsea, the City of London, Barking and Havering.

The next major breakthrough came when Anita Light-stone was seconded in 2003 to the Department of Health to contribute her expertise towards the National Eye Care Programme then under development. This was to include a model pathway for the best treatment of low vision patients, piloted successfully in Gateshead with RNIB's expert guid-ance as input, and later rolled out across the country.

However, the story does not stop there, because of the development of the UK Vision Strategy. This strategy was based on full participation of all organisations and groups from the VI world. One subset (health) which embraced this fully included the ophthalmologists and optometrists as well as others involved in service delivery including the Department of Health: 'The strength of the Strategy is that it has enabled the sector to speak with one voice' (Anita Lightstone, personal communication).

One impressive impact of this unity was the inclusion of an eye health indicator in the Public Health Outcomes Framework – thought to be the first since the formation of the NHS. The then secretary of state for health said: 'Some of you might know that we hadn't originally planned to have an indicator for reducing avoidable sight loss. But because of the links between this indicator and the wider determinants of health, made by the impressive partnership working to the UK Vision Strategy, it's now included' (Andrew Lansley at the launch of the Public Health Outcomes Framework, 23 January 2012).

In 2010 the low vision clinic was still flourishing, under Louise Stalker and within the brand envelope of Action for Blind People, handling over 1,000 patient encounters per year, with each patient having access to a low vision therapist and links to rehabilitation.

Eye Clinic Liaison

The relationship between ophthalmology and optometry and social rehabilitation services in the community needed improving. Patients can get 'lost' in the system between ophthalmologists, social services and local societies for blind and partially sighted people, each with their own rehabilitation possibilities. So, in the 1990s there sprang up the concept of 'eye clinic liaison officers' (ECLOs), based in hospital eye clinics who actively mediated the divide. In addition, they played, and still play, an active signposting role, introducing people with sight problems to resources in the community. Examples are local guiding or reading services, RNIB Talking Books, local talking newspapers and so on. In the 2010s this activity became known as social prescribing. RNIB had been one of the pioneers in the 1990s (catalysed by Chris Croft) when RNIB began to be contracted to run the role from inside eye clinics.

The expanding sub-contracting/outsourcing culture of the New Labour government (1997) provided fertile ground for this initiative. By 2010 RNIB Group (the service had also been transferred to Action for Blind People in 2008 as an RNIB 'delivery agent') had helped 13,400 people in hospital eye clinics through RNIB Group staff presence in 24 clinics in England, all clinics in Northern Ireland, four in Scotland and two in Wales. In 2011, Philippa Simkiss (head of evidence and service impact, whose razor-sharp mind had served RNIB well for the previous 20 or so years) reported that: 'of 185 locations mapped, 122 locations are covered by ECLO or similar roles, of which 66 are covered by RNIB

Group ECLOs' (paper presented to the RNIB Early Reach Programme board meeting, 15 November 2011).

This shows the significant growth of the ECLO model and RNIB's major role in this development since the middle 1990s – a pioneering example of early social prescribing.

Rehabilitation

Rehabilitation is an area where RNIB has long felt comfortable, pioneering rehabilitation for blind people since the beginning of the twentieth century with services (mainly residential) expanding after each world war. Important investigative research in the early 1980s was promoted by Fred Reid and Tony Aston and undertaken by Dr Penny Shore (Shore 1985). In 1985 RNIB founded the RNIB Social Services Consultancy (initially called the RNIB Rehabilitation Consultancy Unit), headed by Penny Shore, as part of the policy-driven expansion into indirect services. By the 1990s this had expanded into direct provision of domiciliary rehabilitation – as demand for residential services declined – with the first local delivery in Rochdale in 1988; and by 2000 RNIB had a number of rehabilitation contracts with commissioners across the UK. By 2003/04 these numbered some 20 in all. For much of the decade the team was led by Deborah Hamlin and Pete Lucas, both experienced officers who inspired confidence in the statutory commissioners. In 2009 these services were transferred to Action for Blind People.

Direct Education Provision

RNIB direct education provision changed its shape significantly during this decade reducing the number of residential establishments by two. In 2007 RNIB New College Worcester, a flagship school for more able blind and partially sighted children, became independent. In the same year RNIB Redhill College closed its doors as a college of further education as employment rehabilitation funding streams dried up. This drop in income coincided with the need, if it were to stay open, for major capital upgrading to modern standards of physical accommodation for all-year-round provision. The departure of these two services reduced charitable expenditure by approximately six per cent. Alongside this, an expanded RNIB Rushton School opened near Coventry in 2002, transferring from its previous location in an isolated rural setting in Northamptonshire – a hugely complex project overseen with great skill by Adam Ockelford. This school had a major capital injection (equivalent to 25 per cent of RNIB annual turnover) to become a state-of-the-art school for children and young people with very complex needs. It was renamed RNIB Pears Centre for Specialist Learning in recognition of the generosity over many years of the Pears Foundation and their executive chair, Sir Trevor Pears.

There were other difficult closure decisions which had some happy and some unhappy endings for individuals and their families. Revenue and investment realities along with some fearsome logic from people, such as Fred Reid, led us to close the Sunshine House School in Southport and Condover School in Shropshire.

Employment

RNIB employment services in the 2000-10 period had to become even more contract orientated. In the typical year of 2003/04 just over 700 people were helped with employment assessment, vocational guidance and training, including ICT training. (Annual Report 2003/04). By 2010 these figures had grown, with RNIB Group helping over 700 people retain work plus over 200 find work – no mean feat given the state of the economy. Of note were two contracts, covering Barclays and Royal Bank of Scotland: here RNIB Group helped almost 100 people in 2010 – supporting the long tradition of bank employment of blind and partially sighted people. However, the overall position of employment prospects for blind people remained grim, with approximately two thirds of working age economically inactive. This prompted more policy analysis to determine the best ways forward (for example, the research work of Reid and Simkiss over the period 2008-12 which was published in 2013).

Organisational Restructuring

During the decade there were two major changes in the organisation of service delivery. The first was in 2005 under the leadership of Lesley-Anne Alexander, supporting the new strategy, *The Future @ RNIB 2005-2009*. With the departure of Jon Barrick, Director of Vocational and Social Services, all the direct services in education, employment, rehabilitation, health and social services were brought together under one director, Eamon Fetton. This was a logical move – although it encompassed a wide span of expertise and control. The UK-wide high-volume services such as customer services, products and publications, Talking Books, technology and research and development were grouped into an access and information services directorate under Stephen King.

The second reorganisation followed in 2008/09 with the impact of the creation of the RNIB Group, including Action for Blind People and the National Library for the Blind. The chief executive of Action, Stephen Remington, joined the RNIB senior management team as a group director, to reflect the redistribution of services between Action for Blind People and RNIB. So, for example, in 2008/09 the management of all RNIB regional services was transferred to Action for Blind People and became part of their brand. Talking Books delivery transferred to the National Library, but under the brand of RNIB National Library Service. In joining the RNIB Board, Stephen Remington brought the benefit of his considerable experience in the sight-loss field as well as his earlier senior experience of management in the arts.

Campaigning – Increased Focus and Investment

The 2000s saw even more active campaigning than the 1990s, with more staff involved, even more priority being applied, and a larger budget (approximately £1 million more per year from 2005/6 resulting in a total of £3.4 million in 2009/10). Fazilet Hadi continued to play a key role, supported by Steve Winyard and his team. An innovation introduced under Fazilet's leadership was a campaign post for a lawyer. First to be appointed was Cathy Casserly in 1999, followed by Sam Fothergill. These two increased the firepower of campaigning, not only on legislation but in negotiations with companies and public bodies to extend their implementation of the Disability Discrimination Act in the provision of goods and services and employment – examples were accessible information by the NHS and talking ATMs.

The long trusted method of underpinning campaign work with solid research continued: examples being reports emanating from the second Needs Survey on which I worked closely with Mark Baker and Polina Obolenskaya (Bruce and Baker 2001, 2003, 2005 and Bruce, Harrow and Obolenskaya 2007); and the research arising from the longitudinal sample of blind and partially sighted people investigated by the Visual Impairment Centre for Teaching and Research (VICTAR) at the University of Birmingham (previously RCEVH). At the end of the decade seminal examples were: *Future Sight Loss 1: Economic Impact of Partial Sight and Blindness in the UK Adult Population* (Access Economics, 2009); and *Future Sight Loss 2: An Epidemiological and Economic Model for Sight Loss in the Decade 2010-20* (Minassian and Reidy, 2009)

The embryonic campaign supporters' network of the early part of the decade expanded massively to a network of some 5,000 people, supported by the appointment of nine regional campaign officers in 2008, each supported by around half a dozen campaign co-ordination volunteers. This initiative enabled RNIB to further strengthen its campaigning voice and to support local campaigning to defend and improve local services, for example, rehabilitation support, Talking Books take-up, school support and concessionary fares. RNIB has had outstanding staff campaigners since the first parliamentary officer was appointed in 1985. One of the most outstanding, as well as longstanding, was Steve Winyard (1996-2016), who led these efforts, supported by many others, including Helen Dearman and Hugh Huddy (amongst the longest serving), Dan Scorer, Dan Vale, Julianne Marriot, Catherine Casserley, Dermot Ryan, Caroline Ellis, Mark Baker,

Richard Holmes, David Mann, Stephen Malcolm, David Groves and Julie Howell.

A major success of the decade was the winning of eligibility for the higher rate mobility allowance element of the Disability Living Allowance in 2008/09 which put an extra £45 million per annum into the pockets of the most severely visually impaired people in the UK. (The lower rate allowance won in 1991 provided £40 million per annum.) These two wins, in hard cash terms, show the benefits of campaigning. The Higher Rate campaign led jointly by Steve Winyard and Colin Low took three years and was underpinned by a research-based campaign report, *Taken for a Ride* (Winyard 2006). As well as behind-the-scenes lobbying, when Colin Low and Steve Winyard met Prime Minister Gordon Brown, this was a high-profile campaign with a petition to Downing Street, two mass lobbies of parliament and the subject regularly reaching the floor of the House of Commons. Blind trustees were active including David Blunkett (vice president), Gareth Davies, Fred Reid, Jill Allen King and Lesley Kelly.

Throughout the decade, two consistent campaigns with many offshoots were, once again:

- the right for, and practical delivery of, access to information
- eye health campaigning.

Access to Information campaigning was vigorous and took many forms including:

- the continuation of 'see it right' persuasion campaigns in several years with a particular focus against the use of small print
- a targeting of pharmaceutical labelling and medical communications, for example, achieving an EU directive on pharmaceutical labelling (2003/04) and having the subject of medical communications raised in Prime Minister's Questions in 2009 (an RNIB first)

- lobbying for the Copyright (Visually Impaired Persons) Act 2002 and amendments to the UK Communications Act 2003
- the Right to Read campaign across the decade among other activities presented a charter to Downing Street supported by 31,000 signatures (2005)
- persuading the secretary of state for culture, media and sport to give vulnerable and older people extra support during digital switchover from analogue TV (2006)
- running an awareness campaign to increase blind and partially sighted people's knowledge that audio description exists, with a penetration level of 72 per cent (2007/08)
- contributing £1 million to the television industry to find a solution to making digital television easy to use for people who cannot see the screen or read the channel changing devices (2007/08)
- Lord Low introducing a new accessible information clause into the Equalities Act (2010).

Eye health campaigning also continued at a very active rate. The loss of free eye tests under the Thatcher government was a severe setback, partly rectified by RNIB persuading the New Labour government in 1998 to re-introduce free tests for the over sixties. Eye tests are extremely important in spotting conditions that might lead to blindness early but price, and the fact that many people do not realise their importance, hinders take-up. Some of the successes of the decade were:

- RNIB Cymru achieved the first breakthrough, achieving free eye tests for vulnerable groups of working age in 2002/03
- RNIB Scotland achieved free eye tests for all in 2004 (not just the over sixties)
- the Open Your Eyes campaign in 2005/06 reached nineteen million people with a message on the importance of having a test

- by 2006/07 RNIB eye health messages were reaching 65 per cent of the population.

Other eye health campaigning included:

- introducing strong new evidence of the link between smoking and sight loss in 2005/06, reaching 26 million people
- successfully campaigning over most of the decade to gain free access to Lucentis on the NHS for the treatment of wet AMD (age-related macular degeneration)
- campaigning in 2009/10 on the importance of siblings of glaucoma sufferers getting regular check-ups.

There were many other campaigns including:

- children's access to the education curriculum, leisure and public transport (2000/01)
- RNIB and GDBA working together on national standards for social care (*Progress in Sight* – Oct 2002)
- jointly campaigning with Action for Blind People in the early decade and again in 2004/05 on access to jobs
- RNIB persuading the government to increase the Access to Work budget in 2007/08.

Underpinning all this campaigning activity was the increased involvement of networks of blind and partially sighted people. As early as 2002/03 the newly developed campaign supporters' network had reached 2,400 members, nearly all blind and partially sighted. The introduction of RNIB membership in March 2002 provided the beginnings of a powerhouse of active constituents lobbying on various campaigns. As mentioned above, this had become very active by the end of the decade, with over 5,000 people keen to be mobilised. As collateral evidence of the quality of RNIB campaigning, in 2008/09 RNIB was voted the charity with the 'most improved parliamentary relations'.

Alongside the public campaigning, throughout the decade there continued the patient work with television manufacturers by a team led by Stephen King. The team worked hard to ensure that what we had learned about making computers and mobile phones usable by blind people was also built into televisions. Initially no one believed TV controls could be made to 'talk', the microchips used were too small and dumb. Nevertheless, RNIB proved everyone wrong by building a prototype and demonstrating it to the industry, enthusing the industry's engineers to come up with solutions. By 2010 Panasonic had launched the first mainstream range of talking televisions in the UK, swiftly followed by Samsung and Sony.

Reading of print books still remained elusive, however. Throughout the 2000s the Right to Read campaign, started in the 1990s and led for most of this history by David Mann, highlighted an uncomfortable fact. Despite services like Talking Books and braille and audio transcription services, fewer than five per cent of books were available to be read independently by a blind person on publication. RNIB campaigned noisily for change, for example through billboards. Also quietly, in the background, RNIB was working closely with partners in the global DAISY consortium to change this at source. (Richard Orme, one of our leading accessibility experts, later became CEO of DAISY.) When e-books burst onto the scene during the decade, we were set for another transformation in access. By 2012 the Right to Read monitor identified that 90 per cent of books published that year could be read on the day of publication by a reader with the right skills and technologies. Very quickly the required speech technologies were built into just about every e-book reader, to the point that reading by listening became a major part of the book reading market. Much of this can be traced back to key investments in very high-quality speech synthesis made by RNIB in the early to mid 2000s. The Right to Read campaign

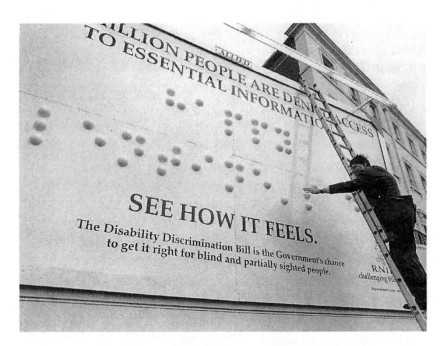

Started in the 1990s, the Right to Read Campaign made great strides in the 2000s. Here, Colin Low tries to read super-sized braille.

became global and culminated in the 2013 Marrakesh copyright treaty under the auspices of the World Intellectual Copyright Organisation (WIPO).

In the mid 1990s RNIB had been told that an amendment to the Berne convention on copyright was impossible. In 2013 the 116 countries of WIPO agreed to do so to enable better access to books by people with print disabilities; the result of a 20-year single-minded global campaign supported by RNIB's David Mann and his successor, Dan Pescod. They used the idea of the global 'book famine' skilfully to build support amongst governments worldwide using the World Blind Union as the vehicle.

International Conference on Low Vision – Vision 2005

The origination of this successful conference was in its predecessor conference in July 2002 in Goteborg, Sweden when, after furious lobbying, we achieved London as the location for 2005 with RNIB as host. Our trump card was offering David Blunkett as the lead speaker. Reasonably, we intimated he might well be the first blind prime minister in the world by then!

Vision 2005 International in London was an amazing success, as evidenced by the numbers attending and the subsequent feedback. It was organised by RNIB's Jon Barrick, Deborah Hamlin and their team, plus international experts in ophthalmology, optometry and rehabilitation.

People – New Leadership

In the late 1990s RNIB further increased its professionalism, monitoring HR data not only on recruitment, training, appraisals and proportions of visually impaired staff, but adding the full suite of diversity data, exit interview information, grievances and tribunals, turnover and so on. By 2003 there were 3,009 employees, 2,075 on the permanent roll – the difference largely accounted for by temporary telephone fundraisers working on locally delivered national raffles, one of our most successful fundraising products.

The decade was one of significant change at the top of RNIB both at honorary officer and director level. Both the chair and chief executive changed. I stood down in December 2003 on my twentieth anniversary of starting. Lesley-Anne Alexander was appointed chief executive of RNIB from January 2004. Previously she had been deputy CEO of the Peabody Trust and before that a director of housing for a north London borough. Outside work she had been Chair of the British Judo Association for four years. Lesley-Anne brought a fresh approach, including merger strategies from the housing movement, greater single-mindedness in concentrating on core business, and a more contemporary outlook to internal markets and internal commissioning. She also reached out more to other service-delivery blindness organisations and groups. This approach, plus the existing close ties with the organisations of blind people, helped to achieve the success of the inter-organisational UK Vision Strategy and bring on board partner charities,

Lesly-Anne Alexander (hands down), CEO of RNIB from 2004 to 2016, with staff outside RNIB HQ.

such as Action for Blind People and the National Library for the Blind.

Continuity was provided by Colin, later Lord, Low as chair from 2000 to 2009, having been vice chair from 1990 to 2000. Colin is one of the most intelligent people I know, progressive and determined in his approach, and a leader in the blindness movement since the late 1960s – therefore, intimately knowledgeable about our movement and its history. His vice chair was Kevin Carey, a creative free thinker with senior executive experience at Sight Savers International, as well as many years' experience as an author and consultant. When Colin reached the end of his term in 2009, Kevin was in many ways his natural successor. He enjoyed keeping RNIB on its toes – and indeed the whole charity sector – with his delight in launching radical thoughts into sector debates. For the first time, however, there was a contested election and the respected Mike Townsend gave Kevin, who was ultimately chosen as the new chair, a run for his money.

Another critical trustee post changed hands, that of treasurer. David Gadbury stood down in 2004. David was a steady pair of hands who took a strong line during some choppy financial waters in 2002 which led to robust debates. (See Harrow and Palmer 2003.) He was succeeded by Terry Moody who served for the rest of the decade – a quiet man with good judgement, who saved his interventions for the moments which counted. A trustee name which featured heavily in the chapters of the 1970s and 1980s returned at the beginning of the decade, Dr Fred Reid, concentrating heavily on his passion – employment of blind and partially sighted people. (He returned after ten years' absence while he concentrated on his university academic responsibilities.)

At the director level there were several changes. Two long-standing directors left in the decade. Perhaps pride of place should go to Barry Gifford, director of finance and administration, who joined RNIB in the late 1970s and became director of finance in 1980. Barry retired in 2002 and this history is littered with references to the crucial role he played. For me the highest accolade for Barry is that he was a director of resources who believed that money was there to be used for the cause – he was a 'how can we do it' charity finance director, quite a rare animal!

Barry would be the first to acknowledge the support he received over many years from the likes of Eve Speare, his assistant, Ken Lavey, Patrick MacDonald, Maureen McMahon, Ian Vickers, Amelia Billington, Paul Hunt, Robin Mann, Giselle Lowe, Tim Stone, Es Parker, Ian Andrew, Tony Fazakerley, Alison Beesley, Barry Goold, Jenny Collis, Howard Platt, Jim Richardson, Kate Stephens, Peri O'Connor, Karen van Dyken.

Barry was succeeded in 2002 by Kevin Geeson, who gave sterling service, including introducing rolling, three-year financial budgeting which transformed our planning. He also played a key role in bridging the change in chief executive in 2004. In 2009 he moved on to become chief operating officer of the NHS Confederation. He was succeeded by

Keith Hickey who joined RNIB from directorship of the Charity Finance Directors Group, a hugely beneficial background to bring to RNIB.

In 2004 the second, long-standing director on whom I also relied heavily, Mike Lancaster, left after fifteen years as director of external relations – a highly successful period of service. Elsewhere in this history I make it clear that he successfully changed the fundraising function to become both more cost-effective and raise much more money – not an easy road. As a manager and leader, he pushed hard, but he always recruited able and loyal senior managers including Pat Orr, Sanchi Heesom, Gill Tishler, Helen Vost, Valerie Morton, Nicky Garsten, Jane Desborough, Lynne Stockbridge, Olivia Belle, Mike Palfreman, Hilary Partridge, Margaret Meyer, Tracey Gregory, Susan Sharp, Sioned Clutton, Paul Hurren, Julian Roland, Theresa Dauncey and Ros Oakley, who became his formal deputy. I have mentioned the fundraisers elsewhere. Crucial also were the communications staff who worked with Mike over those years, including Olivia Belle, Joe Korner, Hilary Todd, Fiona McCarthy, Lynne Stockbridge, Ciara Smyth, Fiona Blakemore, Katherine Eckstrom, Margaret O'Donnell, Madeleine Sugden, Liz North, Ann Lee, Louisa Fyans, Margaret Meyer, Bernard Fleming, Gill Pawley, Fiona Batchelor, Demis de Sousa and Anne Gowan.

Mike was succeeded by a rising star of the fundraising world, Paul Amadi, who stayed until the end of 2009 before he moved to NSPCC. During that time Paul also became chair of the Institute of Fundraising, a powerful and prestigious role. An interim manager, Eifron Hopper, held the fort until the arrival of Wanda Hamilton in 2010. Wanda brought a depth of knowledge of international fundraising which served RNIB well.

In 2004 Jon Barrick left to become CEO of the Stroke Association, which he transformed during his time there. Jon made a major contribution to RNIB over his fifteen years of service, seven as director of community services. He was and is a man of energy who makes things happen and spots winning new launches early, for example, his championing of Talk and Support. He had great support from the likes of Anita Boguslawski, Laura Jacobs, Deborah Hamlin, Sue Grindey, Alison Harding, Charlie Dixon, Andy Barrick, Pete Lucas, Peter Barker, Anne Veart, Chris Croft, Barbara Ryan, Gill Levy Anita Lighstone, Denise Evans, Fran McSweeney, Julie Polzerova, Linda Seru, Malcolm Wood and Andrew Winders.

In 2008 Eamon Fetton, service director, left after ten years with RNIB. His post was created by Lesley-Anne in 2004 to add Community Services Division to his Education and Employment Division responsibilities. His contribution before then was marked by his leadership of a very significant and welcome expansion in RNIB regionally based activity, his resuscitation of early childhood work (children from birth to seven), led by Julie Jennings, and his major contribution to our services supporting mainstream education. Eamonn and his predecessor Paul Ennals were supported by effective senior managers, including Neville Lawson, Richard Botheras, Louise Clunies-Ross, Robert Meadowcroft, Gordon Dryden, Adam Ockelford, Pat Howarth, Olga Miller, Emily Brothers, John Milligan, Sue Hitchcock, John Simpson, Jane Owen Hutchinson, David Sullivan and others. We also benefitted from several long-serving and outstanding school, college and centre heads who had major responsibilities and budgets including Kevin Connell, Brian Hewitt, Judy Bell, Stan Bell, Tony Best, Dave Hussey, Rita Kirkwood, Helen Williams, Lorraine Stewart, Dave Allen, Gillian Eldridge, Elizabeth Clery, Tracy de Bernhardt Dunkin, Kate Storrow, Joyce Deere, Geoff Jackman and Jane Owen-Hutchinson, Gillian Eldridge, Harry Dicks, Ian Bland, Jill Read, Martin Coleman, Nick Ratcliffe, Rob Dyke and Sue Wright.

Eamonn was succeeded in 2009 by Sally Harvey, who inherited a vast portion of RNIB activity to which she applied her flair and calm. Another director who made a very major contribution in the decade to 2010 was William (Billy) Watson, who was director of devolved services, covering Scotland, Northern Ireland and Wales. He left in 2008 to become CEO of the Scottish Association of Mental Health.

There were two other long-standing directors continuing in post when I stood down in December 2003, Stephen King and Fazilet Hadi. Stephen, whom I appointed in 1990, made a Herculean contribution over his 20 years plus at RNIB. Coming from a commercial background, he contributed business acumen which has become so important in modern charity, but he rapidly sensitised himself to voluntary sector values. He contributed in such a wide-ranging way it is difficult to summarise. Apart from having major managerial responsibilities over production and policy functions, he was crucial to RNIB in understanding the strategic and practical impact of the digital online world on RNIB and the people we serve. His empathetic approach helped him to be immensely successful internationally. His leadership and long-term strategic thinking were vital to our successes in, for example, the campaigns on Euro notes and accessible phones and televisions. Managers who supported Stephen in this vastly complicated directorate include Chris Day, John Godber, John Gill (chief scientist), Keith Gladstone, John Crayford, Janice Richards, Malcolm Staniland, Jillian Harvey, Richard Orme, Mandy White, Peter Osborne, Steve Tyler, Wendy Davies, Susan Cuthbert, Tony Gibbs, Joyce Bis, Angela Fuggle, Carol Cotton, Rob Longstaff, Alison Long and others.

Fazilet Hadi, a lawyer, director of policy and later deputy CEO, similarly made a vital contribution to RNIB's achievement and reputation. Like any good lawyer, she has an immense grasp of detail, but she also is very good at seeing the wood for the trees, not always a lawyer's strength! As a negotiator for RNIB and the cause, she was second to none. She acted as the conscience of RNIB, making sure we did the right thing for blind and partially sighted people. She joined RNIB in 1997 in time to make a vital contribution to the implementation of the Disability Discrimination Act. As a blind person, she was particularly well placed to play a vital role in developing deeper connections between RNIB and ordinary blind and partially sighted people. This showed *par excellence* in her commitment to making a success of RNIB membership and the campaign supporters' network, so crucial to our transition from an organisation 'for' to an organisation 'of' blind and partially sighted people from 2001 onwards. Her patience in discussions with other blindness organisations was a critical success factor in bringing the Vison Strategy world together. Everyone who knows her will agree with me when I say she always displays great competence and offers genuine friendship.

During the years of this history Fazilet had the support of a tight professional team including Margaret Alexander, Nicholas Johnston, Jane Peters, Christine Tillsley, Steve Winyard, Alun Thomas, Nigel Charles, Dany Luchmun, Julie Howell, Jan Nesbitt, Kishor Patel, Dan Vale, Evelyn Russell, Fiona McKenzie, James Rogers, Leen Petre, Stella Smith and Stef Abrar.

In 2010/11 under Lesley-Anne Alexander's leadership, the RNIB Group directors were:

- Keith Hickey – Resources
- Fazilet Hadi – Inclusive Society
- Stephen King – Prevention and International Affairs
- Wanda Hamilton – Fundraising
- Sally Harvey – Supporting Independent Living
- Stephen Remington – CEO Action for Blind People.

Finance – Growth through Acquisition

The decade kept RNIB in the top 20 of the UK's public facing charities (Caritas Data 2011). However, 2009/10 income includes a one-off £17.7 million for 'Fair value of acquired net assets'. If this one-off figure is stripped out, the total is £117.2 million giving a seventeen per cent real growth for the decade. The figures for the 2000/10 decade include the considerable income and expenditure contributed from the acquisition of Action for Blind People.

So, the decade was a complicated one financially because of the additions of the associated charities into RNIB Group in 2007/08, 2008/09 and 2009/10.

Table 4b.1. RNIB Income and Expenditure 1999/2000-2009/10

Income (£ millions)	1999/2000	2009/10
Fees for service	28.6	45.7
Voluntary income	41.5	68.3
Investment income	2.5	1.7
Other	0.5	1.5
Total	73.1	117.2
TOTAL at constant 2004 prices	80.2	93.8
Percentage growth, real terms	+47%	+17%
TOTAL at constant 2004 prices, base 100	253	296
Legacies in cash terms (included above in voluntary income)	28.8	38.5
Expenditure (£ millions)	**1999/2000**	**2009/10**
Services	63.5	111.1
Central administration	1.7	
Net expenditure on fixed assets		
Cost of appeals	9.5	17.2
Total	74.8	130
TOTAL at constant 2004 prices	82.1	105
Percentage growth, real terms		+28%
TOTAL at constant 2004 prices, base 100 in 1970a[1]	266	340

[1] UK RPI via the Cleave Calculator

Fundraising – Building Strong, Loyal Relationships

Apart from legacies, which continued to be buoyant, three products continued to deliver during the 2000s: locally delivered raffles (telephone fundraising); major donors and, something new, highly successful fundraising dinners; and direct marketing, particularly direct mail.

As described in detail in the previous chapter the formula for raffles was developed in our northern region. If raffles sound small and old-fashioned, think again, think £7-9 million a year in 2000 prices.

A fundraising breakthrough of the early 2000s was the RNIB finally cracking how to run a fundraising dinner associated with a major donor campaign – another hybrid product. RNIB had previously run a fundraising dinner in 1984, my first year, which raised £250,000, ten per cent of annual fundraised income (see chapter 2a). There followed a long fallow period until a fundraiser in 2002 raised two per cent of annual voluntary income in one evening – £1.3 million. The reason for the success was that it was part of a long-term, relationship-building approach with wealthy supporters and potential supporters, whom we called major donors.

There was a primary reason we lost our way on major donor fundraising and big event fundraising for a period. We did not work hard enough on the importance of building strong relationships with major donors. A turning point was drawing in an outstanding consultant, Jeff Shear, a former social worker who advised wealthy people on how to make sure their gifts were effectively applied. If any of the major donors he advised had an interest in blindness, he was able to introduce us to them. Initially, there was no request for money, only involvement in our work, such as visits to see our services, meetings with the RNIB chair and president – then the Duke of Westminster. Once a relationship of knowledge and trust had been established, donations could be discussed. There were many people on the staff side who made this relationship building a success including Doug Thomson, Mike Palfreman, Ann Paul, Ciara Smyth, John Harvey, Julie Otley, Vinnie Smith, Crystal Chiu, Yolanda Sze, Karen Gold and others. By the time we reached 2002 we had a group of committed and generous major donors drawn from various sources. These included Sir Trevor Pears (Pears Foundation), Lady Joan Jarvis, (widow of Sir Ronnie Jarvis), along with other long-standing donors, such as Sir Mike Rake, Sir John Beckwith, Dermot and Sir Michael Smurfit,

Gerald Ronson, Haruhisa Handa, Richard Brewster, Martin Randerson, the Rt Hon. the Earl of Stockton, Sir Rod Stewart and Penny Lancaster.

The donors become committed to the cause but they also want to feel they can trust the charity and the people they are dealing with day to day. This is an incremental process. For example, I first met Mark Pears at one of the early Savoy dinners. I was invited to the Pears Foundation offices where I also met Trevor (now Sir Trevor), who was about to concentrate on the family's philanthropy. That was the start of a long and fruitful relationship with Pears' Foundation, who were extremely generous, and Sir Trevor, if he had an urgent query, knew that he could talk with me at any time whether I was at work or on holiday. Another example: I met the late Sir Ronnie Jarvis at a reception at the Duke of Westminster's office where Ronnie was fascinated by the display of historic Talking Book machines – one of which he swiftly took apart but had difficulty reassembling! He made a major donation to enable us to open the new Talking Book studios in Camden. Since his death, Lady Joan Jarvis has carried on the family support and brightens all of our events. I always tried to ensure we sat together at dinners, and she is one of our vice presidents.

There were three main draws to our major donor dinner that evening in 2002. First, it was held in St James's Palace, initially in the presence of the Queen; second, it had Andrea Bocelli, the blind Italian superstar tenor, topping the entertainment (*pro bono*); and, third, we had a system whereby loyal major donors would try to bring tables of guests (twelve people). The majority of the money was raised from donations on the night and the auction, with the underlying 'secret' weapon being plenty of wine and conviviality. I helped to whip up enthusiasm for donations at the end of the evening with a rousing call to donate (earlier in the evening a powerful speech from the parent of a blind child had reminded everyone why we were there). The only problem was that the head official from St James' Palace made it clear that I should not ask for money because of the Queen's presence. I pointed out that the 'ask' would be after she had left (we knew that it was not allowed in her presence) but he was adamant. What to do? With my heart in my mouth, I went ahead with my passionate appeal. Would it be the Tower next? Or simply no honour from the Queen when I retired? In fact, the Palace representative, encouraged by Jeff Shear, had surmised that I was going to go ahead anyway and had discreetly left the room. Result – £1.3 million! As with all of these fundraising campaigns, one or two lead donors can transform the result. In this case it was Sir Michael Smurfitt who gave €1 million.

Successive teams have ensured that these gifts continue to come in as more dinners followed: in 2004 with Rod Stewart (knighted in 2016 for his services to music and charity), in 2009 with Sir Cliff Richard and in 2011 with Sir Tom Jones, all raising in excess of £1 million. By the end of the decade there were many major donors contributing reg-ularly, including the Garfield Weston Foundation, Lord Wolfson and the Wolfson Foundation, the Steinberg Chari-table Trust, Lord and Lady Fink, Ruth Rendell, Lily Safra and Isaac and Myrna Kaye. Corporate givers assumed growing importance, including Carmen Butler Charteris, Novartis and Glaxo Smith Kline.

The development of direct marketing was no less important or successful. Essential were painstaking piloting and trialling, building up infrastructure and using creativity. Direct marketing has made a huge contribution towards public awareness of RNIB as well as raising large sums of money.

In successful fundraising new products have to be introduced and one of the most exciting of the 2000s was Read for RNIB Day, combining fundraising and awareness building. It was a series of financial, pledge-based community events, where sighted and blind people raised awareness and money. In its first year alone, it took its place in the Guinness World Records for the longest relay read.

These activities made up what Wanda Hamilton, director of fundraising at the end of the decade (2010) described as: 'RNIB's mature and stable portfolio not only of products but also teams, procedures, infrastructure, supporter care, and timely and supportive database analysis' (personal communication).

Creating RNIB Cymru, RNIB NI and RNIB Scotland

In 1999/2000, following parliamentary devolution in 1998, we set up independently managed RNIB Northern Ireland, RNIB Scotland and RNIB Wales. Each had their own committee and director responsible for RNIB activity in their

Newly launched RNIB Cymru, 1999.

Scotland's First Minister Jack McConnell (L) presents Mike Cairns, Director RNIB Scotland, with a campaigning award, 2002.

country: Susan Reid in Northern Ireland; Allan Murray in Scotland; and Joyce Chatterton in Wales. RNIB was one of the first social welfare charities to devolve independence in this way. This may sound sensible, but easy it was not! A prescient external consultant's recommendations (Mike Hudson of Compass) helped me to push the changes through against some opposition. Most of the national UK directors and committee chairs responsible for 'their' services in the devolved countries had strong views on the desirability of UK-wide benefits of scale. However, the benefits in terms of growth and achievement quickly shone through as donors, commissioners and governments looked much more favourably on charities with a distinct Northern Irish/Scottish/ Welsh identity.

Some of the first examples of the success of this strategy were:

- The rapid growth in income from the three devolved governments and from the public in all three countries outstripped that achieved in England throughout the decade.
- All three countries produced much more active campaigners, successfully lobbying their parliament/ assemblies and civil services in a way they could not before (Scotland excepted, which set up its identity earlier).
- RNIB Cymru achieved free eye tests for at-risk groups, including African Caribbean and Asian communities.
- RNIB Cymru opened a child and family centre.
- RNIB Scotland successfully tested CD-ROM technology (DAISY) with the simultaneous production of audio, large print and soft braille texts to improve curriculum access (2003).
- The largest Scottish society for the blind merged into RNIB Scotland.
- RNIB Scotland was one of the founding partners of the first radio station for blind people (November

2003) which eventually became RNIB Insight Radio in 2007.

- Over the whole decade there was a growth of direct and indirect services, with highlights being accessible information, reaching younger blind and partially people, as well as upping the agenda for eye health and sight loss services.

Moving HQ to a State-of-the-Art Service Centre

In March 2002 the RNIB moved from its home of 86 years at 224, 226 and 228 Great Portland Street to 105 Judd Street. Its headquarters in Great Portland Street had become

RNIB in the late 60s at 224 Great Portland St.

External view of Judd St TBC

**Judd St Resource Centre, leading to the new
Low Vision Clinic.**

overcrowded. Action had to be taken. A major refurbishment
would release a lot of space trapped in grand style, spacious
corridors of the early 1900s. We would have to move out while
this happened. However, the space planners advised that it
made no sense to move out into another building for two
years and then move back – a double move; far better to

move only once into a new site. We decided on this, but not without much heart searching. Number 224 was built specific-ally as the home for RNIB in the 1910s, with its concert organ and concert hall and the five-storey, basement book stack for braille storage dropping deep into the earth to reach the buried River Fleet (which occasionally flooded the lowest floor). Losing the Armitage Hall with its size, height, glorious wooden panels and plaster cornices was a big wrench.

Finding a new location was difficult but finally the Salvation Army's building near King's Cross at 105 Judd Street was chosen. It had a number of advantages. It was very near so many train, tube and bus routes – far better than Great Portland St; it was relatively cheap because the area was still undesirable to all except those with an eye for the future; it was large enough and had the potential for an additional floor which we planned to sublet for rental income; and the structure itself was well built and capable of being sub-divided. We did have a wobble as we moved towards decision time, with several senior staff and trustees having last minute doubts, primarily because of the area. Kings Cross was still then a red-light district. (To confirm the safety of the area at night, I drove slowly around there one evening at around 10pm, seeing how safe it appeared. A little while later a very prominent civil servant was arrested for kerb crawling near to where I had been slowly reconnoitring!) In recent years, it has been gentrified and I am pleased we went ahead with the move.

Here I want to pay huge credit to our consultants and to Barry Gifford and the staff who were on the planning committee, including estates staff, Paul Hunt, Robin Mann, Patrick MacDonald and Es Parker. As a charity, we felt we had to go open plan to save space and money and we wanted to create small communities on the floors and encourage meeting points to support cross-departmental interactions. We also took advice from my colleague at Bayes (then City University) Business School, Professor Clive Holtham. So instead of banishing the photocopiers and print and braille printers into 'tucked away' black holes, we placed these near the lifts, regular entry and exit points. We created adjacent kitchen areas with fridges, sinks and tables and chairs for people to use at lunch time. These placements created concentrations of informal interaction in the centre of each floor. To accommodate the views of staff who worried that they might need to make confidential telephone calls regarding clients, we created tiny telephone rooms, three or four to each floor. We also located meeting rooms on each floor. Those few offices which were designated for personal occupancy were located on the internal lightwell, so that the open plan areas had priority 'light rights' from the large externally facing windows.

Recruiting More Volunteers

Large charities in England are seldom good at involving volunteers in any sizeable quantity unlike smaller charities (Jas *et al.* 2002) and RNIB has been no exception. Some areas have traditionally been strong, such as Talking Books (some 3,000 volunteers up to the end of the last century) and fundraising (a few hundred or as high as 200,000 plus if you count the volunteers selling raffle tickets). Nonetheless, throughout the 2000s RNIB did focus on volunteer development, with Rob Jackson playing a leading role. At the end of the decade numbers had risen to some 4,400 and policies had been translated into safer operational procedures, led by Lynne Green in the Resources Group. Some 95 per cent of customers were satisfied with the support they received from RNIB Group and the volunteers contributed £6 million per year in equivalent value – a major development over the decade (RNIB 2011).

Sustainability – Early Adoption

Another theme of the decade was reducing RNIB's impact on the environment, led by Joe Rodrigues, and focussing on five of ten priorities identified in Bioregional's One Planet Living framework of 2003, namely, reduction in carbon waste, reducing travel by air and road, developing sustainable pro-curement policies, increasing staff satisfaction and reducing staff sickness levels.

Planning, Impact and Service Evidence

Strategic planning and measuring impact had been priorities in RNIB for 25 years, arguably longer, but the decade saw an increase in priority, as outlined earlier in the chapter. On the impact side, a long-standing advocate, Philippa Simkiss, joined the outstanding line of strategic planners RNIB recruited – Steve Cooper, Deborah Jack, Jean Barclay, Jane Peters, Karen Allsop, Debbie Hyslop, Nicholas Johnston, Mark Meller and Stella Smith – ensuring that RNIB remained at the cutting edge of planning for, and achieving, impact.

Conclusion

The first decade of the new century was for RNIB one of renewal and growth based on new alliances. Some services were closed or spun off, but the overall performance was one of growth with an even greater focus on campaigning. This combined with the structural and systemic changes described in the first half of this chapter, added up to a very strong position from which RNIB could encounter the economic and political challenges facing the UK in the second decade of the century. As Lesley-Anne Alexander put it:

> RNIB is a fantastic organisation with a clear mission rooted in the needs of our beneficiaries. We are constantly changing and adapting, but we do so in a planned and evolutionary way. We are incredibly proud that we are led by blind and partially sighted people and this gives the organisation great confidence to face the future. (Personal communication)

Part II

Forty-year Trends in the Charity in Socio-Political Context

Part II draws out themes and conclusions which cover most or all of 1970-2010, locating RNIB within the wider society, the social welfare sector, charity in general and the world of disability organisations

Chapter 5

External Impacts 1970 to 2010

This span of history has seen significant social change: from the end of the swinging sixties to the world financial crisis and transformative social media of the 2000s. In the book's introduction I suggested a list of changes in non-profit organisational behaviour. Here I focus on those changes that had a major influence on the world within which RNIB operated: as a social welfare charity, as a disability charity and as a sight loss charity. Within these contexts, what were the external and internal factors shaping RNIB's development and what were RNIB's initiating and responsive actions?

Society-wide Impacts

Such a heading opens a Pandora's box which would reveal changes in family structure, disparities of wealth, demography and so on. Two changes, in particular, impacted hugely on RNIB: the digital information age; and Britain engaging with what would become the European Union.

The Digital Information Age

For blind people much of the analogue world was obscure but often tactile and thus accessible. Not so the brash, fast moving digital world which put its foot in the door in the

1970s and by the middle of the 1980s had forced its way in, powered by visual images on smooth digital displays which were inaccessible to blind people. At best, in the late twentieth century systems and devices such as computers and phones were designed to be capable of access and, at worst, frequently were not capable of adaptation at all. Due to the foresight of John Gill from the 1970s onwards and the leadership of Stephen King and his team, our original work, and our preparedness to form and join international alliances, we made a major impact. (See chapters 3b and 4b.) Increasingly, accessibility was built in from the start rather than always having to be retrofitted.

European Union

As early as 1980, a leading trustee, Tom Parker, had spotted the income potential from the European Union but this was just the start. RNIB helped to form, and became the major resource supporting, the European Blind Union's Commission for Liaising with the EU. Why? Not only for grants, but because some 60 per cent of UK legislation emanated from Brussels and Strasbourg (as estimated by House of Commons Library research in 2014). It was vital for UK people with sight loss that we were in on the ground floor of the preparation of EU

The UK delegation at an EBU General Assembly, Poland 1993.

directives and legislation such as the Amsterdam Treaty. The EU had major funding programmes and also could call for numerous practical requirements such as braille on medicine labels. There were other welcome knock-on effects of EU engagement. The EU favoured pan-disability approaches led by disabled people, not their advocates. So, this view supported our activity in the UK working with organisations of disabled people, such as BCODP, in alliances, such as the Disability Benefits Consortium, co-chaired by Richard Wood and me. This view was also one of several important factors nudging RNIB to become, legally, an organisation 'of' people with sight loss in 2001 by requiring more than half of our Board to be visually impaired. Impact on the EU also required inter-member country alliances which was a driver of RNIB active support and leadership in the European Blind Union and within the EBU, its commission for liaising with the EU.

Social Welfare Sector Impacts

Here there were many more obvious changes which impacted RNIB.

Marketisation of Service Delivery

This history starts with the 1970s, the last decade of the 'welfare state consensus' between all the main political parties that the welfare state needed to grow to meet all reasonable need. Beveridge's (1948) hopes for an expanded voluntary contribution was neglected or ignored. The image of the voluntary sector was not one of major service provider but as Cinderella looking after a small, old-fashioned, patronising rump of services. Its only positive role was to innovate new services, which, if successful, should be transferred to the state to run. Examples of these transfers were: advice to benefits claimants passed to statutory social services, family planning to the NHS, and support to disabled people to get jobs to the Department of Employment.

So, when I left Unilever to join the sector in 1970 to relaunch an old people's charity, my fellow managers thought I was mad for several reasons: for one, giving up my salary prospects; the other was that charities were seen as *passé*, insignificant in their contribution and in decline – worthy, but a waste of a career.

On the contrary, however, arising out of the activism of the second half of the 1960s, for example, opposition to the Vietnam war, student revolts and occupations, the touch paper of voluntary sector growth had already been ignited, in particular, of lobbying and campaigning. For example, there was the launch of the Child Poverty Action Group (1965) and Shelter (1966), and the relaunch of the National Old People's Welfare Council as Age Concern (1971) and the National Association of Mental Health as Mind (1972). The voluntary sector was on the march, literally in some cases.

The stagflation of the 1970s slowly strangled the dream of a comprehensive welfare state but the final blow in policy terms was in 1979 with the Conservative Thatcher government. In practice, marketisation only kicked in from the mid 1980s and continued through the Blair government. Major in this policy change was the system of outsourcing, commissioning and competitive tendering. Social welfare charities might have previously competed for funds from the public but they tried to co-operate on service delivery (or so the accepted wisdom said – I never managed to get local old people's welfare committees and local WRVS groups to share the details of which of 'their' old people received annual Christmas food parcels to prevent duplication and omission). With competitive tendering, service co-operation went out of the window and charities had to learn from business, applying techniques such as competitor analysis. Statutory grants gave way to contracts with their earned income from successful competitive tendering – which could be against other businesses as well as other charities. By 1995 total earned income (from government and the public) was 33 per cent of total general charity sector income, by 2000 it was 39 per cent and by 2009/10 it had reached 55 per cent (Hems and Passey 1996; Clark, Kane, Wilding and Bass 2012). Marketisation was firmly established, charities had become more businesslike (Eikenberry and Kluver 2004; Bruce and Chew 2011).

Rights, Not Welfare

The Race Relations Act 1965 and the subsequent iterations of 1968, 1976 and 2000 gave all disadvantaged groups a sight of what a rights-versus-welfare approach to status and provision could do. The British permissive approach to provision (nuanced but often prejudiced) was influenced by the more aggressive demand for rights not permissions. Campaigners in the UK learned from the United States through watching the civil rights movement in the 1960s, the feminist movement in the 1970s, and the movements for disability rights in the 1980s and gay rights in the 1990s.

Nowhere did this US influence show itself more clearly than in the field of disability rights where the activism of American disabled people was significant in showing the

Campaigning for greater rights across Westminster Bridge, Nov 1989.

British movement what was possible: the Americans with Disabilities Act 1990. We in RNIB, the National Federation of the Blind and the National League of the Blind and Disabled felt it from our contacts with blind people in the United States, particularly the American Federation of the Blind (AFB) and the regular visits here of their long-time president, Dr Kenneth Jernigan. These interactions were not always comfortable. I received the singular honour of being invited to address one of the AFB national conferences in Dallas with 3,000 blind attendees. As the only sighted speaker at the conference, I felt somewhat under pressure to prove myself; it took ten of my allocated 20 minutes to win the regular applause and bugle calls that were normal from the rumbustious audience. Going to the outside restaurant in the evening there was no question of me guiding a blind speaker. As many as five abreast with their very long American white canes out in front, they swept unaided down the sidewalk and woe betide any sighted person who got in their way!

The influence of the Americans with Disabilities Act (ADA, 1990) was inspirational in our disability movement, setting goals for the UK Disability Discrimination Act, achieved some five years later. This act was and is a civil rights law, far distanced from the earlier legally permissive welfare-ism on which UK disabled people previously depended.

In the UK, RNIB was active in the pan-disability alliance co-ordinating with and lobbying allies in parliament, with our parliamentary officer, Alun Thomas, providing much of the legislative process advice to the voluntary sector alliances.

From Specialism to Integration, to Inclusion

From the start of this history there were strong signs that the trend was moving away from special provision for disadvantaged groups, separate from the mainstream. Initially, this posed challenges to specialist charities such as RNIB who were viewed as out of step. However, as time went on specialist knowledge came to be valued again in the new generic world. RNIB developed a range of advice and consultancy services for social services and education departments, jobcentres, the NHS and the commercial world on how the needs and wishes of people with sight loss could be met by the mainstream – the social model.

One of the earliest signs pinpointing the shift towards genericism/integration/inclusion (the descriptors change according to the time and setting) was the Local Authority Social Services Act 1970. This arose out of the Seebohm Report of 1968. The thrust of this policy abolished the long-established separate local authority childrens' departments, welfare departments (for older people), services for 'the mentally handicapped' and so on and created integrated social services departments with 'generic' social workers serving 'families' within their communities. Social workers for the blind held out for a while but then became generic rehabilitation workers. Mobility officers lasted longer, giving newly blind people training to get around independently, primarily with long white canes, a revolutionary technique imported in the 1960s from the United States.

In the field of education, the name was not Seebohm but Warnock in 1978 with the publication of her report on Special Educational Needs. The thrust to integrate (later, include) was there, this time disabled children into mainstream local education. Unlike Seebohm, Warnock introduced an element of a rights-based approach with families having the right to an assessment of their child's educational needs in the form of a statement.

Once again, the impact of this report on disabled people and charities working in the field was profound. Like other charities for children with hearing loss and learning difficulties, RNIB had separate schools for blind and partially sighted young people. Most were residential and most were with children who had problems in addition to sight loss. RNIB's schools survived and flourished for two almost three decades more. How? By concentrating on the two ends of the developmental curriculum. Most RNIB schools concentrated on more profound and multiple learning difficulties (PMLD) but, at the other end of the spectrum, Worcester College (which became RNIB New College after it merged with Chorleywood School for Girls) concentrated on very intellectually able young people with sight loss – young people whose ability might have been underserved within mainstream education. For example, Chorleywood, under head Peggy Markes and her staff, pioneered teaching practical biology including animal dissection and computer programming in the late 1970s.

There was a similar story in the field of employment although not in this case with one seminal transformational report. Since the early twentieth century integration/ inclusion existed for blind lawyers, clergy, physiotherapists, telephonists, factory workers and basket weavers. However, other professions and occupations were difficult to breach. Throughout the 1970s and 1980s there was increasing demand from blind people to be able to access any career path in an integrated fashion and gradually this was achieved, although numbers placed remained stubbornly small. From the 1970s onwards, in parallel with these demands, blind persons resettlement officers (BPROs) were merged into generic disablement resettlement officers (DROs).

Residential to Day Provision

At the same time, there was a concomitant shift from residential provision to day provision. Very obviously inclusion or integration could not be achieved in residential provision. In 1970 RNIB had 23 residential schools, colleges, rehabilitation centres, hotels and homes. By 1990 there were eighteen and by 2012 there were nine. These bald figures hide the heartache and despair that some parents and children suffered through the massive disruption of their lives. For others, it is to be hoped, a majority, it was the start of a happier more fulfilling future. Nor was it easy for staff – even if they knew it was the right decision.

Trends in the Charity Sector

From Subservience to Forceful Player

The 1960s were a low point for the voluntary sector (Davis Smith 2019). As has been mentioned above, the post-Second World War consensus between the political parties was that the welfare state needed to grow to meet all reasonable need, gradually taking over services pioneered by charities. For example, RNIB since 1942 had run a successful job-finding service. In 1963 this placement service for blue-collar workers was transferred to the then Ministry of Labour to run. RNIB managed to keep hold of the placement service for white-collar workers but for a while that was in doubt. However, in the 1970s RNIB, with its major specialist services, was largely impervious to the statutory colonisation of the sector. Even the state was cautious of taking on schools for multi-handicapped blind children, Talking Books and specialist aids.

Nevertheless, moving into the 1970s confidence that the welfare state could meet most, if not all, need was high. Bob Hudson, professor of partnership studies at Durham University, at the time, was among the first members of Sunderland local authority social services committee in the early 1970s at the height of Seebohm reorganisation euphoria: 'Everyone on the committee felt they were on the brink of a new era; we were genuinely carried away by the sheer excitement of it all [and] there was money to spend' (Hudson 1972).

The increased public and institutional confidence of the 1960s was also picked up by charities such as Oxfam, Shelter and Age Concern, who began to reject their subservient role to the welfare state. In the very late 1960s and early 1970s charities started to become much more pushy. Charity amelioration was no longer sufficient nor even cure, we wanted prevention – to stop bad things happening. Charities increased their pressure group and campaigning activities, trying to persuade others, the general public and professionals, to change their behaviour in favour of their charitable purposes. Just after I had led the relaunch of the National Old People's Welfare Council as Age Concern, the then secretary of state for health and social services, Sir Keith Joseph, spoke at Age Concern England's AGM in 1972. David Hobman (CEO) sent his own speech in advance to the secretary of state's private office to warn Sir Keith that he would be arguing for charities to be openly campaigning on behalf of their purposes. We waited with bated breath for the minister's response. As if to confirm the developing role, he acknowledged the right of charities to campaign, but that campaigns should not be 'shrill'! While 'shrill' sounds arcane now, deciding insider/outsider tactics for achieving social change is a crucial charity choice (Purkis 2020)

Another sign of charities' increasing confidence was the growth in the 1970s of their information services aimed particularly at beneficiaries. Here was this growing welfare state, particularly, in social security and social services, but people did not know of many of the benefits to which they were entitled. Charities such as Age Concern, CPAG, Mind, NACAB, Shelter and Scope brought out a raft of booklets on how different groups of people could claim or trigger benefits and services from the state. Age Concern England's *Your Rights*, written in 1973 by Patricia Hewitt (then a public relations officer fresh out of university and working in my department but later to become a Labour secretary of state for health) was an early classic of this trend.

In the early 1970s, RNIB and its associated charity, the Sunshine Fund, with its active trustee leader, Lady Astor, had no need to relaunch and reinvigorate because they were continuing strong public brands with massive incomes – RNIB was in the top ten largest English service charities measured by voluntary income (Wells 1971). However, this confidence was misplaced.

As someone active in the voluntary sector throughout the 1970s, I regarded RNIB as a giant but not very modern or nimble, with its brand oriented towards fundraising rather than campaigning. This restricted involvement in campaigning was buttressed by the organisations of the blind insisting that campaigning was their job, not RNIB's. This view was still prevalent in the 1980s when I joined, especially within the National League of the Blind and Disabled (personal communications from Tom Parker, Mike Barrett, Gwen McCready and others). Meanwhile, the leading charities in the sector were becoming much more active as campaigners and lobbyists – for example, Scope and Age Concern appointed parliamentary officers who gained easy access to parliament by legitimately becoming research assistants to MPs. Campaigning required and gained active public awareness – for example, Scope's advert, 'Public Conveniences, not public, not convenient', featured a person in a wheelchair outside a down-stepped public lavatory.

So RNIB was behind the curve in these developments, a conclusion reached by the RNIB Sunningdale Conference in late 1980. Benedict Nightingale (1973) in his book on charities called RNIB 'venerable'.

Chair Duncan Watson was keen to rectify our weak lobbying position and to appoint a parliamentary officer which we did successfully with the appointment of Hugh Lawrence as our first parliamentary officer in 1984 By the end of the 1990s RNIB had 35 public affairs staff and was winning awards for this work. In the second half of the 2000s under the leadership of Colin Low and Lesley-Anne Alexander the emphasis on campaigning was even greater.

During the 1970s and 1980s there was also a decline in the 'god-like' role of caring and curing professionals in the welfare state who became more prepared to listen to and co-operate with beneficiary representatives. This was another important factor contributing to the rise in influence of the social welfare charities. For example, in our field the Royal Colleges were initially very prickly if RNIB gave out any information on eye conditions as this was regarded as an exclusive prerogative of medical professionals. By the early 1980s we were jointly publishing with the Royal College of Ophthalmologists (RCOphth) information for people with different eye conditions such as glaucoma, macular degeneration and so on. By the middle of the 1980s these leaflets were flying off the shelves of eye clinics all over the country and increasing RNIB's standing and usefulness to newly blind people. This change in attitude of professionals was critical to social welfare charities' expansion of power, especially RNIB. Professors David Hill and Alistair Fielder deserve special mention because of their work to build a bridge between RNIB and the Royal College of Ophthalmologists.

Quite apart from the growing realisation in the statutory services of the near impossible task of meeting all need and the changing attitudes of professionals, the 1979 shift in government policies signalled a decline in the 'monopoly' position of statutory welfare services and the growth of outsourcing to the charity and commercial sectors. For RNIB this was nothing new and thus presented an easier shift which enabled us to grow substantially. Local education authorities had been subcontracting us over many decades by paying fees for 'their' children to attend our residential schools. Some other charities such as Action for Children (then known as National Children's Homes or NCH) grew enormously through local authority contracts.

These changes increased the space within which charities operated and gave RNIB opportunities to expand, perhaps pre-eminently in the field of eye health from 1987 onwards. This was critical. Eye health should have been RNIB's core 'business' but its history and the earlier attitudes of eye health professionals had prevented this move (see chapter 4b).

Causes Change – from Religion and Age to Arts and the Environment

Which causes and their charities were waxing and waning especially in the public's mind over the 40 years to 2010? Where the public chooses to donate can be a hard expression of this popularity. Ranking by voluntary income also gives us some insight into the popularity of causes over time. Pharoah, Walker, Goodey and Clegg (2004) gives us a comparison of fundraised income by cause in 1978 and then in 2003.

Pharoah *et al.* (2004, Fig. 2.3) ranked the top 200 fundraising charities by voluntary income in 2003, compared in real terms with their income in 1978:

	1978	2003
International	3	1
Cancer	2	2
Religious (general services)	10	3
Heritage/Environment	8	4
Disabled including blind	1	5
Children	4	6
Arts	23	7
Animals	1	8
General social welfare	7	9
Religious/missionary	5	10

Causes for the disabled, including blind people, dropped in popularity from first to fifth. Superficially, it looks as though charities in the disability field were less effective than others in raising voluntary income. However, a moment's reflection suggests this is unlikely. Some might be so but, given that they constitute approaching around 20 of the 200, it is statistically unlikely they are all less effective. It is more likely that public sympathy has shifted and donations followed. Why might this be? Disability charities were very effective in this period in lobbying government and commerce to improve goods and services for disabled people, for example, achieving the Disability Discrimination Act 1995. Advances were very visible: for example, braille and audio in lifts, trains, on medicines etc.; dropped kerbs on pavements and slopes for wheelchair access into buildings. It is a reasonable hypothesis that the public noticed or at least sensed these changes and improvements and concluded the needs of disabled people were being met better than before. Remember also the long-standing, Labour government minister, David Blunkett, who for a period was so successful that he was tipped in 2003/04 as a future prime minister. He showed *par excellence*, with other successful people such as the broadcaster Peter White and Britain's first appointed blind judge John Wall, that blind people could succeed at the highest levels.

Two risers in the voluntary income charts were arts and environmental charities and two major losers were religious and missionary charities and those for old people. This perhaps suggests a dual-factor explanation: improvement versus danger. Improvement in the situation of cause bene- ficiaries at one end of the continuum versus danger of extinction of the cause at the extreme other end. Charity supporters, including the public, perceive the position of disabled people and older people as having improved. Whereas the environment and the arts were seen as in an increasingly perilous state.

What this data and part explanation does not show is the impact of campaigning and pressure group activity of chari- ties of and for disabled people behind the scenes, leading to the disability rights legislation. This was alluded to in 'Rights, Not Welfare' in chapter 5 above and will be returned to later in this chapter in the section on changes to disability policies.

So, my (defensive?) explanation is that the real growth in voluntary income, but the drop in ranking order, of disability and sight loss charities was in significant part due to the successful lobbying for rights and improved provision for disabled people, in general, and people with sight loss, in particular.

Diversity Enriches

From at least the 1980s, the charities sector was starting to take diversity seriously, including RNIB, but prioritising visual impairment.

Looking at employment diversity: on gender, a majority of RNIB staff were women. The percentage of senior managers who were women rose from a third to a half between the middle 1980s to 2003, as judged by attendance at the biennial senior management conferences. However, the picture at the top was very unrepresentative: none of the elected trustee standing committee chairs throughout this history were women and it was not until 1997 that RNIB appointed a woman director (Fazilet Hadi), followed by two more in 2000 (Susan Reid, RNIB Northern Ireland, and Joyce Chatterton, RNIB Cymru), making three out of nine. In 2004 Lesley-Anne Alexander was appointed as chief executive and by 2010 four out of the six senior management team were women (Fazilet Hadi for inclusive society, Wanda Hamilton for fundraising, Sally Harvey, independent living, plus Lesley-Anne Alexander as CEO).

People from minority ethnic groups were hugely under-represented among senior managers rising from zero to four per cent over the 40-year period and in 2003 still only made up around five per cent of the workforce (RNIB 2003).

People with disabilities were highly represented in RNIB because of the active recruitment of employees with sight loss. In 2003 disabled people made up 7.3 per cent of the workforce with 5.7 per cent having sight loss. Senior managers with sight loss declined from fourteen per cent in 1985 to ten per cent in 2003, largely explained by senior field fundraising posts ceasing to be protected for blind people only.

On LGBTQ+, one of the senior managers and one of the trustee standing committee chairs were openly gay but we collected no data.

There were other ways in which our services were unrepresentative, for example, geographic diversity. In the 1970s and 1980s we proportionately underserved Northern Ireland, Scotland and Wales. By the late 1990s we had largely rectified this both in share of resources and, importantly, with devolution of decision making through establishing autonomous bodies – RNIB Cymru, RNIB Northern Ireland and RNIB Scotland, each with their own directors responsible for in-country services.

Growth in Income

Perhaps the most striking structural change in the whole sector over the 40 years was the massive growth in real terms in total sector size and importance.

RNIB income trebled in real terms. How did this major growth **compare with all charities**?

RNIB's rank income position in the charity world (excluding technical charities such as the Arts Council and the British Council) stayed in the top 20:

1970 (Wells 1971)	– 5th
1980 Charity Statistics (CAF 1983)	– 12th
1992 Top 3000 (Henderson 1993)	– 12th
2000 Top 3000 (Caritas Data 2001)	– 17th
2010 Top 3000 (Caritas Data 2011)	– 19th

(The Wells result is likely to be over positive, given that it was the first attempt by anyone to try to capture the information and did not include dominantly, earned income charities such as Mencap.)

So, against a general decline in the popularity of disability charities overall (Pharoah *et al.* 2004), RNIB managed to retain a position in the top 20 of all charities up to 2010. This was no mean feat against a background in which seven charities dropped out of the top 20, including Christian Aid, Scope and Guide Dogs for the Blind Association, and the decline of disability as a charitable fundraising cause.

In **comparison to the largest disability charities**, in the early 1990s these were the Spastics Society (now Scope), RNIB, Leonard Cheshire and GDBA – all having a place in the top 20. As mentioned, by 2010, two of these had dropped out by some distance, Scope and GDBA, and one had entered, namely, Mencap.

In **comparison to the blindness/visual impairment charities**, RNIB (nineteenth) had outgrown the only other large blindness charity, GDBA which by 2010 had dropped to 69th behind a growing Sight Savers International (35th) and Sense (46th).

So, from an RNIB perspective, the charity trebled in size in real terms over the 40 years to 2010 and maintained its position as one of the country's largest 20 charities.

Improving Charity Effectiveness?

Over the years 1970-2010, there were recognisable developments in how charities operated, it is to be hoped, for the better. In some of these RNIB led the way, in others, we joined the norm and in some we bucked the trend, arguably falling behind.

As a generalisation, when I became involved in the sector in the late 1960s, it was underpaid, significantly populated by managers who accepted these conditions, often women and retired forces personnel on a generous pension. Management training was virtually non-existent. The sector lagged behind the commercial and statutory sectors in developing staff professionalism of operation in areas such as strategic planning, marketing, HR (called personnel then) and to a lesser extent in areas such as finance, estates management and social work. Over the decades the sector caught up.

RNIB was a charity leader in implementing strategic planning and marketing (see chapters 2a and 2b) going through five different iterations of the strategic plan over 40 years and setting up our in-house marketing training. We were also among the leaders in finance and HR, for example, Barry Gifford played a leading role in the early years of the Charity Finance Director Group. RNIB HR developed some of the earliest internal, management training courses in the sector which were externally accredited (which I shall discuss later) and complemented by external management training such as the PGDip/MSc in Charity Management which I founded and led at City University London. In fundraising, RNIB was a leader in the 1960s, lost momentum in the 1970s and early 1980s but was re-invigorated in the 1990s. An exception was RNIB's effective legacy fundraising which was a continuing mainstay of voluntary income throughout the time period, boosted by thoughtful promotion.

As a charity, service delivery to people with sight loss was always the reason for RNIB's existence. Throughout 1970 to 2010 standards were high and always evaluated.

In the case of schools, colleges and residential homes, inspections were either wholly or partly independent. Staff were professionally qualified and often participated in training people in statutory services and other sight loss charities.

If growing staff professionalism was a trend across the 40 years, so was trustee governance. For most of the time there was a higher than charity average involvement of trustees, especially ones with sight loss. There were never fewer than four committee support staff ensuring efficient organisation of meetings and follow-up, all recorded in accessible media. Governance reform waxed and waned having high spots in the 1970s and 2000s (see chapters 1a and 4a). From the late 1980s there was a sector-wide trend supported by the Charity Commission to increase the power and authority of trustees in relation to the paid officers or executive. A key recommendation to effect this was to reduce trustee numbers. Some would argue RNIB was late with its reforms in governance at the beginning of the 2000s, reducing trustees from around 100 to 24 (in 2002) and, subsequently, even further. In RNIB's case the focus of power and decision making was historically on the smaller Policy and Resources Committee (fourteen people). However, larger trustee numbers gave more opportunity to involve blind and partially sighted people in running RNIB and made it easy to develop expertise and competence through informal mentoring of the less experienced by the experienced trustees. Nevertheless, in my view, Colin Low, as chair from 2000, was correct to press for trustee reduction as the 100-person trustee body had become an anachronism. The change gave Colin and me the opportunity to press for and introduce the practice for at least 50 per cent of trustees to be blind or partially sighted. This was one of my proudest moments and in 2001/02 was a first among blind and other disability service charities. This change converted RNIB from an organisation 'for' into an organisation 'of' blind and partially sighted people – philosophically and practically hugely important.

Disability Politics

Significant but insufficient progress on the place of people with disabilities was achieved over the 40 years, especially in the 1980s and 1990s with social security reform and the Disability Discrimination Act. Within this context it was an exhilarating period when disabled people forced their way into the driving seat of disability politics and the major charities for disabled people increasingly welcomed them. More importantly society, government and the charities changed their attitudes away from ones of pity, to recognition of the rights of disabled people, and recognition of institutional disablism in our society and its institutions

Who Were the Players?

Disability politics during this period is a minefield to describe, such were the trenchant views held by different interests. This was particularly apparent between and within organisations of disabled people, charities largely founded to provide services for disabled people, and government and parliament where the politics were finally arbitrated.

Disabled people's organisations 'of'

BCODP became the most powerful and radical established group but was widely regarded as led by the wheelchair lobby. Its interests and views were disparate. They ranged from the Disability Action Network (DAN), led by Alan Holdsworth, which mounted guerrilla raids on Downing Street with red paint and wheelchair users lying on the ground, through to the Association of Disabled Professionals. Their views diverged as well as coalesced. For example, organisations of people with sight loss initially opposed dropped pavements for wheelchair users because dropped kerbs make it hard for blind people to sense where the pavement stops and the road starts. Sections of organisations of the blind were also highly sceptical of the radical disability lobby's dogma that all problems of disabled people could be solved if barriers to their participation were removed.

Then there were the more explicitly focussed groups such as the British Deaf Association (BDA) of sign language users or NLBD, the trade union founded in 1899, affiliated to the TUC and the Labour Party. In the blind world alone, there were dozens of groups such as the NFB, the Association of Blind Asians, the Association of Blind Piano Tuners, the Association of Visually Handicapped Telephonists, ABAPSTAS, BCAB, COGDO, the Organisation of Blind Africans and Caribbeans (OBAC) and many, many more. Throughout the period there was a range of active organisations of blind and partially sighted people, fourteen of whom had formal representatives on RNIB's trustee council.

At the same time, the number and range of organisations of disabled people increased significantly. More importantly, their power and authority increased. Conservative and Labour governments listened carefully to the most influential groups. Very importantly, the EU gave preference to the views of organisations of disabled people over those of organisations for the disabled.

Organisations 'for'

The second grouping in disability politics consisted of the hundreds of national, regional and local disability charities providing services for people with different disabilities. They had always been relatively influential in parliament and local government. In the 1970s they were generally resistant to the rise of organisations 'of'. I remember a former CEO of RADAR in private conversation being very dismissive of organisations 'of', especially the more radical ones. Even RNIB, which had many organisations of blind people on its large trustee body, initially fiercely opposed more joining in the early 1970s (see chapter 1a).

By the 1980s charities 'for' were beginning to recognise the legitimacy of the 'of' lobby and its growing power and authority, and the human presence it could muster. Several alliances combining of and for organisations grew up.

Ironically, the problem facing RNIB was not gaining acceptance of sight loss organisations 'of' because they had been
the most powerful bloc inside RNIB since 1975. Rather, the
problem for the blind "of" and "for" lobby was their joint dis-
trust of other disability groups which they felt had stabbed
them in the back with the Labour Party of the early 1970s – a
Labour Party which they felt was warming towards the idea
of a blindness financial allowance. Luckily, the National Federation of the Blind had already buried the hatchet and
joined a pan-disability coalition in the early 1980s, the Disability Alliance, chaired by Professor Peter Townsend and
ably led for many years by Lorna Reith. So, with the support of
trustees Fred Reid and Colin Low, by the middle 1980s I was
able to persuade RNIB that we had to get inside the pan-
disability tent, as all the policy and practice trends were
towards pan-disability approaches not single disability ones.

RNIB's key role in founding the DBC, a pan-disability
coalition on disability benefits with me as co-chair with
Richard Wood of the British Council of Disabled People, was
a manifestation of this repositioning and brought our cause
many benefits (see chapter 3a).

Many government ministers have been involved: pre-
eminently Alf Morris (see chapter 1a); Sir Norman Fowler
(now Lord Fowler), whose reviews in the 1980s led to
reformed social security for disabled people in 1991 which
benefitted blind claimants but was heavily criticised in some
other respects; and Nick Scott, whose daughter criticised
him publicly for his role in 'talking out' a Private Members'
Bill on disability rights. On disability legislation at least one
backbencher deserves mention, Roger Berry, who gave
much support to disabled activists. David Blunkett inspired
us all as a successful blind politician.

Models of Disability – Medical, Social and Interactionist

Emerging in the middle 1970s and full blown in the 1980s,
the disability charity world was engaged in a fierce policy
debate within itself and with the outside world, especially

government. For the movement 'of' people with physical disabilities, the 'social model' became dogma: that is, disabled people do not have a problem; society has/is the problem by not adapting itself to include people with disabilities. They rejected what they called the medical model: disabled people have a problem which medical science can mitigate and, it is hoped, in due course cure or prevent). They later also resisted an RNIB revision, promulgated by Colin Low, which he called the interactionist model: society needs to adapt radically but disabled people need skills to take full advantage of these adaptations.

In my observation, the heart of the social model movement was disabled people's valid wish, graduating into a demand, to be in control rather than be 'sorted out' by well-meaning non-disabled people – 'nothing about us without us'. I worked hard to build bridges to the radical disability movement because of its validity, energy and capacity. One of the best compliments I ever received was from a (physical) disability leader who said 'Ian, it is a pity you are not disabled because then you would be one of us.' One of the worst came when RNIB had been a prime organiser of a larger pan-disability rally in Trafalgar Square packed with disabled people. Our chair John Wall was one of the speakers and, when his time came, he had to walk across a wide platform (easy), not deviate and fall off a two-metre-high stage (not too difficult), then find and not knock over a tall, thin tripod microphone with no podium (very hard if you are totally blind). He took my arm and I walked/led him across parallel to the severe drop and placed his hand on the mic – standard practice in the blind world where walking is easy but getting to an exact intended location is not (no chance of echo location in Trafalgar Square). The audience booed me for helping – and, possibly, John for accepting help.

It could be argued that the social model was not integrated fully until the RNIB governance changes in 2001/02 with the adoption of membership and more than 50 per cent of the trustees being blind or partially sighted – formally putting them in charge. Nevertheless, my observations in the 1980s suggest that there was no doubt that the dominantly influential group on the RNIB trustee body was the combined 'organisations of the blind' group of trustees. If they wanted something strongly, they got it; and, if they did not, it did not pass Executive Council.

Oliver (2013) argues that the publicly stated position of the social model of disability emanated from a joint publication by the Union of Physically Impaired Against Segregation and the Disability Alliance, 'Fundamental Principles of Disability', in November 1976. It was subtitled: 'A summary of the discussion held [between UPIAS and the Disability Alliance] on 22 November 1975'. The seminal nature of this meeting ties the social model into this RNIB history because three of the leading members of the Disability Alliance were from the National Federation of the Blind (NFB) – Charles Taylor, who was a speaker at the November meeting, and Fred Reid and Betty Veal. All three were active leaders in the NFB in the contemporaneous and successful struggle to increase blind people's representation on the RNIB Executive Council (chapter 1a) – an important step in the struggle to turn RNIB into an organisation in which blind people had majority control.

UPIAS put it this way in the 1976 publication: 'it is society which disables physically impaired people. Disability is something imposed on top of our impairments by the way we are unnecessarily isolated and excluded from full participation in society. Disabled people are therefore an oppressed group in society.' In 1983 this came to be labelled as the social model.

While the social model of disability found greater agreement among many organisations of disabled people, a key reason that organisations of the blind had reservations came from from the different impairment attributes. A person in a wheelchair can gain full access to a building if the steps barrier is removed by the installation of a sloped entry. A blind person's access to a book can be achieved by publishers producing it in braille. However, learning to read braille takes a lot longer than learning how to take an electric wheelchair up a slope. Hence, Colin Low developed the concept of the interactionist model to indicate a combination of removing the barriers created by society and empowering the individual disabled person through skills acquisition, and a recognition that some impairments cannot be overcome via the social model. For example, despite audio description, as Fred Reid put it to me: 'I desperately want to see a painting but I know I never shall' (personal communication 2019).

The social and interactionist models of disability had a strong resonance with other rights-based models, for example, those put forward by the civil rights movement and LGBTQ+. In all of these, the focus is on society needing to change its attitudes and behaviour. By the time the UN Year of the Disabled Person arrived in 1982, the social model was well recognised. When the decade of the disabled person was over, the United Nations Standard Rules on the Equalisation of Opportunities for Persons with Disabilities (1993) was established, which entrenched the social model, but also ensured the place for skills acquisition of the interactionist model. In 1992, by invitation, Sir Duncan Watson (RNIB's immediate past chair and then president of the World Blind Union) addressed the General Assembly of the United Nations and underlined the importance of this widened definition of the social model.

Key Legislation

Disabled people, including those with sight loss, are people like anyone else and so are affected by all legislation. RNIB, as do other charities, has to spot disparate legislative proposals that at first reading appear to be of little importance. Examples are: proposals for changes to the postal service which might impact on universal delivery (braille books go post free); or changes to the design of bank notes (differential size and clarity of design). However, over the years there were specific legislative changes which had major impact on the RNIB's concerns, for good or ill.

Chronically Sick and Disabled Persons Act 1970

This act, often called Alf Morris' act after the Labour MP who introduced it, is arguably the first piece of legislation worldwide on disability. As it resulted from a Private Member's Bill, it was weak in one sense in that it could not increase government spending but it did raise disability, including blindness, up the public agenda.

Mobility Allowance 1976

The introduction of the Mobility Allowance in 1976 was seminal legislation focussed on disability. It was a cash benefit to help disabled people with the extra costs of getting around. The anger and disbelief of the blindness lobby at being excluded was massive. The 'blind people can walk, can't they?' attitude took no account of how a person with sight loss might safely find his or her way along an unknown route to an intended destination; he or she needed help (e.g. a taxi or a guide). Theories, perhaps conspiracy theories, abound about the reasons for the exclusion. First, it was the height of pressure for a blindness allowance and the blind lobby might have taken its eye off the Mobility Allowance proposal or, indeed, regarded it as a competitor to be opposed or at least ignored. Second, the Mobility Allowance proposal was led from the pressure group side by the physical disability lobby and there was little love between the two groups. Third, the fact that people with learning difficulties (then called mental handicaps) were also excluded suggests that the Labour government was relieved at the lack of solidarity. Also, the costs to the Exchequer were much lower if visual impairment and learning disability were excluded from the Mobility Allowance.

Social Security Contributions and Benefits Act 1992

It would take eighteen years for this injustice to be corrected via the Social Security Contributions and Benefits Act. This was one of the major outcomes of the various reviews of disability begun by Norman Fowler, when he was the Conservative government's secretary of state for health and social services (1981-87), and groundbreaking research by the Office of Population Censuses and Surveys (Martin, Meltzer and Elliot 1988). This 1992 Act introduced the Disability Living Allowance with its two components, the Care Allowance and the Mobility Allowance, each with a higher and lower rate. This time the relevant wording on the MobA, as it came to be called was: 'cannot walk outdoors on an unfamiliar route without guidance or supervision from another person most of the time'.

This wording included blindness and learning disability and put £40 million into the pockets of blind people under 65. How was this achieved? Until quite late in the day it was not a done deal for either of the two new groups. A civil servant told us that research RNIB had undertaken, showing that blind people got out and about less than disabled people, in general, was critical (Bruce, McKennell and Walker 1991, with the early results shared with the government department in 1989/90). This finding surprised us as much as the civil servants but, seemingly, was a clincher. It was particularly convincing because our sample was a sub-sample of the government survey of disabled people (Martin, Meltzer and Elliot 1988) run by the Office of Population Censuses and Surveys (the forerunner of the Office of National Statistics). Particular credit for much of the behind-the-scenes work must go to Andy Barrick.

So, from 1992 the blindness lobby (RNIB, NLBD and NFB) had achieved a blindness allowance in all but name by access to both components of the Disability Living Allowance (DLA), albeit at the lower level. It would take until 2009 to win the higher rate. Our leadership role in the pan-disability Disability Benefits Consortium was vital. It tied us in with the blindness lobby's opponents of 1975/76, the organisations of physically disabled people; and gave us frequent and legitimate links with government ministers and civil servants while the benefits were being designed.

Disability Discrimination Act 1995

In the year of DLA success, 1992, Rights Now, another pan-disability alliance was set up to press for comprehensive disability discrimination legislation. Given the radical/ traditional organisation partnership within Rights Now, our acceptance was greatly enhanced by Alun Thomas (RNIB parliamentary officer) as our key representative. His sight loss gave him enhanced credibility with the 'ofs' and his acute understanding of the parliamentary process, so critical during the drafting of the legislation, made him indispensable to Rights Now: 'Success was achieved after a coalition of more radical disability-run organisations joined forces with some more traditional charities to form the Rights Now group' (Vanhala 2011: 206)

The resulting Disability Discrimination Act 1995 introduced the requirement on providers of goods, services and employment to make 'reasonable adjustments' for people with disabilities. The impact on goods and services is very significant and there for all to see – sloped access to buildings, dropped kerbs, staff guides for blind people at rail stations, braille on medicines and so on. The impact on employment is harder to discern. A well evidenced article in the *Journal of Health Economics* (Bell and Heitmueller 2009) argued that it had no impact on employment rates and may possibly have worsened matters.

EU Treaty of Amsterdam 1997

Less well known but crucially important was the Treaty of Amsterdam 1997, which made substantial changes to the 1992 Treaty of Maastricht. Under the new treaty, member states agreed to transfer certain powers from national governments to the European parliament across a range of areas. The treaty was fundamentally important for disabled people in all EU countries because, for the first time, it provided a legal basis for the EU to work in the area of disability. The previous consensual agreement to do so was breaking down and without this formal agreement the history of disabled people in Europe would have been far worse and many important disability programmes would not have happened.

In 1996 I was with RNIB Brussels' staff when an EU civil servant suggested a worrying development in relation to the anticipated treaty revision. It was known that powerful political elements in Germany wanted to restrain EU growth by halting much of EU's permissive activity which was the basis of EU activity on disability. What we had not appreciated was that in their sights was reducing support for disabled people. A permissive activity in an EU programme would fall if just one country were to veto it.

The disability campaign was led by the European Disability Forum (EDF), chaired by the dynamic Johan Weseman from the deaf lobby. However, it had no funds and no income in prospect. The campaign was at the point of collapse less than a year before the Treaty negotiations would be concluded. At this critical point our RNIB EU team (Sally Kneeshaw, Barbara McLaughlin and Kate Seymour all supported by our long-time EU expert, Jane Peters.) persuaded me that RNIB must put £20,000 (1997 prices) into the pot for a last push. This sounds easy and logical now. Back then, persuading RNIB would be difficult. Why should RNIB out of hundreds of EDF members accept total responsibility for the rescue? There was no time for this argument, so I used the method 'better to do it and apologise afterwards'.

By late 1996 the EDF thought we had support from nine of the fifteen EU member states but way short of what was needed. What was even worse, the British Conservative government, seeking to clip the EU's wings, was against our campaign. Nevertheless, there was a general election in prospect on 1 May and the polls were indicating a likely Labour victory. To the delight of disability charities in the UK, on 6 March, two months before the election, their spokesman on foreign affairs, Robin Cook, stated clearly that the position of a Labour government would be to include the social protocol in the Treaty together with a chapter including protection of disabled people.

However, after the Labour win, when we, RNIB, made contact with the new government (not an easy task in the frenetic atmosphere of the new government!) our hopes were dashed. The Labour election promise not to spend more than the previous Conservative government in its first two years, made the new government reverse the Cook promise. RNIB parliamentary staff managed to get the message through to the political advisers that an EU budget line had existed for several years so no new money was needed. Second, it would allow the prime minister, Tony Blair, an immediate, international leadership opportunity, in pressing for inclusion with a good chance of success (we had not realised how attractive that would prove to be to him). The UK government was known to be cautious about any expansion of Brussels' powers, so, if the UK said adding disability was alright, then other waverer countries might be persuaded.

He did and they were so persuaded. Six countries changed their position. Disability was included unanimously in the Amsterdam Treaty agreed on 18 June 1997, seven weeks after the Labour government was elected and four weeks after we got our message across to the new Labour government.

Equality Act 2010

The last piece of disability legislation for this history is the Equality Act 2010, consolidating all rights legislation (that is, age, race, sex, sexual orientation etc.) and updating it in line with EU law. RNIB supported Lord Colin Low's work in the Lords to ensure the legislation had explicit provision on accessible information, so fundamental to people with sight loss.

Chapter 6

Trends within RNIB

The previous chapter identified outside forces impacting on RNIB and its interaction with these. This one examines the trends within RNIB and their impact on the external world, primarily on blind and partially sighted people.

Over the years 1970-2010, priority activities remained focussed on accessible information (including braille, audio and digital), education and employment. However, RNIB added many activities by way of new methods, new areas of need and new kinds of VI people served and, above all, many more people served.

A crucial trigger for these changes was one of the policy directives (number two) in the 1987 strategy: 'To reach more and a wider range of visually handicapped people, in particular, older as well as younger, multi-handicapped as well as single handicapped, ethnic minorities as well as the majority, and those with low vision as well as those who are totally blind.'

Discovering and Reaching Many More People

Services direct to the people with sight loss expanded exponentially over the 40 years, especially in the form of information provision: via publications, telephone and, since the middle 1990s, via digital communications.

From 150,000 to Two Million

One of the main drivers of this expansion was the paradigm shift in RNIB's view of the numbers of blind and partially sighted in the country. In the 1970s the dominant guide to numbers was the statutory register, which indicated around 150,000 blind and partially sighted people. RNIB's focus within that number was on the 95,000 who were blind. Many of RNIB's services were residential (high-impact but low numbers) and some were mass services such as Talking Books. Then, we had few information services. A reasonable estimate would be a penetration of 40,000 blind and partially sighted people, albeit with major individual impact. For example, the average RNIB Talking Book member spent twelve hours a week listening to Talking Books (our audio books).

Part of my induction in 1983/84 was talking to ophthalmologists and social workers for the blind. It was clear that significant numbers of eligible people were not being registered, but how many? In 1985 RNIB commissioned a demographic review (Shankland Cox 1985) which concluded that between 20 and 30 per cent of eligible people were being missed. This was enough to trigger the second policy directive in the RNIB strategy (RNIB 1987) demanding that RNIB should reach many more blind and partially sighted people.

The more evidence-based RNIB Needs Survey (Bruce, McKennell and Walker 1991) drew the even more dramatic conclusion that there were not merely 150,000 but around three quarters of a million registrably blind and partially sighted people. By the 1990s, adding in people who had uncorrectable sight loss but insufficient to reach official partial sight levels, the estimate became two million. The additional sight loss numbers included people who were ineligible to drive through to those unable to read a car number plate at 20 yards while wearing glasses.

More, Empowering Information Services

So, these facts required a massive expansion in information services. In the early 1970s RNIB information and advice was reaching only tens of thousands of people each year and the activity hardly featured in annual reports. After the policy shift of the middle 1980s, expansion in the 1990s and 2000s was rapid and, by 2010, RNIB was answering over 400,000 requests a year for help covering a staggeringly wide range of subjects, particularly on sight problems, benefits rights, rehabilitation and everyday living.

Reach – to New Kinds of People

Writing a history, it is so easy to write down a heading listing a new group of people a charity has decided to work with. In practice it is a huge decision, not to be taken lightly if the group are to be well served and engaged with.

Partially Sighted in Addition to Blind

In practice RNIB had included partially sighted people in some of its services, pre-eminently Talking Books but the official policy position and practice was to focus on blind people. However, early results from the RNIB Needs Survey (Bruce, McKennell and Walker 1991) confirmed that this group had more problems than had previously been generally recognised. In the second half of the 1980s the policy position changed when the trustee body (the Executive Council) decided that partially sighted people were formally part of the target group. In the 1990s this coverage was extended to cover campaigning for all people with uncorrectable sight loss.

In retrospect, the decision to expand to do more for partially sighted people looks obvious and overdue but it was not an easy one to take. The dominant organisations on the trustee body were organisations of blind people who were voting to share resources with another large group of people which common sense indicated had less of a problem than totally blind people. Second, the extension was opposed by the Partially Sighted Society who felt the RNIB would not understand the needs and wishes of partially sighted people and, in political terms, did not want their territory invaded. Such was the delineation between the two sight levels that the Partially Sighted Society was not represented on RNIB. Their leader, Bob Greenhalgh was on RNIB committees representing a social work constituency and so could fight a rearguard action. The clinching arguments were in the needs survey research showing the extent of unmet need of partially sighted people. In addition, support for the extension came from registered blind people with residual vision as well as progressive totally blind people, dominant in the RNIB trustee leadership.

Widening the target group not only helped the newly included people, it also helped the many registered blind people with some residual vision who were able to benefit from campaign wins. These wins also became easier to achieve through the increased lobbying power of two million people with sight problems as opposed to the earlier smaller number.

Minority Ethnic Groups

As for services to minority groups, RNIB, like most charities had a lot of progress to make. We finally recognised this (arguably too little but first among disability charities) in the 1987 RNIB Strategy.

To expand and improve our service delivery to minority ethnic groups we appointed in 1987 RNIB's first development officer to encourage greater focus, Gladwell Msimang, followed by Kishor Patel in the 1990s. This was the only operational post accountable to me as director general which was not a divisional directorship. This seniority of report was in order to emphasise the priority of the role. Practical changes included: producing significant numbers of Talking Books in Asian languages; a major campaign on

Mrs Nimi Handa knitting while testing our new Talking Books in Hindi 1991.

the increased likelihood of glaucoma amongst people of African and Caribbean heritage and actions which needed to be taken; and development officer advisory visits to our schools and colleges where we thankfully had proportionate numbers of minority students. The development officers also gave support to two mutual aid groups which emerged: the Organisation of Blind Africans and Caribbeans and the Association of Blind Asians.

Very importantly, Kishor ran workshops for staff, helping us to recognise our prejudices both institutional and personal. From 1997 on Fazilet Hadi, in her role as director of policy and, subsequently, deputy chief executive, did much to improve our performance in this area. However, in common with most, if not all, British institutions at that time, RNIB should have done much more to combat what in retrospect was at least conformity bias which must have led, in effect, to institutional discrimination in many of our services and employment activities.

Here is an anecdote which hints at the broader British society's split attitude towards black and minority empowerment. Gladwell Msimang used to save up his holidays to use them for urgent requests for relatively short periods of time off (*circa* five days). It did not affect his work but I was worried he might be shouldering undue home responsibilities and it was somewhat exasperating 'yet again' to have an urgent request for personal leave with no clear explanation as to why. Once we had built up a relationship of trust, he shared with me that he was active in the African National Congress (ANC), fighting apartheid in South Africa. These urgent requests for time off allowed him to travel to Zimbabwe to attend ANC Executive meetings arranged at short notice. This was in the 1980s when national political attitudes to the

ANC varied widely and he did not wish his association with the organisation to complicate his work with us. In earlier jobs he had found that these associations had counted against him.

Multi-handicapped Visually Impaired Adults

RNIB had a tradition of residential education and care services for the growing number of what were then called MHVI children. These services were pioneered in the early 1950s by Oscar Myers, head of Condover Hall School, which educated children and young people who would previously have been called ineducable and often kept in long-stay hospitals.

The extension to work with visually impaired adults with learning difficulties was prompted by the little-known fact at the time that a disproportionate number of adults with learning difficulties had undiagnosed visual impairments. These exacerbated the assessments of the extent of learning difficulties. Providing visual aids and visually impaired rehabilitation produced startling improvements.

The extension into work with this group of people was two pronged. In the late 1980s RNIB launched an indirect service to persuade and support other providers of the benefits of assuming multiply disabled adults had a visual impairment until shown otherwise. The second prong was a much larger direct service in Scotland championed by Tony Aston as director of vocational and social services. When RNIB Scotland was established, it came under Allan Murray and later Mike Cairns. RNIB Springfield Centre (founded in 1994) in Glasgow was pioneered by Frances Miller with important championing by Allan. It provided groundbreaking day-care and outreach services for adults with learning and physical disabilities that included visual impairment; supporting people to live as independently as possible by providing services where the person needed them, whether it be in the home, community, college, employment or at RNIB Springfield Centre.

One of the UK leaders in this field, the RNIB worked to get recognition of the needs, aspirations and abilities of visually impaired children/young people/adults with severe or profound and multiple learning difficulties. We did this in our schools (Rushton, Condover, Northwood and Southport), through our outreach service with our network of Education and Employment Centres, and through adult multiple disability services as described above as well as through publications and videos. With groups such as Sense, Whitefield School and the Royal Blind School in Edinburgh, RNIB pioneered new approaches to understanding and communication, through 'objects of reference' (Ockelford 1994), that are now found in every special school that caters for children with learning difficulties. A key figure in RNIB who helped to develop and weave all this activity into a coherent strategy was Adam Ockelford.

Older People

RNIB had realised for years that the formal registers of blind and partially sighted people underrepresented the older population. A significant reason was that ophthalmologists judged that there was little to be gained by diagnosing an

Older guests at one of our four hotels enjoying Eastbourne.

older person as blind. The early findings of the RNIB Needs Survey (Bruce, McKennell and Walker 1991) showed that two thirds of registrably blind and partially sighted people were over 75 years and most had lost their sight later in life. Looking at this age demographic and the balance of existing services, the conclusion was clear. RNIB had to do more to help older people with newly acquired sight loss. As with the partially sighted extension debate, the decision was a tough one. Most of RNIB trustees with sight problems had had this condition for most or all of their lives and RNIB services had coalesced around the needs of this demographic, not newly visually impaired over 75. Once again, they made the selfless decision to try to reach more older visually handicapped people (RNIB 1987).

Here, unlike services for minority ethnic groups, RNIB was building on existing services which had already proved effective, such as our hotels and Talking Books, of which half the members were over 60 years. The driver was to invest subsidy more into services for older people. Results were initiatives such as: Talk and Support (championed by Jon Barrick), a telephone service whereby groups of newly visually impaired could talk together on the phone and thus supported mutual aid; a campaign for free eye tests for the over sixties; big button telephones developed with BT; and audio description on TV.

Conclusions

The most cost-effective initiatives tended to be those which reached more than one of these extension target groups at the same time, for example, Talking Books in Asian languages. Here, we reached mainly older people who were partially sighted, could not read print and came from a minority ethnic group. Designing bank notes which had highly differentiated colours between denominations and had high contrast within the notes, particularly on the large denomination numeral (e.g. the £20 note) helped all four groups.

New Ways of Working

Over 40 years there were many changes in RNIB ways of working but one stands out, the shift to indirect services, including campaigning. This was a trend one can observe across the wider charity sector. I define indirect services as a charity working with others in the statutory, commercial, voluntary and informal sectors (family friends and neighbours) to persuade them to meet the needs and wishes of their cause or group.

Partly though tradition and partly through the narrow interpretation of charity law in the middle of the twentieth century, most charities, including RNIB, concentrated primarily on helping their target groups directly, for example, running their own schools, residential homes, libraries for blind people and so on.

The trend over the last 40 years away from primarily concentrating on direct services, towards indirect ways of working is reflected widely across the charity sector, for example, in the National Trust, Oxfam, Save the Children, Barnardo's, Mencap, Cheshire, Cancer Research UK (CRUK), Scope, Christian Aid, NSPCC, Help the Aged, British, Heart Foundation, Macmillan, RSPCA. More specific examples of this trend are: in 1972, the newly independent, relaunched Age Concern persuaded Tesco to sell smaller 250g packets of butter designed for older people living alone; or, at the end of the period, the National Trust and the National Federation of Women's Institutes joined a wider campaign against the expansion of Heathrow Airport because of its feared adverse environmental impact.

RNIB Indirect Services

In the middle 1980s RNIB decided to increase greatly the amount of indirect help it would give through persuading others to do more.

The 1985 policy guidelines and, in particular, the 1987 strategy (recommendation number six) put it this way: 'To increase the number and scale of our indirect services so as to improve support to visually handicapped people through the statutory, voluntary and commercial sectors and via the informal sector – family, neighbours and friends.'

In essence, this is persuading mainstream service and product providers to adapt their ordinary activities to better meet the needs of people with sight problems – persuading them through information, advice, training, consultancy and lobbying, campaigning and, in the extreme, direct action. The theoretical underpinnings of this way of working can be found in social marketing theory.

One major example was pressing and supporting mainstream education to be more accepting of, and competent in, educating blind and partially sighted children. Other examples were: persuading drug companies to put braille labels on medicine packets; persuading local authorities to lay bubble pavement warnings at street corners with dropped kerbs; persuading the Bank of England to increase the size, colour and contrast differentiation on bank notes; training train station staff in guiding techniques.

In education there was a discernible development path starting with direct services, mainly residential, moving to direct in the community, into indirect – for example, starting with the RNIB Sunshine Schools and Condover and Rushton Hall Schools – all initially residential, then RNIB Education Advisory Service (EAS) (direct) for parents and young children in their own homes in 1972, and then the RNIB Education Support Service (ESS) in 1986, supporting staff in mainstream schools and helping them with integrating (including) children with sight problems through consultancy, training and publications.

One of the publications from ESS was *Play It My Way* (RNIB 1995) using the experience of the earlier EAS advisers who visited families with very young blind children. This exercise was moderated by Louise Clunies-Ross and also drew in outsiders for a broader perspective from mainstream education (Tina Bruce and Linda Pound from the School of Education, University of Roehampton). Next came a series of videos

Discovering the fun of music and movement at RNIB Sunshine House School in Southport 1988.

produced by Adam Ockelford and his team. In this way, our practical experience of direct service provision provided the basis of advice to those in mainstream education – 'We know what we are talking about because we have done/ are doing it'. The counter argument was 'They are stuck in the RNIB method', an argument which, of course, we strongly rejected.

This dual approach of direct provision, supported by indirect provision, in the same area had its tensions – some RNIB school heads felt that our work supporting blind children in mainstream schools was reducing demand for residential places in their schools. However, this was the tide of social policy moving towards mainstreaming. As a consequence, we began to segment recruitment in more appropriate ways. For example, our residential schools shifted more towards those with profound and multiple learning difficulties (PMLD) at one end of the spectrum and advanced learning development at the other – at RNIB New College Worcester where it was normal for children to progress to university. Mainstream schools found it difficult to meet the needs of children at either end of the spectrum.

From 1986 onwards, RNIB's indirect services extended also into the commercial world and included ones aimed at publishing, retail, transportation, construction, leisure (especially television and film), sport and so on. In the public sector RNIB focus turned to persuading the statutory sector to do better in helping blind and partially sighted people – in the NHS, social services, social security, education, employment and environmental services.

One of the most important areas where RNIB invested heavily in order to encourage others to make their activities accessible was digital communications. This was pioneered initially in the 1980s by Dr John Gill (early for the voluntary sector but logical for a blind charity) and, subsequently, under the leadership of Stephen King. RNIB concentrated in research and development and leadership. As a result of these and others' efforts, combined with the digital world seeing commercial opportunities, accessing electronically-based information and culture became feasible. Nevertheless, the cost to the person with sight loss is still high – hence, the need for subsidy or a costs allowance. Furthermore, there is still the challenge that many people do not have the necessary access skills and most sighted people do not know that access services exist. So, at the end of this history, in the 2010s, the strategy shifted to benefits realisation.

From the moment the broader strategy was decided in the middle 1980s, indirect services grew dramatically. From the 1990s they became a normal way of working for RNIB and from 2005 under Lesley-Anne Alexander they grew even further.

Supportive External Trends

With the benefit of hindsight, I would say that RNIB, and other charities, experienced several trends which helped charities to expand indirect services – points covered in more detail earlier in this chapter.

There was the decline in the power and authority of professionals. On the one hand, they were attacked by some politicians and the popular press who took their gloves off when dealing with professionals, such as social workers. In a more positive mode, professional associations became less arrogant about their knowledge, less defensive and more prepared to listen to and co-operate with beneficiaries and their representatives.

Additionally, through the new policies of the 1979 Conservative government there was a reduction from the 1980s in the 'monopoly' of welfare state provision and a growth in outsourcing, which allowed RNIB and other charities to practise what we were preaching to local and national government. This trend was actively promoted by the NCVO (Davis Smith 2019), with Nicholas Hinton and their head of policy Francis Gladstone espousing the detail (Gladstone 1979).

Third, from the 1990s the Charity Commission broadened its view on the legitimacy of campaigning as a charitable activity, which really took off under the leadership of CEO Andrew Hind (2004-2010). Charity Commission guidance, *Campaigning and Political Activity Guidance for Charities* (CC9), says that charities can campaign for a change in the law, policy or decisions where such change would support the charity's purposes.

Fourth was the growth from the 1980s in the legitimacy of the social model of disability.

Lastly, there was the field of opportunity opened up by the Disability Discrimination Act 1995 which required all providers, whether from the commercial, statutory or voluntary sectors, to make reasonable adjustments in the provision of goods and services.

New Needs, New Needs Markets

Some readers will bristle at the terminology in this section. I use it because some of these terms and their background theories and assumptions may help charities to analyse better what is happening and when to act on behalf of their cause.

When I entered the sector full-time in 1970 the widely held view was that the welfare state alone could, should and would meet all reasonable need. This view began to erode during the 1970s primarily, but not exclusively, through lack of money. Then came the Conservative (Thatcher) government of 1979 with its policy intention to reduce the size of the state and to introduce more free market practice, i.e. outsourcing often associated with contracting via competitive tendering. While the Thatcher policies were momentous, outsourcing and contracting had taken place previously, for example, RNIB would be contracted by a local education authority to accept a child in one of our residential schools; or the Manpower Services Commission might contract a charity to accept a placement under its employment programme (Davis Smith 2019).

This presented the charity sector with an opportunity and a dilemma: the opportunity to enter that free market; and the dilemma of how to do this without undermining and reducing welfare state provision, so important to their beneficiaries. In practice, the choice could be stark. NCH Action for Children entered and grew enormously, the Children's Society hesitated for fear of undermining the state and dropped from the list of top 20 charities. In practice, most charities have entered the market or continued to operate in it as RNIB did, with provisos:

- The statutory call had to be in line with RNIB policy.
- The likely contract fee would achieve breakeven, or near breakeven.
- RNIB would be reasonably accountable to the statutory commissioner, i.e. the activity was still the state's responsibility, but the terms were not so restrictive that we could not apply our expertise on beneficiary needs and wishes.

Has this widespread charity entry undermined the welfare state? In brief, I would argue 'No'. First, while contracting has increased charity income substantially (see chapter 9), as a proportion of state, social welfare spending it is miniscule. On the contrary, charity campaigning has massively increased state spending. To take one example only, state spending on disability benefit has increased greatly in real terms through charity lobbying on the shape of Disability Living Allowance, and through largely successful campaigns against proposed cuts by Labour and Conservative governments. (Although spending is still not enough to meet need.)

In summary, the 1979 government policy change, which has continued under all successive governments to a greater or lesser extent, has seen shifting boundaries between social welfare provided by the four actors: state, charities/non-profits, commercial organisations and the informal sector (family, friends and neighbours).

Charities have benefitted, as have their beneficiaries. (For a more extensive discussion of these issues, see Davis Smith 2019.)

Market Entry

This still leaves the question: 'Which areas of need?' Traditionally RNIB concentrated on accessible information, employment and education and technical aids. Was this enough? No, it was clear that people with sight problems had additional needs which were not being addressed by RNIB. In the 1980s, the combination of the existence of money to invest, the desire of trustee leaders, such as Watson, Wall, Parker, Low, Reid, Poole, Morton and Dunn, to progress, my arrival and finding a highly motivated senior management team and a legacy from my predecessor (Eddie Venn): all resulted in RNIB entering into several new areas of work (markets). We launched a variety of new services, most of which survived and grew over the period covered in this history. Between 1985-1991 the following new RNIB services were launched:

- benefits rights;
- social services consultancy;

- NHS consultancy;
- mainstream education support service;
- arts and sports advice;
- accommodation advice;
- mobility and access unit (aimed at architects and developers);
- eye health consultancy;
- a UK parliamentary unit; and
- a European Union unit.

Later examples include multi-media bills and bank statements, Talk and Support, RNIB Radio, family mutual support events, Audetel, accessible televisions and many more (see chapters 2b, 3b and 4b).

Example of Market Entry – Eye Health

The term 'new needs markets' is used because the needs themselves are seldom new, for example, partially sighted people have needed magnifiers for centuries. What is new or changing is: who should meet those needs; in what combination of the four sectors (private, state, voluntary and informal)to best expand provision; how best to meet these needs. To over-simplify: how to supply the magnifiers, what kind of magnifiers and, most importantly, how to use them easily, effectively and in a socially acceptable manner – for example, using a mobile phone camera magnifier rather than a magnifying glass (which will likely stay in the partially sighted person's drawer because of stigma).

So, how does a charity analyse these opportunities or, for the sake of this discussion, what I would call 'needs markets'?

If, how and when to enter a new needs market is an extremely complex decision for a charity with lots of unknowns and uncertainties. In RNIB's case, let us look at the field of eye health. Entry into this field became very successful and with the benefit of hindsight was very obvious – eye health should be core business to a charity centred on blindness and partial sight. So, it is perhaps surprising that until the

**Campaigning against charges for
eye tests, 1989.**

middle 1980s after 117 years of existence RNIB had little or
no service delivery involvement with eye health other than
minor funding ophthalmic medical research. One can develop
hypotheses as to why this was. First, the voluntary sector was
keen not to inadvertently reduce statutory responsibility for
service provision, especially within the NHS. Second, in the
twentieth century relationships between ophthalmologists
and optometrists were often tense and the last thing that was
needed was RNIB entering the fray and creating even more
boundary disputes. Finally, optometrists, and, in particular,
those specialising in people with partial sight (low vision as
the professionals call it), were very defensive of their patch.
They saw any incursion by RNIB as a threat to their area
of professionalism. Such a small step as exhibiting back-lit
magnifiers in our resource centre in 1984 was challenged by
some leading optometrists as an ignorant excursion into their
area of expertise. However, a traditional role of the voluntary
sector is to pioneer new services; and new service forms
were sorely needed in the world of partial sight/low vision
where services were not reaching many people who needed

them and too many of those prescribed, low vision aids stayed in people's drawers, unused through lack of support and training.

With the policy guidelines (Bruce 1985) and the first strategy (RNIB 1987), RNIB bit the bullet and launched the health consultancy and the regular eye health campaigns. We were blooded in the field of optometry by our campaign opposing the 1989 Conservative government decision to start charging people for eye tests. The government's majority was reduced to eight votes in April 1989. (See the campaign case study in Bruce 2011: 147-50). Also, by the late 1980s professionals were becoming more inclusive and consultative. First to lead on this for RNIB came Carolyn Wardrop-White heading an Eye Health Unit, later Sue Grindey (now Browning), Barbara Ryan and Anita Lightstone, all guided for much of this time by Deborah Hamlin. By the late 1990s there were over a dozen staff and we had moved into low vision optometry services for six London health districts.

By the early 2000s RNIB staff were working closely with the Department of Health on low vision policy. Eye health was a key part of the UK Vision Strategy of the middle 2000s and the unity of effort this encouraged led to the inclusion of an eye health indicator in the government's Public Health Outcomes Framework (launched in 2012). This achievement shows the effectiveness of long-term professional lobbying. This was a rapid rise for RNIB from outsider to insider in the world of eye health and low vision optometry.

In conclusion, in 1970 and for previous decades RNIB's main markets were accessible information, employment, education, technical aids and social rehabilitation. From 1987 onwards eye health was introduced and became an additional core activity by the end of the 1990s. Arguably adding eye health in 1987 was the most important strategic extension made by RNIB in over 80 years since the first decade of the twentieth century and the RNIB's predecessor organisation expanded from embossed literature into education and employment (Thomas 1957).

Reduction in Residentially-based Services

The policy and practice trend over 1970-2010 towards integration and inclusion of disabled children and adults into mainstream society had a major impact on RNIB. Nowhere was this clearer than in the field of residential services which declined in favour of community focussed initiatives. This shift was typical of the social welfare charity sector and included others, such as Barnardo's, Action for Children, Scope, Leonard Cheshire and Mencap.

In 1970 RNIB was dominated by establishment/building-based services, all requiring clients to be residential, some 23 establishments; whereas by 2010 that had been reduced to nine. The number of residential beneficiaries also declined. This shift was brought about by statutory social and commissioning policy changes, making many of our previous building-based services inappropriate, as well as too expensive. However, three kinds of building-based activity expanded – headquarters service buildings in Northern Ireland, Scotland and Wales (there were none in 1970, only fundraising branches); production buildings moved out of London (for example, to Peterborough, Tarporley and

Table 6.1. RNIB Residential Establishments 1970-2012

RNIB residential establishments	1970	1990	2012
Sunshine House schools	5	2	1
Primary provision	1	1	1
Secondary provision	3	2	1
Further and Higher Education	3	3	1
Rehabilitation	2	3	2
Residential homes	4	3	3
Hotels	4	3	0
Hostel	1	1	0
Total	23	18	9

Stockport); and, lastly, small offices, either locally- or region-ally-based, for multi-purpose service provision (education, employment, information), often of an indirect service nature.

Out with the Old, In with the New: Minority Specialisms versus Volume Services

The shift of national social policy towards integration/inclusion had unintended negative impacts on the provision of charity specialist, minority services, in general, and visual impairment ones, in particular. Theoretically, the impact of integration opened new expansion possibilities. Take education: every mainstream school with a newly arrived blind child needed extra specialist support from RNIB and other specialist workers, for example, not only general Braille but the special codes for Mathematics Braille. However, many mainstream professionals knew too little about the specialist area of disability and sight loss, in particular, to know what special support might help or was available, so demand for Braille dropped. Also, 'easier' access methods were adopted. Recording text onto voice recorder (tape recorder or, later, smart phone) was easier for the teacher. The pupil (and teacher) did not have to be taught Braille – but, arguably, the quality of engagement with text of the subject of study was less than if the pupil could read and write Braille and have the text in a form they could 'see'. Another vital minority service, tactile maps, survived, supported powerfully for many years by Sue King. In the area of music, RNIB transcription of print music scores into Braille for blind musicians and students in specialist education had been served by a brilliant succession of knowledgeable blind musician leaders – John Busbridge, Bob Hoare and Roger Firman. These drops in external demand for highly specialised services meant defending them inside the RNIB became harder. RNIB's response was to try to open the eyes of professionals in the integrated settings through music promotional work from the likes of Adam Ockelford, Sally Zimmerman and Simon Labbett. Nevertheless, it was hard because of the tension between the twin effects of (false) reduced demand for specialist services and the necessary attention demanded to supply more, much needed, high-volume services with associated income streams, such as Talking Books, social rehabilitation and low vision services.

One anecdote might serve to lighten this discussion. Mathematics Braille is extremely complicated and precise. One dot in the wrong place destroys the desired meaning, regrettable for literature but disastrous in a mathematical calculation. RNIB had traditionally found it difficult to train up and retain Maths Braille transcribers. In a mysterious (semi-secret from me at least) part of RNIB Braille transcription we had trained up long-serving prisoners in the Maths Braille code. This way we achieved long-term, high-quality Maths Braille for teaching purposes and exam papers. At the same time, prisoners committed to sentences of a minimum of ten years in prison had a worthwhile outlet for their time.

This decline of some minority specialist services can probably be generalised across much of the social welfare charity sector and was perhaps inevitable. Nonetheless, I was uncomfortable with it and tried to slow it down for fear of 'throwing out the babies with the bath water'.

Chapter 7

Strategic and Structural Change

While there were many strategic changes over the period 1970-2010, the dominant and consistent theme was always trying to increase the focus on the needs and wishes of people with sight loss, particularly with their involvement – 'co-creation', in the jargon.

This section looks at governance and management within that context. 'Governance' refers to the setting in which trustees and other unpaid committee people determine RNIB's policies and activities as required under charity law. The 'executive' or 'officers' refer to the (largely) paid managers executing the policies: for example, running the schools, hotels, eye clinics, drafting the detail of the lobbying positions, organising the fundraising dinners, working with advertising agencies etc. The organisation structure describes the operational framework in which the trustees and executives and managers work.

Governance – Fewer Trustees, Half to Be Blind or Partially Sighted

Over the period, RNIB returned to the principles of its foundation (1868-79), namely, the pre-eminent role of blind people in its governance. At its foundation and for the first nineteen years RNIB required all its trustees to be blind but thereafter, and especially from the 1920s until the 1970s, this dominant role of blind governance slipped down the agenda. This is not to say that some blind people were not trustees, there as of right, but they represented a small proportion. Progressive changes from the 1970s onwards raised this proportion until in 2001/02 the legal constitution was changed to require once again a majority of trustees to be blind or partially sighted. Also, the policy intent was enlarged to introduce voting membership, predominantly of people with sight loss. RNIB became formally the Royal National Institute of, not for, the Blind – cementing a major philosophical and political change. This was one of my proudest moments. RNIB was a leader among service delivery charities in making this shift, with other charities following, such as Mind, Mencap and Action on Hearing Loss. Others made much less of a shift during 1970-2010, for example, Leonard Cheshire and Guide Dogs for the Blind Association. Interestingly, the word 'people', as in Royal National Institute of Blind People, was not added until later in the noughties, having been deemed unnecessary political correctness by organisations of the blind in 2001.

While the composition of governance changed significantly (more blind people), from 1970 to 2000 the structure of governance remained remarkably constant. There was a large trustee body (the Executive Council) of 100 plus people and many committees and sub-committees – approximately 45. In 1987, a typical year, there were six main standing committees (Policy and Resources; Education and Leisure; Vocational and Social Services; Publications and Equipment; International; Finance and General Purposes) and 40 sub-committees, which met a total of 110 times in one year! All had agendas and were minuted. The set up was similar to the way local government operated throughout much of the twentieth century. Probably, many people in the twenty-first century would regard this structure with incredulity, verging on ridicule, but the system had strengths as well as weaknesses. It is worth noting some of the advantages. Major decisions only took a maximum of four months (the committee cycle); the sifting of proposals by the committees exposed weaknesses which could be corrected especially important as the majority of committee members had sight loss. Also, the focussed sub-committees on minority interests, often with budgets, helped to defend minority areas of work, for example, the Music or Blind Clerics Groups or the deaf/blind sub-committee. Finally, the democratic/participative system of committees gave participation and professional development opportunities to new cadres of beneficiary representation. These provided a supply of visually impaired, experienced, future trustee leaders.

However, as described in chapter 4a, in the early 2000s the advice from the Charity Commission, and best practice advice across the sector, was for lean governing structures. These were also seen as mechanisms for rebalancing power towards trustees away from senior managers.

This charity-wide trend in governance restructuring gave RNIB the opportunity to introduce increased power and authority to people with sight loss, something the then chair, Colin Low, and I were keen to do for reasons outlined previously, primarily the rights climate. Consequently, there were dramatic systemic and structural changes to governance between 2000 and 2002, in summary:

- An RNIB membership was created of (primarily) blind and partially sighted people with democratic elective rights (2001/02).
- RNIB changed from being an organisation 'for' to being an organisation 'of' blind and partially sighted people – by requiring (legally) that a majority of trustees and members be blind or partially sighted. (2001/02)
- Trustees were reduced from 120 on the Executive Council to 24 on the (new) RNIB Board (2001/02).

As will be readily appreciated, all three structural changes were challenging. The last was extremely difficult and took all of Colin Low's powers of persuasion and determination to ensure that the Executive Council of trustees voted itself out of existence to become a non-trustee advisory assembly. The outgoing trustees characterised the process as turkeys voting for Christmas!

By 2009/10, under Kevin Carey (who succeeded Colin Low as chair in July 2009) and Lesley-Anne Alexander's, watch the committee structure looked very different. Gone were the committees of Policy and Resources, Education and Leisure, Vocation and Social Services, and Technical and Consumer Services, reporting to the Board; they were replaced by four committees: Executive, Governance, Audit and Remuneration; and three subcommittees: Education, Care and Safeguarding; Human Resources; and Investments. Common to both structures were the three country committees (Northern Ireland, Scotland and Wales) plus boards of governors of schools/colleges – all with some powers of independence.

Organisation Structure – Mainly Evolution, Latterly More Dramatic

Just as governance remained structurally unchanged so did RNIB's main organisation and management structure from 1970 until 2004/05. Activities and staff were grouped functionally around services. (See Appendix, Organisation Chart 1990.)

We had regular discussions on other desirable configurations, particularly in the light of the inevitable silo effect of structured groupings. Because of our mission and our concerted efforts to be focussed on the needs and wishes of people with sight loss, there was one frontrunner basis for reorganisation: a structure based on beneficiary segmentation, that is, one part of the organisation serving children and young people, one serving adults of working age, and another serving older people. As a marketer, wedded to market segmentation, this alternative had great appeal to me but here I must declare a strongly held managerial view. In my observation, major reorganisation produces chaos of the new, destroys the old informal connections developed to make previous structures workable and, initially at least, drastically reduces effectiveness. Boards and new chief executives like restructuring because they seem concrete and real; you can look at organisation charts and observe the mass of new job descriptions and appointments to the new roles. It looks busy and active but it promotes high levels of staff anxiety with hard-working staff having to apply for new roles. The most able, if feeling too threatened, leave for jobs in other organisations. The less able remain or are made redundant, which impacts on morale.

There were between five and seven similar looking groupings up to 2005 (mostly called divisions, see the organisation chart in the Appendix). However, functions within these groupings changed significantly reflecting:

- the growth of day/community services;
- the decline in residential facilities;
- the growth in new service functions, such as information, policy development, social security advice, eye health, social rehabilitation, audio description, prevention etc.; and
- the growth of new resource functions to support telephone lotteries within fundraising, or HR and internal audit within resources, strategic planning and marketing in the director general's office.

Given the major governance restructure of 2001/02, and the length of organisational structural stasis, Lesley-Anne Alexander's restructures of 2004 and 2008 were timely and chimed with the current views of good practice. So, by 2009/10 the structure was based not so much on services (education, employment etc.) but on strategic foci, namely: Prevention and International Affairs; Supporting Independent Living; Inclusive Society; Fundraising; Resources; and Action for Blind People, the latter showing pragmatic realism of the absorption of this charity.

Increased Role of Marketing and Strategic Planning and Implementation

It would be wrong to assume strategic planning was not taking place in the 1960s and 1970s. One example was Director General John Colligan's report from 1968, in which he laid out in visionary terms the expansion goals for the 1970s. However, it is true to say that the time, breadth and depth of effort which went into such planning and implementation increased dramatically from 1980. This was the first decade where I could find evidence of formal strategic plans, not simply at RNIB, but anywhere among the large charities with the exception of World Wildlife Fund (see chapter 2a).

Marketing to Meet the Needs and Wishes of Blind and Partially Sighted People

The 1985 policy guidelines were important because they signalled a marketing orientation (putting the blind consumer first) as opposed to a production orientation (putting efficiency first) which was more prevalent in RNIB than I would have liked. For example, in the mid 1980s, as an RNIB Talking Books member you could not order the specific title you wanted to read next. You had to submit a list of between 50 and 100 books you fancied. The book you got next was whichever of your 50 titles had been returned from another reader the day before and had not yet been returned to the book stacks. This was very efficient in production terms, developed by the then TB manager (Squadron Leader) Harry Walton and Don Roskilly, because it cut out staff time returning books to the stacks and then being pulled out again later. However, it was frustrating to our beneficiaries and only just about acceptable to them.

Coming originally from Unilever and Courtaulds, I was keen for RNIB to take advantage of marketing theory, and through my work at Bayes Business School for it to benefit the wider charity and non-profit sector. Marketing is an ideal framework to support charities to run effectively where they

10,000 Talking Books returned each day to RNIB in Alperton and the same number despatched, 1989.

do not have the drivers of profit. It is a pity that the term marketing in much of the commercial as well as the charity world has become synonymous with communications and how to run digital media campaigns. When I am teaching I define charity marketing as 'meeting the needs and wishes of customers', with customers segmented between beneficiaries, supporters, stakeholders and regulators. Being even more precise, charity marketing is 'meeting customer needs and wishes through co-creation and within the objectives of the charity'. To be effective charities must involve their customers in solutions that meet their needs and wishes. To be effective, and without the driver of profit, they must restrict the needs they meet to those within their charitable objectives. So marketing is a framework to run a charity, and it provides tools such as market segmentation, marketing research, other player analysis (competitor analysis) and the marketing mix.

This history has already shown the importance and usefulness of segmentation and targeting with regard to increasing reach and how to prioritise – in our case between the partially sighted, older, multi-handicapped, minority ethnic groups and so on. The tools contained in the marketing mix can be crucial to improving services. (see Fig. 11.1 showing a check list of concepts which need to be considered to run an effective activity). I have described their use elsewhere (Bruce 2011) but here two examples will give an indication of how this works. 'Price' would not seem initially applicable as so many charity services are free, such as residential rehabilitation was at our centre in Torquay. On the other hand, the centre had spare capacity and market research revealed that families did not believe their newly blind family member would be able to cope alone on a six-week residential course. How could we reduce this psychological price? We started to invite prospective rehabilitees and their families down for taster residential weekends to show how we would care as well as rehabilitate. These weekends reduced the psychological price and numbers attending rose. Under 'Processes', the requirement is to make sure they are as customer friendly as possible. RNIB was one of the first charities to introduce payment for items by credit card over the phone. Blind people cannot write cheques but they can remember credit card details. Another process first at RNIB was the early adoption of email. While blind people can type letters, they cannot read incoming letters or memos. Email with voice output meant that, at a stroke, they could listen to their incoming mail via voice output without having someone having to come in and read out their post to them.

The techniques that were key to gaining managerial attention to marketing, a business method initially regarded with suspicion by staff such as teachers or rehabilitation workers, were market research and, especially, promotion. (See Fig. 11.1). Which manager is not interested in the services of her unit being better known? This in turn immediately promotes a dialogue on what they should be known for, among which people, and how they are best reached and their opinions ascertained etc.

So, gradually interest in using marketing theory built, starting up immediately in the fundraising and the press office with Lucille Hall in the early 1980s, then in technical aids and equipment with Maurice Wright in charge, gradually seeping into education and employment services in the mid 1980s. Structurally, it was a struggle to know where best to place

Fig. 11.1

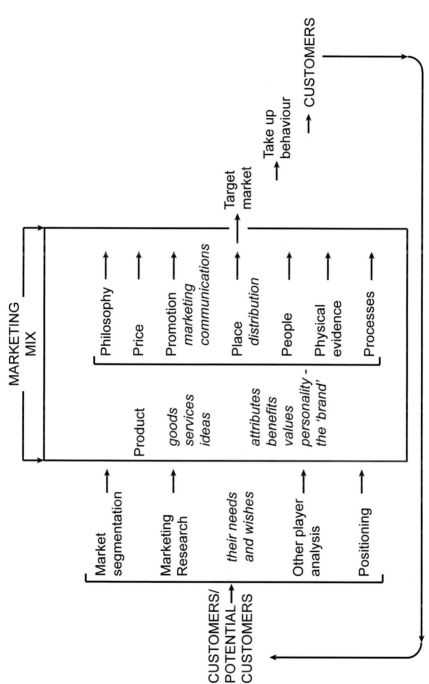

Charity marketing framework and tools (Source: Bruce 2005, reframing Borden 1964, and Booms and Bitner 1981) © Ian Bruce

the marketing function. Initially, it went into the fundraising and communications division corporately to advise the whole organisation. However, that fundraising provenance made it difficult for the education and employment divisions to accept. So then we put marketing advisers into each service division at a senior level to respect the specific professions, such as teachers and social workers, but that still created a 'Them' (marketers) and 'Us' (teachers and rehabilitation workers). The final conclusion was that, for professional services such as education, marketing skills had to be put in the line: for example, it is for the headteacher and his or her staff to decide on the needs and wishes of pupils, their families and funders (ideally co-created), not some non-teaching marketer. To do this, in the mid 1990s we developed a formal marketing training course led by Deborah Jack which gained traction, training the majority of middle managers in marketing theory and practice. By the last decade of this history, 2000-10, a marketing approach was pretty well embedded as the 'way we do it round here', with RNIB being one of the charity marketing leaders.

Strategic Planning – All Pulling in the Same Direction

The start of systematic attention to strategic planning was the 1980 Sunningdale Conference under Director General Eddie Venn's and Chair Duncan Watson's leadership. This was followed, after my arrival in 1983, by the service reviews of 1984/85, the policy guidelines and RNIB's first formal strategic plan (RNIB 1987), one of the first in the voluntary sector, with its timeframe and evaluation mechanism (see chapter 2a). There were further strategic plans in 1994, 2000, 2005 and 2009; all had formal final reviews of achievement and failure and most had mid-term strategy reviews to check on progress.

Development and implementation techniques for RNIB strategic planning evolved, absorbing a marketing approach and focussing on the needs and wishes of customers, be they beneficiaries, supporters, stakeholders or regulators. In

1985 there was a first residential staff conference of some 80 managers to help to develop the plan, but it is fair to say the first plan (RNIB 1987) was fairly 'top down' with broad goals used to distribute development finance and dictate action. (I wrote the first draft while on a management course at Ashridge Business School.) The second strategic plan in 1994 was interesting as it not only had greater staff involvement, but new resources were distributed via an unusual decision-making technique. Senior and middle managers co-operated to make costed proposals. These proposals were presented to trustees via the Policy and Resources Committee and compared against their contribution to the strategy goals. Finally, they were voted upon by the senior staff management team (eight people) and the Policy and Resources Committee (seventeen trustees), with the projects getting the most votes being selected. For the time this was unusual because of using voting and particularly for including the senior management team in the voting.

In 2000 there was another unusual development in plan implementation techniques. In those days it was common practice for close-ended objectives (targets) to be set by the charity leadership. In 2000 RNIB middle and front-line managers were delegated to come up with targets and plans (methods) in their areas of responsibility, in order to implement the six priority directional themes of the central strategy. Cross-divisional project/goal groups were asked to oversee this implementation. The organisational leadership was centralised 'hands on' with overall goals but 'hands off' on targets. This approach was based on the paradigm of the organisation not as a car with a driver (leader), but as an organism (Hatch 1997). The centre/top was assumed to be less well in touch with the fast-moving outside world. This new delegating approach was progressing well until we hit the UK recession of the early 2000s, and the Board as well as the senior management team, felt the only responsible way forward was to call the decisions back into the centre whereby the expenditure could be more tightly controlled. A pity, but at least the treasurer became more relaxed!

In the 2005 strategic plan (RNIB 2005) under Lesley-Anne's leadership with Colin Low as chair, there was a much more concerted effort to change the structure of RNIB in order to fit and support the strategic imperatives of the plan. Structural change had been relatively minor in scope over the previous three decades.

In 2009 internal commissioning and bidding for work predicated on the strategy was introduced as a method to ensure that RNIB activities reflected strategic policies (RNIB 2009).

The process of strategy creation should have a catalytic effect. Its purpose is to galvanise action but here the science of strategy is weak. For example, the majority of literature on strategy is concerned with its creation rather than implementation. RNIB provides an interesting case study of progressive attempts over nearly 30 years to ensure an effective connection between strategy planning and strategy implementation. Between 1984 and 2014 there were five strategies created and, while there were strong commonalities and evolutionary change to content, each had different approaches to implementation (see also Bruce 2003).

While strategic planning in charities was virtually non-existent in the early 1980s, it spread across the sector with courses and conferences galore in the 1990s and by the early 2000s it would have been hard to find a major charity which did not have a strategic plan, including vision, mission, values and strategic directions.

The Brand

Marketing has taught us that the brand is the fundamentally important asset of any organisation or product and nowhere is this as important as for a charity. Why? A commercial organisation selling a car or a packet of soap, or an electrician installing a new lighting system or other service, provide offerings which the paying customer can judge through experience – the lights either work or they do not. The additional challenge most charities face is that many of its paying customers (supporters and donors) do not experience the primary offerings of the charity. The primary offerings go to the charity beneficiaries (blind people, villages in Africa etc.). So, donors are essentially 'buying' an idea, not a physical good or service that they will consume directly. To buy an idea which is necessarily intangible, requires that you, the donor, believe it will be faithfully translated into action. This belief means the donor has to have a great deal of trust and confidence in the honesty of the charity and confidence in its capacity to deliver. Public trust and confidence in charities is so fundamentally important that the Charity Commission measures this longitudinally every two years. In this context the 'brand' and 'brand image' are the terms marketers use to describe how the customer (donor or beneficiary) perceives the charity and its offerings. The brand is the very personality of the charity; it encapsulates how the people regard the charity – how much they know about it, trust it, rate its competence and believe in its cause. Perhaps the most important trigger of a charity brand is its name. If I list charities and non-profits concerned with the environment, in an instant you will have a distinct image of their different approaches to the issue – Greenpeace, Friends of the Earth, the Council for the Protection of Rural England, the National Trust and the National Federation of Women's Institutes.

At the beginning of this history in the late 1960s/early 1970s, charities were still trying to discard their Victorian, Poor Law, censorious and institutional (brand) images associated with the time before the welfare state's expansion in the late 1940s. When I started to work in the charity world in the early 1970s, I would regularly encounter older people who were still bitter towards the old hospital charities. They remembered the humiliation they felt, caused by the processes they had to go through to access free or affordable health care from charities before the establishment of the NHS in 1948. Charities with names like the National Old People's Welfare Council or the Hospital and Home for Incurables did not sit comfortably in the optimistic, modern world of post-Second World War Britain of the Swinging Sixties.

So, what to do with the charity brand at the beginning of this history in the 1970s? When I joined the National Old People's Welfare Council in 1970 as head of fundraising and PR from a marketing role in Unilever, the answer seemed obvious – rebrand and change the name. I led its relaunch as Age Concern in 1971 after extensive market research. It is now Age UK having merged with Help the Aged. Several other charity rebrandings followed, such as Mind (formerly, the National Association of Mental Health) and Scope (formerly, the Spastics Society).

For a charity like RNIB the answer was not nearly so clear. The name might have seemed old-fashioned but it was one of the leading charities in terms of raising funds from the public. It was (and is) trusted, seen as reliable and doing a good job for a worthy cause. It had good brand awareness, both of the Royal National Institute of the Blind and RNIB. In other words, it had strong 'brand equity'. To change the name and endanger that brand strength could have been a disaster.

Our market research in the 1980s showed that RNIB was still trusted, seen as effective in a good cause but was felt to be old-fashioned and not at all nimble-footed. In our more relaxed moments this was very much what we as trustees and senior managers thought too and the first RNIB strategy began to address this, calling for a 'major Increase in public awareness' (RNIB 1987, para. 6.4).

We worked hard on this and initially succeeded in raising spontaneous/unprompted awareness up to one third that of Oxfam, the gold standard, and ahead of charities such as the British Heart Foundation, GDBA and Age Concern. However, from the beginning of the 1990s this success started to slip. Declining public awareness can be dangerous and precede a decline in public donations and, even worse, a decline in service take-up by beneficiary customers – people with sight loss.

In the early 1990s, in order to address this issue, Sanchi Heesom persuaded us that we needed a public relaunch of RNIB, of our brand (as described in chapter 3b). This was partly prompted by the awareness of slippage but also by some disturbing market research which showed that, despite the significant modernisation and expansion of RNIB, the public still saw us as old-fashioned and distant. This pointed to a classic marketing solution, the relaunch. This means building on what you have, making it more memorable, distinctive and relevant while keeping it flexible (Berry and Parasuraman 1991).

We seriously considered changing the name, which Sanchi and I were against primarily because of RNIB's significant brand equity including its relatively high public awareness. Even so, this was a difficult decision to defend. While so much of our name was positive to some people, i.e. 'Royal', 'National' and 'Blind', for others these words were negative and the word 'Institute' had few defenders. RNID changed its name to Action on Hearing Loss in 2011 but I take a certain sense of satisfaction that nine years later, in October 2020, Action on Hearing Loss announced it was changing back to RNID: 'brand research involving 6,000 people found that the old name [RNID] was still more popular and more trusted, even after almost 10 years' (Civil Society News, 'Action on Hearing Loss to change its name back to RNID', 12 October 2020).

So, what did we change for the relaunch? – the logo and the introduction of a strapline. The old logo was of a stiff representation of a blind male figure tentatively and cautiously stepping forward. With the new RNIB philosophy of bringing rights and empowerment to the fore, the logo figure became more androgenous, much more determined, striding along using a long white cane not only as an aid, but as a symbol of confidence not dependency. The accompanying strapline was 'Challenging blindness' with its double meaning emphasising the empowerment, rights and campaigning stance RNIB wanted to expand.

The next major brand change came in 2001/02 and was perhaps the change I was most proud of: we changed our name from the Royal National Institute for the Blind to the Royal National Institute of the Blind, a seemingly small change but one of huge significance. The paper I wrote arguing for this change emphasised several points including:

- The new policy atmosphere we had chosen during the 1990s was of 'rights (of) not welfare (for)'
- We were changing so that more than 50 per cent of our trustees would be people with sight loss which qualified us to make the 'of' claim
- The European Union, at that time so very powerful in influencing UK legislation, was increasingly wanting to partner and hear the 'of' disability lobby and not the 'for' and the change would signal our new positioning (the British government was also following this path although more tentatively)
- The name change and the reality would strengthen our partnerships with disability organisations 'of' in this country and abroad but would not lose co-operation with the 'fors'.

Also suggested was the addition of 'People' at the end of the name but the organisations of the blind on the trustee body, at that time, rejected this. Why? I suspect they were confident in their power and influence inside RNIB and regarded the addition of 'People' as simply a genuflection in the direction of political correctness.

This relaunch had a more modest budget but Lynne Stockbridge, head of communications, and Ros Oakley, assistant director, external relations, ensured it happened smoothly and made powerful impact through being integrated into contemporaneous campaigns such as Right to Read.

The modest budget in this case exemplifies a conundrum which charities face over rebranding budgets – how to justify them when there is still significant unmet need among the charity's beneficiaries? While this was a fundamental RNIB repositioning which justified significant spend, it came at a time when we knew we would have to close an RNIB school. Closure was for several reasons, only one of which was affordability, shown through major annual school deficits.

Financial strategy can easily justify a one-off spend on a relaunch, of the order of just one year's school deficit, but a service's deficit will repeat year after year. However, I challenge anyone to explain that justification to parents whose child will no longer be able to go to a school they and their child love. On top of that, factor in the reputational and donation damage when the story hits the news media.

The final rebranding in this 40-year history was in 2007, led by Fiona Blakemore, with the support of a design agency, The Team. The white cane was dropped from logo and 'People' was added to the name – Royal National Institute of Blind People, but remaining RNIB. As Ciara Smyth said on BBC television on 27 February 2007, describing the background to the rebranding:

> the logo as it stands [i.e. with a white cane] promotes the idea that we are a charity that only helps blind people, rather than also partially sighted people … and the reality is that a lot of blind people get around without a white cane, so it seems to represent an organisation which is not in touch…

To reflect this conclusion, the cane was dropped from the new logo and the new strapline became 'Supporting blind and partially sighted people'.

So, successive staff 'brand managers' over the period 1970 to 2010 had built RNIB brand equity and had resisted calls for more fundamental changes in the name, which the

2007 rebranding, dropping the white cane figure of 1993.

experience of RNID between 2011 and 2020 showed, would have likely been disastrous. Remaining RNIB kept us in the second group of charities as measured by public awareness after the small market-leading group of charities, such as Cancer Research UK and Oxfam. From the 1980s on, we shifted our positioning from one of exclusively welfare more towards one of the rights supported by welfare activity, which reflected the reality of our approach. While we made progress in softening our brand image and signposting partial sight as well as blindness, all of us would have liked to have achieved more.

Chapter 8

Friends and Foes –
Campaigning and Lobbying

Relationships – from Brave and Alone, to Disability United, to Sight Loss United

An area of policy which showed remarkable change and development over the four decades was RNIB's attitude and behaviour towards other associated groups and lobbies. The key ones were the organisations 'of' disabled and 'of' blind people; other service delivery charities in the blindness field; and similar ones in the broader disability field. This section shows the importance RNIB ascribed to 'Other Player Analysis' (Bruce 1994) in achieving our goals, i.e. how did changing activities of other relevant organisations from the statutory, commercial, voluntary and informal sectors impact on RNIB. This process is an expansion of what in the commercial world is called 'Competitor Analysis'. These analyses were important factors in RNIB's assessment of the most useful alliances from which to achieve benefits for blind and partially sighted people. Our critics would no doubt be less generous and ascribe our positions to organisational self-seeking or advantage. It would be naïve to reject that assessment completely. Charities are not saintly in their organisational behaviour just because they have a saintly cause. Marketing, in general, and other player analysis, in particular, are value neutral and can be used for good or ill.

A summary of our relationship policy changes towards other groups over the 40 years could be characterised as follows:

- 1970s – RNIB linked with key organisations 'of' the blind in a somewhat colonial way and stood aloof from other service delivery blindness charities and was largely hostile to other disability organisations and their 'competitive' causes.
- 1980s – RNIB strengthened links with organisations of the blind, stayed aloof from other blindness service charities but reached out to other disability charities (e.g. deaf, learning disabled etc.), creating and leading the pan-disability Disability Benefits Consortium.
- 1990s – RNIB reached out half-heartedly to blindness service delivery charities and further embraced disability charities, proposing and co-forming the Disability Charities Consortium.
- 2000s – RNIB maintained relationships with other disability charities but reached out more and, post-2004 embraced, other blindness charities and visual impairment interests; and played a major role in creating and leading a cross-VI-sector, UK Vision Strategy and, within this, formally associating/merging with several, key, sight loss charities.

Looking at this progression in more detail: despite the all-encompassing composition of RNIB's Executive Council, we started the 1970s with fairly poor relations with most groups. The outcome of the battle over governance representation of blind and partially sighted people described in chapter 1a, eventually brought RNIB and the key organisations of blind people much closer together. This was cemented as the blind leaders of the revolt became chairs of committees within RNIB– for example, Tom Parker (NLBD), Bill Poole, Colin Low and Fred Reid (all NFB).

Relations with other disability organisations were fraught, largely brought about by RNIB, NLBD and NFB in the early 1970s pressing actively for a special allowance for blind people, opposed by the other separate disability groups. When chances of a blindness allowance failed at the end of the 1970s, RNIB felt let down, 'stabbed in the back' by other disabilities' opposition was how Tom Parker, former NLBD general secretary, described it to me in 1983.

When I arrived in 1983 it seemed clear that this tactic of 'blind going it alone' was doomed, but the momentum and rhetoric to continue alone was still strong. Changing this approach became a key priority for me. The external policy environment had transformed from 1970 to 1983, from single impairment orientation to pan-disability. (See earlier references to Seebohm, Warnock and government employment services reorganisation.) However this trend was not so easy to discern at the time and, where we could see it, it was not easy to know whether the trend would last. Consequently, when, in 1987, Amanda Jordan, policy officer of Scope (then the Spastics Society), and I proposed to the disability movement that we should form a cross-disability alliance on benefits (see chapter 2b), there was both opposition and support inside RNIB.

Nevertheless, the result was the formation of the national Disability Benefits Consortium in 1988 with Richard Wood of BCODP and I as co-chairs. The organising committee contained the four leading disability co-ordination groups – RADAR, Disablement Income Group, Disability Alliance and BCODP – and co-opted representatives of the main disability service charities such as RNIB, RNID (Action on Hearing Loss), Mencap, Scope and Mind. These 'for' organisations were crucial because we had the money, the press officers and the capacity to organise lobbies and demonstrations. The 'of' organisations provided particular legitimacy, encouragement to take stronger positions and disabled members prepared to take to the streets.

The DBC rapidly became a powerful unifying, united front on disability benefits, able to meet ministers and civil servants whenever necessary and able to gain airtime on programmes such as the BBC Radio 4 *Today* programme, television news and BBC *Newsnight*. It was a crucial period, covering the creation of a major new benefits structure for disabled people in 1991 under a Conservative government (including the Disability Living Allowance). Those were exciting and heady times and I really enjoyed working with the other organisations' representatives on the DBC, working hard to build camaraderie and trust – so necessary for any multi-interest lobby.

The formation of the DBC strengthened campaigning for disabled people in general but at a stroke RNIB and the sight loss lobby had repositioned itself. No longer was RNIB an isolated 'for', it became a leading member of the pan-disability lobby and closely associated with the growing power of the pan-disability 'of' lobby.

On the sight loss front, proof positive of the success of this approach showed itself with RNIB's ability to influence the Conservative government during its disability reviews 1985-90 under Norman Fowler, then secretary of state. In turn this led to our success in drawing blind people into the eligibility criteria for the Disability Living Allowance, from whose predecessor benefit they had been earlier deliberately excluded in the 1970s. Without our leadership role in the DBC, we would simply not have had enough meaningful access to civil servants to get the detail of our research across and establish ourselves as a powerful part of the lobby. Andy Barrick and Errol Walker deserve special mention here.

Another crucial alliance which bound us further into the pan-disability movement, especially the 'of' sector, came when we joined Rights Now in 1992. The Rights Now campaign resulted in arguably the biggest win of the 40 years, the Disability Discrimination Act 1995 (see chapter 5).

The 1990s also saw RNIB further consolidate its links with the wider disability lobby through the formation of the Dis-ability Charities Consortium of the leading disability service charities (the 'fors'). I persuaded my fellow CEOs of RNID, Mencap, Mind, Scope and RADAR that such an alliance was necessary if we were to form a successful (social enterprise) approach towards helping/ensuring that commercial and public organisations fulfilled their responsibilities under the new Disability Discrimination Act by making 'reasonable adjustments' to make their services and jobs accessible (see chapter 1b). Charity lobbies often make the error of assuming that once their demands are enshrined in law, the job is done – far from it. Charities must follow up, encouraging take up of new laws.

With the arrival of the Labour government in 1997, we were caught off guard with its early attempts to cut disability benefits. The DBC found out about the cuts proposals via a leaked letter, which was sufficient evidence to get me on Newsnight. This in turn, combined with good relationships with government, was enough to secure a meeting on 16 February 1998 with the Prime Minister, the Secretary of State Harriet Harman and the Minister for Disabled People Alan Howarth. As a result of the meeting (we believe) the

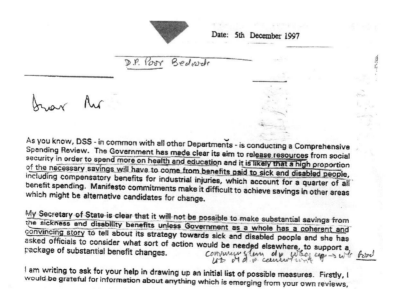

Disguised leaked letter tipping DBC off about proposed cuts to benefits for disabled people, Dec 1997.

The DBC delegation meeting Tony Blair, Harriet Harman (Sec. of State at DSS) and Alan Howarth (Minister for Disabled People) to oppose the cuts at No. 10, 16 Feb 1998.
In the Delegation were (L-R) leaders of MIND (Judi Clements), Disability Alliance (Lorna Reith), SCOPE (Richard Brewster), Rights Now (Rachel Hurst), RNIB (Ian Bruce), BCODP (Richard Wood), RNID (James Strachan with an interpreter), and RADAR (Bert Massie).

After meeting with the PM, Richard Wood and Ian Bruce, DBC Co-Chairs, give a press briefing. The cuts were postponed by 2 years.

cuts were postponed. We explained the extra costs that disability brings to our various constituencies. On behalf of blind people I had a Perkins brailling machine by my feet. During the meeting I asked the PM roughly how much he thought a decent ball point pen cost a sighted person, then carefully put the brailler (in front of me in the picture) on the highly polished table and explained that a blind person's ballpoint (the brailler) cost over £100.

However, there continued to be a strongly held view amongst influential Labour government political advisers (SPADS) that there was widespread fraud in claiming disability benefits, when all the research showed it was minor. The SPADS wanted to show the voters that the Labour government was tough on benefit fraud, but their proposals would be cutting genuine claimants. In 1999 there were cuts, successful this time but not without some degree of misinformation. The Times on 17 May 1999 claimed that 40 percent of those in receipt of Incapacity Benefit who were retired on an occupational pension, were in the top 40 percent of income distribution. We calculated this could only be justified if money given to cover the extra costs of disability (for example to pay for carers) was counted as income. On that basis the prime Minister would be one of the top earning millionaires as the annual costs of his security would be counted as income. Despite this confusing information, three days later an amendment opposing the government's proposals from Labour backbencher Roger Berry resulted in the government's majority of 178 being reduced to 40 through the largest revolt of the early years of the Labour government – 65 Labour MPs voted against and 14 abstained.

Co-operation in the later 1990s between the blindness service charities gained some support from an unlikely source, Guide Dogs for the Blind Association. One of their trustee leaders was Lord Patrick Jenkin, former government health secretary. (see chapter 4a). He persuaded the blindness charities to form a committee of co-operation. We worked hard on this and the group produced some significant reports and, most importantly, the Jenkin initiative laid the groundwork for the next decade when co-operation between sight loss agencies rose up the agenda.

The 2000s produced some electric developments of co-operation between charities and other organisations with interests in the sight loss field. These started with discussions by Vision 2020, a loose co-ordination body under Mike Brace's leadership, for sector-wide co-operation. In the first years of the century, RNIB's director of policy, Fazilet Hadi, represented RNIB on this group which was chaired by Stephen Remington of Action for Blind People. Lesley-Anne Alexander, RNIB's new CEO (2004), had fresh, strong views on what she saw as the inefficiencies brought about by the lack of active co-operation within the sight loss field. She saw an opportunity to implement a strategy of consolidation in the sector, to bring about a focus of aims, more co-operation to reduce duplication and make efficiencies through sharing back-office functions. In 2007 Lesley-Anne, on behalf of RNIB, formally proposed the idea of a UK Vision Strategy and offered initial funding of £300,000 a year for its sector-wide development. By the time of the launch in 2008 she and RNIB were in pole position as leaders of the implementation of the Vision 2020 Strategy. Rather as in the 1980s with the DBC, full support for a new alliance transformed RNIB's position from outsider into core leader in a very short time. Also, Lesley-Anne's experience of methodologies of active partnerships in the housing field brought new intellectually-based solutions for the closer co-operation which had eluded those of us on the Jenkin committee. These solutions were covered in chapter 4a but essentially offered a joint working formula between two previously independent charities, a formula adopted from the housing charity sector.

Campaigning and Lobbying

The growing importance of campaigning by RNIB over this history cannot be overstated and the detail of campaigns are threaded throughout this book. RNIB had campaigned in the early 1970s for a blindness allowance using methodologies recognisable today – petitions to the prime minister, mass lobbies of parliament. However, the time and resources devoted were small and the lead was taken by the National Federation of the Blind and the National League of the Blind and Disabled, with the support of RNIB. This was a powerful model, but the number of campaigns which the organisations of the blind could lead were necessarily small because the organisations 'of' had few resources. Despite this, the protocol was that RNIB provided the services and the organisations 'of' did the campaigning.

This was the understanding as late as 1983 held by the

Campaigning for free treatment for wet Age-Related Macular Degeneration (AMD) 2007

NFB and the NLBD. I knew the chair, Duncan Watson, was keen for RNIB to establish a post of parliamentary officer which suggests at least his wish for RNIB to be more pro-active on campaigning. Indeed, one of the reasons I suspect I was selected in that year to be director general was because of my campaigning experience in Age Concern England and Volunteering England. In my early expansion plans one of the first posts to be established and filled was that of parliamentary officer (Hugh Lawrence, previously a parliamentary correspondent and just the person to estab-lish the role). When the post was proposed, there was push back from the NFB and NLBD which took Duncan Watson's

The 'take an eye test' campaign team – the eye test can spot blinding conditions early.

firm backing to break down. From then on lobbying and campaigning capacity grew rapidly. While the League and the Federation retained the nominal lead on the blindness allowance, many other issues were identified and driven by RNIB.

By the 1990s we not only had two parliamentary staff but also supporting corporate public policy staff, plus experts in education, employment and accessible formats in the RNIB service divisions.

Our ambitions and campaigning horizons widened to Europe. By 1992 we were already active in lobbying to ensure the proposed Euro notes and coins would be designed to be identifiable by the blind and partially sighted. By 1994 we were leading the Europe-wide campaign to ensure that Euro notes introduced in 1999 would be size differentiated by value with good colour contrast between denominations. European legislation assumed increasing importance overall and by the late 1990s we had three professionals working in Brussels, more than any other UK disability charity (see chapter 2a).

At the same time in Britain over 30 different campaigns were underway in addition to the daily lobbying around service delivery. By 2000 there were 32 staff in the public policy department, headed by Steve Winyard, under divisional director, Fazilet Hadi.

This growth trend in lobbying and campaigning expanded even further when Lesley-Anne Alexander became chief executive in 2004 under Colin Low's chairmanship. Up until then, when money was short, direct services budgets were more protected and campaigning budgets waxed and waned depending on overall income. From 2005 to 2010 there was a rebalancing away from direct services towards lobbying and campaigning (chapter 4b).

This campaigning growth was greater than in most other charities but was going with the grain of trends in the disability charity sector. RNIB came from behind though, for example, appointing its first parliamentary officer in the middle of the 1980s compared with Scope and Age Concern in the middle 1970s, among the first to do so. The expansion also went with the grain of the development of the interpretation of charity law related to campaigning. In the 1970s the Charity Commission acted as a restraint on what it saw as illegitimate campaigning. For example, in 1977, I tried to register a Centre for Social Action Broadcasting as a charity to promote good practice among broadcasters and to include services such as the BBC Action Line (now a standard part of BBC responsibility and service). The proposal was rejected because it was 'too political'. When I protested that it was like an NCVO for the broadcasting field, the response in the meeting was that, if the NCVO had tried to register itself as a charity at that point, it would also be refused! While the Charity Commission representative was replying off the cuff, he was not joking. This restrictive Charity Commission view softened in the 1980s and 1990s, not least to stay in touch with the expansion of charities speaking truth (as they saw it) to power. For example, from the late 1970s onwards government ministers increasingly had bruising encounters with charity representatives on BBC Radio 4's *Today* programme to the point that by the 1990s ministers were refusing to be interviewed alongside them. By the 2000s the more proactive campaigning role of charities was not only happening in practice but had also been legitimised in Charity Commission guidelines: 'Charities can campaign for a change in the law, policy or decisions where such change would support the charity's purposes'.

So, the expansion of lobbying and campaigning as part of the development of indirect services by RNIB was one of the most major, organisational, functional developments over the 40 years of this history. This trend benefitted blind and partially sighted people and gave RNIB a major boost in its awareness raising of the cause and the charity – a major support to fundraising from the public, and towards increasing public empathy for positive social change for the cause. This was part of a trend in the charity world over the period of increasing emphasis on not simply amelioration but towards cure and prevention.

Chapter 9

Resources – People and Money

People and People Policies

I have already mentioned my scepticism about the significance of restructuring and reorganisation as a means of improving organisational effectiveness. I now go even further and say that functions close to my heart, such as marketing and strategic planning, come second to developing an organisation's people – through inspiration, support, delegation, and occasionally reining in, of staff, volunteers and trustees. These activities have to happen in the line, through management and leadership across the whole organisation. However, the functional support is crucial. Human resources statistics and policies are discussed chronologically in Part I. In this chapter I pull out more personal reflections on what has made RNIB function over the years 1970-2010.

The transformation and development of HR inside RNIB, and, I suspect, most charities, was revolutionary. In the early 1970s the personal assistant to the director general was the only corporate person with personnel responsibilities apart from payroll. As far as I can find out, all other personnel functions such as they existed were undertaken by line managers. By 2000 the corporate personnel/HR department numbered 23 posts. In earlier chapters there are more statistics on staff make up and staff development practices.

In this section I describe more the ambiance of RNIB and how this changed over the period.

Relationships were much more formal in the 1970s. When I arrived in 1983, long-standing support staff still called me and other senior managers by our surnames, that is, 'Mr Bruce'. Until I could abolish the system in 1984/85, we had two staff canteens at headquarters, one for senior managers and one for the rest of staff. Intriguingly, my primary opponents to their merger were not the most senior but those newly arrived in the senior managers' dining room (as in, 'I have spent ten years waiting to be allowed in and now you are abolishing it!').

As late as 1983, while there was detailed corporate supervision of holiday entitlement, there was still virtually no corporate personnel or staff development function – only 1.5 posts under pressure as reported by a consultant (Walsh 1984). We quickly consolidated resource functions (for example, finance, personnel and estates management) under the director of finance and administration. Barry Gifford held this post for over half this history and appointed Ken Lavey as personnel officer in the mid 1980s. They made an outstanding team, together building up the substantial HR function as one of our most important critical success factors over the period. Staff training and development was impressive, way ahead of most other charities as I could observe through founding in 1992 and running (*pro bono*) the postgraduate charity management programme at City University London's Bayes (then Cass) Business School, attended by many hundreds of charity managers. Equally impressive were the RNIB professional development programmes and appraisal systems. Regular reporting included summary information on appraisals, diversity, training, recruitment, turnover, exit information, grievances, disciplinaries and tribunals (see, for example, RNIB 2003).

Personnel was associated with a shift in RNIB culture to become a less cautious, more ambitious organisation. On arrival, I found an organisation where the culture favoured being cautious. Fred Reid, a long-standing trustee and reliable commentator in my experience, told me this had been around for many years – he cited the initial opposition of RNIB to white canes and guide dogs as examples from before the start of this history. My mantra was 'let a thousand flowers bloom', don't blame the gardeners when some of the flowers die and certainly don't say, 'I told you so'! It is just so difficult to be sure in advance which initiative is going to succeed. If you plant many seedlings, some will blossom gloriously. Examples from the period are eye health services and benefits rights advice which started out as just two equals among 20 or so development projects in 1987. Along with this push to have as much a 'no blame' culture as possible was a concerted effort to build on people's strengths rather than criticising weaknesses. It is often said that it takes at least half a dozen pieces of praise to wipe out the hurt and disincentivisation of a single criticism. The aim should be for all staff to be both excited and confident when they come to work.

At various points in the text I have mentioned individuals who have been involved in various initiatives but I am conscious of the many thousands whom I have not named. They are in this book because they have created the work described. Allowing for staff coming and going over the 40 years, probably in excess of 10,000 people were employed by RNIB, in addition to the many hundreds of thousands of volunteers, including fundraising volunteers in telephone raffles. For most of the period there were between 2,500 and 3,500 full- and part-time staff in RNIB. One of the things you learn as you get older is that organisations are dependent on all the people in it. However, wherever we are located in an organisation, we tend to assume that is the focus of attention. Also records tend to be made by staff and volunteers further up the hierarchy. For ordinary blind and partially sighted customers of RNIB, the most important people are the staff and volunteers they meet at the front line who are often further down the hierarchy. It is those people they will want acknowledged and I can think of no way of doing this individually, so I can only do so in spirit, with examples. Anyone who feels left out should please contact me via RNIB.

An example of these front-line services were those which have variously been called customer services, the helpline, the resource centres – all those who speak or otherwise communicate with blind and partially sighted people and their families, in our education services, homes, hotels, benefits rights, eye clinics, libraries, employment support etc., etc., etc. Our visually impaired customers are often going through a traumatic period of one sort or another and the information, support and practical help these staff and volunteers give can be crucial – from explaining to someone who has macular degeneration that she will, almost certainly, not go totally blind, retaining some peripheral vison, through to helping someone claim a substantial social security benefit because of his blindness, through to making sure a customer gets a replacement white cane quickly because his current one is broken.

Another group which goes, undeservedly, unsung are the porters, receptionists, telephonists, secretaries and assistants and others at information points. Take the example of the porters in RNIB's headquarters and national service centre in Kings Cross and before that in Great Portland St. The traditional name, 'porter', does not nearly convey the range of duties. For the tens of thousands of blind and partially sighted people and their organisations who have held meetings at RNIB headquarters in the evenings over the 40 years, the porters were and are vital. They are the ones who stay at night to keep the rooms open, to help people to the correct room, especially when several groups are meeting at once, to clear up after a guide dog if it is sick on the floor, to get more chairs if extra people turn up. Over the years, in the evenings RNIB headquarters regularly had between 10 and 150 blind people meeting in various rooms with just one sighted porter and the occasional staff member working late. It was a blind world and the face of RNIB was not the director general or chief executive, it was the porter.

Another group I would single out in this history are all the RNIB professional staff, examples of which are the optometrists, rehabilitation workers, teachers, physiotherapists, social workers, as well as the policy workers and the myriad of other professionals in communications, planning, finance, surveying, HR, IT and so on. For anyone who is still under the illusion that charities are somehow less efficient than the private or public sector, I can correct them. Having worked in all three sectors, my experience is that charities are just as efficient (or inefficient).

I have struggled to find a fair way of acknowledging individuals and have failed, except to mention a very small proportion in the preceding chapters. Here, in this overview chapter, I mention one or two more in contrasting positions in the formal hierarchy to whom I have been close. Writing about the porters reminds me of two of our porters – Mick and Jim Mahoney, father and son, who between them cover the whole 40-year period of this history (and more). I remember vividly in 1983 coming anonymously to RNIB, prior to applying for the CEO post, to check it out to see whether it was the kind of organisation I should like to work in. Exiting Regents Park tube station, I was unsure which direction to walk to find RNIB. I rang from a public call box (no mobiles then!) and reached Mick (whom I obviously had never met). I think he assumed I was blind and immediately he offered to walk a quarter of a mile round to where I was and fetch me. That alone convinced me RNIB was an organisation I wanted to work for!

At the other end of the conventional organisational hierarchy, we have the titular heads of RNIB, two above all others, our Patrons Her Majesty The Queen for this whole history and Her Majesty Queen Elizabeth, The Queen Mother for much of it. We have been well served over the years by our presidents, Lord Cobham, Lord Head, the Duke of Devonshire, the Duke of Westminster and, from 2012, Dame Gail Ronson. For most of my time the president was the Duke of Westminster. He arrived with a completely unfounded reputation as a young unformed figure, not particularly committed to public life. I cannot believe that was ever a reality because like all our Presidents he threw himself into helping and encouraging RNIB. He immediately started visiting our establishments and services, raising morale through his evident interest in what the staff and volunteers were doing. He was always there for me if I was troubled or in need of advice, as I am sure his predecessors and successors were and are for other RNIB leaders.

Over the years RNIB was also well served by its trustees, several of whom have been mentioned earlier. Many, and from 2001 a required majority, were blind or partially sighted. The Executive Council (until 2001/02) and the Board (from then on) always had a mix of long-established members and new blood: outstanding examples of the former were Lord Low of Dalston, Sir John Wall and Sir Duncan Watson who served as trustees or equivalent for the whole 40 years as did Bill Poole. Many other people served for several decades in various roles, showing the richness and depth of outreach, including Jill Allen-King, Mike Barrett, Richard Bignell, Carol Borowski, Kevin Carey (chair from 2009), Derek Child, Lisa Charlton, David Clark, Hans Cohn, Michael Crowther, Gareth Davies, Cindy and Rilan Cash, Peter Wilkins, Gill Gorton, Bob Greenhalgh, Benny Foxall, Des Kettle, John Claricoat, David Clark, Jackie Hicks, Steve Plumpton, Jimmy Cook, Gill Burrington, Alan Suttie, Margaret Bennett, Cindy and Richard Godfrey-Mckay, Ray Hazan, Vidar Hjardeng, Don Jackson, Anna Lawson, Janet Lovell, Terry Moody, Tom Parker, Wally Kinder, Arif Khan, Amir Majid, Gwyn O'Grady, Paul Questier, John Ramm, Dr Fred Reid, Terry Robinson, John Spence, Janet Stonehouse, Norma Town, Mike Townsend, Dafton Robinson, Terry Robinson, Careen Bradbury, Louise Wright, Karl Farrell, Profs Fielder and Hill, and many others. Ellie Southwood (chair after Kevin Carey) joined the Board in the last year of this history. Conventional wisdom is that trustees and committee members should not stay too long but I would argue for balance recognising the value of their organisational memory. Their continuing presence was family-like and most knew when to withdraw from active roles.

Someone else at RNIB for virtually the whole period, and whose job spanned meeting porters and presidents to help make things happen, was Carol Bird who joined RNIB in 1961 and retired in 2005. For over 30 of her 44 years there she was assistant to the chair or chief executive and she helped to manage transitions between incumbents, a critical role if organisations are to maintain momentum as well as stability. A fount of knowledge and wisdom on RNIB's development, she was invaluable in helping me to construct the RNIB chronology of events (Bruce and Bird, in preparation). Examples of other senior support staff who operated similarly were Viv Barnes, Eve Speare, Lisa Godsalve, Jean White, Penny Foulkes, Julie Shephard, Betty Brown, Wendy Graham, Jillian Harvey, Andrew Hodgson and Ruby Underhill.

A more wide-ranging list of senior staff who all made a major difference can be found in the Appendix entitled: 'RNIB Management Conference Attendance – 1985, 1991, 1997 and 2003'. It lists over 250 people who played important senior roles, as selected by their divisional directors. Please note that people's titles related to the year in question and were not necessarily their most senior role with us. These biennial conferences were residential gatherings of senior RNIB staff. I instigated them in 1985 to help us harness a wide range of thoughts and reflections, create a positive atmosphere and galvanise action. They were powerful in all these respects but I rapidly learned they also had unanticipated consequences. One was that, for some, released from the work pressure cooker, it offered an opportunity to let their hair down, as well as work hard. This was particularly the case for heads of residential settings who normally were responsible for keeping vulnerable children and adults safe at all times – a significant stress and pressure from which they were released for three days. At our 1997 conference in Cambridge one of them (David Teager I think) somehow 'borrowed' a pullover from Barry Gifford, the director of finance and administration, and promptly organised a secret raffle with the pullover as the prize and the proceeds going to RNIB. Luckily, Barry took it in good heart!

My last comment here may appear to be through rose-tinted spectacles, but it is a view I have held ever since my early days in RNIB. I have worked in or around more than a dozen charities in my time. None can match RNIB for the feeling that you are joining an extended family – loyalties, bonds of friendship and, yes, occasional rows – but there is a pulling together. This feeling applies particularly to the blind and partially sighted community within RNIB. During the period when we had a 120-person Executive Council with a very large number of blind members, later a Board with a majority of blind members, I had a sense of being welcomed into a community, almost a family, and being inspired by them to achieve my best. We know and knew why we were there because in RNIB there were and are blind and partially sighted people all around, in governance, staffing, volunteers and customers. The secret of creating this family feeling in a charity is to ensure it is normal to have beneficiaries involved as trustees (or in other roles of governance), staff and volunteers.

On a more light-hearted personal note, while sorting my files, I came across a letter from the time in 1970 when I was preparing for my departure from Unilever before entering the charity world. I had been offered jobs by what I subsequently relaunched as Age Concern and by Mind, but the courteous reply from RNIB (Ruby Underhill, assistant to the then director general, John Colligan) said that at RNIB there were 'no openings within my sphere of interest'.

On reflection, I believe it showed that RNIB was one of my preferred charities some thirteen years before I did actually join as director general.

Finances

So, from people to money, quite a contrast! However, to rephrase a song, 'you can't have one without the other'!

Growth – Three Times Larger

RNIB finances fared well over the 40 years (1970-2010), income and expenditure approximately trebled in real terms – with most of this growth in the1980s and 1990s. In cash terms they rose by 40 times but so much of this was the impact of inflation. For the organisation to be three times the size it was 40 years before is no mean feat, especially as the amount spent on services also trebled in real terms. Over this period both the primary income components of earned income from service fees (*circa* 39 per cent of the per annum total) and voluntary income (*circa* 56 per cent) trebled also and stayed in near constant proportion to each other.

The income table below (Table 9.2) gives the percentage income growth rates by decade in real terms: namely, eleven per cent growth in the 1970s, 56 per cent in the 1980s, 47 per cent in the 1990s, dropping to seventeen per cent in the 2000s. This last decade's lower growth rate is explained in part by: the increased emphasis on lobbying and campaigning after 2004 (with little associated fee/earned income); and the significant reduction in direct service delivery from 2005 onwards with the concomitant loss of fee income (for example, spinning off RNIB New College Worcester in 2008, which comprised three per cent of RNIB income).

In 2009/10 income was boosted by the absorption of Action for Blind People (which represented fourteen per cent of RNIB in income).

Growth Compared to Other Charities Working with Sight Loss

Throughout this period RNIB was by far the largest charity helping blind and partially sighted people in the UK (measured by total income, Wells 1971 and Caritas 2011).

Maintaining its pre-eminent position was not a foregone conclusion. For example, in 1970 the top 50 voluntary income charities contained four UK blindness ones –RNIB, St Dunstans (now Blind Veterans UK), the Jewish Blind Society and the Greater London Fund for the Blind. Of these only RNIB (nineteenth) remained in the top 50 by the end of this history (Pharoah 2011).

Growth Compared to Other Disability Charities

In 1970 RNIB was the largest disability charity (measured by total income), roughly equal to Scope, then called the Spastics Society. (Wells 1971). By 2010 Scope had dropped back to fourth, RNIB to third, with both overtaken by Mencap (first) and Leonard Cheshire (second) which were powered by earned income from the statutory sector, constituting over 80 per cent of their income (Caritas 2011). The significance of this will become clear in a few pages.

Growth Compared to All Charities

RNIB retained a position in the top 20 of all charities measured by total income for the whole of this history. This was no mean feat against a background of seven charities dropping out of the top 20, including Christian Aid, Scope and the Children's Society (Caritas Data 2011) and the decline of disability as a charitable fundraising cause (Pharoah *et al.* 2004).

The importance of staying a major income charity is emphasised by the extraordinary income distribution among general charities shown in the NCVO Almanac. In 2009/10 only 500 charities out of 151,000 commanded nearly half (46.4 per cent) of all charity income (NCVO Almanac 2012). This pattern remains the same today. Small and medium-sized charities need more help to grow, perhaps building on their relatively greater involvement of volunteers (Kendall, Mohan, Brookes and Yoon 2018).

The NCVO Almanac has been mentioned several times in this history and provides essential market data for the charity sector. It was a major innovation in 1996 under Sir Stuart Etherington's watch; he was an outstanding chief executive (1994-2020) of the influential National Council for Voluntary Organisations. Until the Almanac arrived there had been virtually no longitudinal sector data.

Sources of RNIB Income

There were two main sources of income for RNIB throughout the 40 years. These were voluntary income, such as legacies, direct mail, telephone raffles, major donors and so on, and fees for services, sometimes called earned income.

Examples of fee income include: contracted work undertaken on behalf of the NHS; school fees from local authorities; Talking Book memberships; individuals with sight loss buying, for example, white canes or watches; and the commercial sector buying consultancy and training (for example, on DDA implementation).

Most large charities have income from both of these sources but RNIB consciously tried to maximise both in order to have two 'legs' of income on which it stood. If fees/earned income suffered a hit, it was hoped that this would be cushioned by voluntary income and vice versa. The split between these two sources stayed remarkably constant over the 40 years, always within the following ranges:

Fees/earned income	38-40 per cent of total income
Voluntary income	53-59 per cent of total income
Investment income	one to five per cent of total income

Growing both earned and voluntary income threefold in real terms and keeping them in proportion was not inevitable. I remember well in the 1990s when voluntary income was doing well, there was a strong internal argument for keeping fee/earned income growth low, below inflation. For example, 'How can we justify raising fees when legacies are doing so well?' This is an attractive argument but would have soon led to fee income declining in real terms with less money to grow services to meet unmet need. The extra voluntary income would have been swallowed up further, increasing donation subsidy of fee/earned income services. Even worse, as so much of fee/earned income was from the state (local or national government), we would have been using voluntary (donated) income to subsidise the statutory contracts. Many donors, especially major givers, are opposed to charities that they support subsidising statutory contracts. They argue that they have paid their taxes and they do not wish their donations to subsidise the state; they see this as a 'second tax'. They want their money to be doing something extra. Second, as business people, they noted the growing trend of state outsourcing. Charities can be competing with commercial bids and entrepreneur donors can be uncomfortable with their donations having the effect of subsidising a charity bid and so 'undercutting' a commercial bid.

Earned Income

That RNIB maintained a fairly constant balance between the three sources of income makes it look 'normal'. However, in comparison with the wider charity market RNIB was an outlier. In summary and generalising, for 1970-90 the sector as a whole had a smaller proportion of earned income than RNIB's 38-40 per cent. Starting from 1979 in policy terms and the middle 1980s in implementation effect, statutory grants to the general charity sector were increasingly replaced by contracts or fees for services. By around 2000 the sector had increased average earned income such that it constituted 39 per cent and RNIB and the sector were at the same level. By 2010 the sector as a whole had increased its reliance on earned income even further; it now represented 49 per cent, significantly above RNIB's 39 per cent. The sources of these figures are RNIB's accounts and the NCVO Almanac.

This was a dramatic shift which RNIB anticipated in its strategy review of 2001 (RNIB 2001):

> The other disability charities have achieved their significant service income growth through rolling out largely new services which are beneficial

Table 9.1. Charity Sector Earned Income

	2000	2010
Voluntary Sector	39%	49%
RNIB	39%	39%

to their end customers and are paid for by the statutory authorities …

So one conclusion is that we need to identify a shortlist of services that are needed by blind or partially sighted people; are being under attended to currently in the statutory sector but for which we believe statutory funding can be grown; and where we have the capacity in terms of knowledge, skills, distribution potential to meet need.

(Bruce and Milligan 2001, pp. 219-20)

What were these shortlisted services? One was eye health services. The decade saw the major expansion of contracts for low vision services and for eye clinic liaison workers who help people newly diagnosed with sight loss to steer their way through the range of services there to help them at a time when the patient is at her or his most vulnerable. Another was the contracts for low vision clinics set up to help people use their residual vision more successfully. Then there was the JMU, the unit which brought in income from training and contracts to advise statutory and commercial organisations on how better to serve people with sight loss and other disabilities under the auspices of the Disability Discrimination Act. A third was the expansion of RNIB local rehabilitation services under contract to local authorities.

Why did these earned income initiatives not steer the percentages in the direction of the wider charity market? This would take further investigation, perhaps examining the following hypotheses: from 2004 RNIB shifted priorities significantly in favour of investing more in campaigning and lobbying; the income market for the growth of RNIB direct services was not there; and/or the loss/closure of mature direct services (e.g. RNIB New College and RNIB Redhill College) outstripped the growth of new earned income such as eye health and ECLO services.

Voluntary Income

On voluntary income, often called fundraised income (legacies, donations, collecting tins, fundraising events etc.), RNIB remained a major player across 1970-2010. In 1970 its voluntary income was the tenth largest after the following in order of rank: Joint Palestine Appeal, Christian Aid, Barnardo's, Oxfam, Imperial Cancer (now CRUK), the Spastics Society (now Scope), Save the Children, RNLI, Cancer Research (now CRUK) and RNIB (Wells 1971).

Forty years later RNIB voluntary income was fifteenth following in order: CRUK, British Heart Foundation, Oxfam, RNLI, NSPCC, Macmillan Cancer Support, British Red Cross, RSPCA, the Salvation Army, Sightsavers International, PDSA, Marie Curie, Save the Children, RSPB and RNIB (Pharoah 2011).

The fact that six of the original 1970 top ten are, 40 years later, still in the top fifteen shows the strength and longevity of the leading charity brands.

Fundraising is a highly competitive business in the charity world. In the 1960s and the early 1970s RNIB had a very successful fundraising operation perhaps because the then director general, John Colligan, came from a fundraising background. In the late 1970s and 1980s non-legacy fundraising became lacklustre – good solid performances but few spectacular successes. Introducing a strong marketing approach, Mike Lancaster, a commercial marketer with a penchant for risk and investment, loosened up fundraising thinking amongst staff during the 1990s and early 2000s and the situation was dramatically improved. This position was driven further forward under the leadership of the successor directors, Paul Amadi and Wanda Hamilton.

How did the make-up of our voluntary income develop over the period? The star in the firmament across this history and earlier has been legacy income which contributed over half of voluntary income throughout: 52 per cent in 1969/70; 64 per cent in 1979/80; 69 per cent in 1999/2000 and 56 per cent in 2009/10. RNIB has traditionally worked hard on promoting its need for legacies. However, it is salutary to remember the apocryphal adage of the advertising world: 'Half of advertising is a waste of money but which half?' From 1975 RNIB's blind chair, Duncan Watson, wrote 'from one solicitor to another' to all English solicitors about the helpfulness of legacies to our cause. In the early 1980s, under Barry Gifford's prompting, we produced a legacy leaflet. By the early 1990s, under Mike Lancaster's leadership, we had one then a team of legacy officers holding information receptions for potential legators, who had responded to RNIB advertisements. Yet, despite this work and regular research trying to connect legators' names to lists of people who had used our services, we could never find a causal link between us and our largest legators.

Over the same period fundraised income (that is, non-legacy voluntary income) changed dramatically. In the early 1970s RNIB relied on two major methods, local (mainly blind) fundraisers with guides (often their wives) and national press advertising. By the beginning of the 1980s local fundraising was showing a decline, with costs ratios rising unacceptably. Started by Barry Gifford in the late 1980s and then driven much further by Mike Lancaster in the early 1990s, local fundraising was wound back but with much higher income targets per fundraiser. This was a difficult time, especially for those fundraisers who lost their jobs, amongst whom were blind employees. Mike introduced, or radically developed, newer methods, such as capital appeals, telephone promoted raffles

RNIB supporters pull a jumbo jet 100 yards at Gatwick (a world record) and raise £50,000 in 1990.

(pioneered by Kath Howard in the north of England), direct mail, major donor fundraising and expanded legacy fundraising.

Over 2000 to 2010 Mike Lancaster was in post until the middle of the decade, succeeded by Paul Amadi and Wanda Hamilton by the end. All the aforementioned methods were in place but by then we had grasped the central importance of instituting a relationship fundraising approach. At the smaller donation end, this was driven by how much more cost effective it is to retain and develop an existing donor than to recruit a new one.

At the major donor end, banged into us by Jeff Shear, it was about stewardship, earning trust and so building commitment and loyalty. Critical to this process of relationship building over the period were the RNIB president and the chair of the fundraising committee. The presidents were Lord Cobham, Lord Head, the Duke of Devonshire, then the Duke of Westminster and, lastly, Dame Gail Ronson. Appeal committee chairs were Sir John Beckwith, Sir Mike Rake, Guy Sangster, Jeremy Bull and Dame Gail Ronson. These committee chairs were hugely important in their leadership roles and in reaching targets, so empowering help to blind and partially sighted people. Vice presidents at the end of this history in 2010 were Sir John Beckwith CBE, the Rt Hon. David Blunkett MP, Richard Brewster, Professor Ian Bruce CBE, Jeremy Bull, Haruhisa Handa, Dr Euclid Herie, Lady Jarvis, Penny Lancaster-Stewart, Lord Low of Dalston CBE, Sir Mike Rake, Dr Dermot Smurfit, Rod Stewart CBE, the Rt Hon the Earl of Stockton and Sir Duncan Watson.

In conclusion, all this time and effort led to the tripling of voluntary and statutory income in real terms over the 40 years. We maintained RNIB as one of the UK's largest charities as measured by total income, earned income and voluntary income, throughout this history – 1970 to 2010.

Service Expenditure Growth

Income growth for its own sake was not the objective and perhaps the most important set of figures across the years were those recording expenditure on services to blind and partially sighted people and this is also a good news story – which I hope is evident from the detail laid out in earlier chapters. Here we look only at the overall financial picture. Expenditure on services grew from £2 million in 1970 to £111 million in 2010, which meant in real terms, the tripling of service growth. Indirect services (influencing others – see earlier in this chapter) grew massively. Expenditure on direct service also grew, with significant shifts away from residential services to day provision, and away from education (with the rise of inclusive state education).

Reading and writing Braille at Rushton Hall school in the 70s. Later pupils had learning disabilities and would use other communication methods.

There was major growth in expenditure on direct services in the area of eye health, accessible digital information (especially online) and information and advice generally, for example, on benefits rights and social security. The major income gainer was lobbying and campaigning for improved conditions for blind and partially sighted people.

Financial Data in More Detail

The table below gives the actual cash figures and the inflation adjusted total income and expenditure in constant 2004 prices for valid comparison across the 40 years. Why 2004? I could have picked any year but 2004 was the latest available year when I started this first element of the history. The important point is that the decade changes in income and expenditure can be validly compared because each pound has a constant value, that is, equal purchasing power. When we compare like with like, we can see that RNIB

Table 9.2. RNIB Income and Expenditure 1969/70-2009/10

Income

Income (£ millions)	1969/70	1979/80	1989/90	1999/2000	2009/10
Fees for services	1.16	4.7	14.3	28.6	45.7
Voluntary income	1.61	6.25	19.9	41.5	68.3
Investment income	0.16	0.73	2.7	2.5	1.7
Other	0.13	0	0	0.5	1.5
Total actual	3.04	11.68	36.9	73.1	117.2[1]
TOTAL at constant 2004 prices [1]	31.7	35.1	54.7	80.2	93.8
Percentage growth, real terms		+11%	+56%	+47%	+17%
TOTAL at constant 2004 prices to base 100 in 1969/70	100	111	173	253	296

[1] Excluding £17 million one-off for 'Fair value of acquired net assets'

Expenditure

Expenditure (£ millions)	1969/70	1979/80	1989/90	1999/2000	2009/10
Services for blind and partially sighted people	2.29	10.13	32.4	65.2	111.1
Cost of appeals	0.67	0.92	4.3	9.5	17.2
Total	2.96	11.05	36.7	74.8	130
TOTAL at constant 2004 prices (£millions) [2]	30.9	33.2	54.4	82.1	105
Percentage growth, real terms		+7%	+64%	+51%	+28%
TOTAL at constant 2004 prices to base 100[1]	100	107	176	266	340

[2] UK RPI via the Cleave Calculator

income grew in the 1970s by eleven per cent, in the 1980s by 56 per cent, in the 1990s by 47 per cent and 2000-10 by seventeen per cent, including the absorption of Action for Blind People's income in the second half of the decade. The expenditure figures show a similar growth pattern. See the previous sections of this chapter for the commentary.

Chapter 10

Milestones – but a Long Way to Go

Decade-by-Decade Developments

In this history I worry I may have created for the reader a feeling of not being able to see the wood for the trees! So here are my subjective choices of the most significant milestones over the period. If you wish to be reminded of the detail, you can return to the relevant chapter of the book. Please tell me of important developments I may have missed. In all of these milestones RNIB was either the sole actor, or at least a decisive leader.

1970s

- Major governance changes during 1970-75, strengthening the role played by blind representatives
- Education Advisory Service launched (1972)
- RNIB School of Physiotherapy opened (1978)
- Garrow House hostel opened (1978) – accommodation for blind people seeking work in London
- Braille production transferred to Braille House in Islington (1979)
- Thompson Auto Braille press

1980s

- Creation of the European Blind Union, leading to the World Blind Union 1984
- Creation of one of the first charity corporate strategies (1985-87)
- Ever-improving campaigning and lobbying effectiveness, especially in parliament
- Creating nineteen new direct and indirect services (1985-90) including: parliamentary office; benefits rights; (education) integration unit; arts and sports advice; eye health; ethnic minorities adviser; marketing unit; and a European office (Brussels)
- New build, rebuilding, refurbishing and relocating fourteen services in RNIB's largest ever capital programme (1987-90) totalling one year's total income at the time (RNIB Production and Distribution Centre, Peterborough, RNIB Vocational College in Loughborough, RNIB New College Worcester, RNIB Redhill College and ten other major capital refurbishments)
- Founding and leadership of the national Disability Benefits Consortium (1988) of over 500 organisations of and for disabled people
- Publicity impact in 1989 of reducing the government's Commons majority from over 100 down to eight in defence of free eye tests – as more people began to understand that the eye test also checked for eye disease
- The influence RNIB had on technology, in its own right and as part of national and international consortia (1989-2010)

1990s

- The first needs survey and the way it changed RNIB's practice and provided evidence for RNIB campaigning (Bruce, McKennell and Walker 1991) and, similarly, the children's needs survey (Walker, Tobin and McKennell 1992)

- Achieving the inclusion of blind people in social security (Disability Living Allowance), putting £40 million per annum into blind people's pockets (1991 prices)
- Providing the funding, and being a key part of the leadership of, the pan-EU campaign which achieved the inclusion of disability issues into the remit of the EU as part of the Amsterdam Treaty (1997)
- Successfully campaigning for accessible Euro bank notes – differentiation by size, colour and contrast (1992-99)
- Fighting hard and successfully to save the BBC Radio 4 *In Touch* programme (1994-97) – despite the grief it often gave RNIB!
- Winning back free eye tests for older people in 1998
- Launch of the RNIB Helpline in 1997 and its rapid growth – by 2010 it handled 400,000 enquiries per year
- Launch and expansion from 1998 onwards of contracts for local social rehabilitation services, Talk and Support (telephone mutual aid groups), eye clinic liaison officers and low vision ophthalmic services
- Campaigning from 1998 to defend Access to Work benefits and Disability Living Allowance
- Lobbying for and achieving significant percentages of audio description on television and films (1989-2010)
- Campaigning, training and consultancy work to improve services for multi handicapped visually impaired adults

2000s

- Re-launch of Talking Books in digital format 2000-04
- Governance changes of 2001/02 and becoming formally an organisation 'of' blind and partially sighted people
- Purchase, conversion and move from old RNIB headquarters at 224 Great Portland Street to 106 Judd Street in 2002
- Supporting a successful Private Member's Bill to achieve exemption of copyright for audio, braille and large print, and lobbying on the Communications Act (2002)
- Vision 2005 International Congress on Low Vision, London, 4-7 April
- The Vision Strategy (2007) drawing together voluntary and statutory agencies into a co-ordinated effort
- The rapid rise of mergers and associations with other visual impairment charities in the second half of the decade (2005-10)
- Achieving higher rate Mobility Allowance for blind people in 2008, gaining £45 million per annum
- Opening the RNIB Pears Centre a special, non-maintained school for 2- to 19-year-olds and a children's home (2010-11)
- Achieving an eye health indicator in the government's health strategy (2010-12)

1970-2010

- The tripling of services to blind and partially sighted people
- Becoming one of the UK's most successful lobbying and campaigning charities
- The massive change from a dominance of residential direct services (e.g. from residential schools,

social and employment rehabilitation and hotels) to community-based services, and consulting, lobbying and campaigning through indirect services
- From the mid 1980s the opening up and expansion of eye health services and campaigns to join other RNIB priorities of employment, rehabilitation, education, leisure and accessible information.
- Our work making computers, mobile phones and televisions accessible
- The transformation of RNIB's resource side, finance, HR and fundraising
- The tripling of RNIB income and expenditure in real terms between 1970 and 2010 and its application to RNIB aims and objectives

Conclusion

The years 1970 to 2010 saw a dramatic change in the fortunes of charities in Britain, from subservient bit players in a powerful welfare state, to significant service providers campaigning confidently for more state and societal action on their causes. When I left business for the charity sector in 1970, my Unilever manager colleagues thought I was stupid – in their view, the age of charity was over, the welfare state was the total solution. However, since then, the sector has grown enormously, fuelled significantly not only by growing donations but by exploding earned income, primarily from statutory sources – to the extent that one could argue the state has infiltrated the sector, were it not for, perhaps the most dramatic change of all, the growth in campaigning for causes. Charities are no lap dogs of the state. Take the example of climate change. The UK could be doing more, but we would be doing a lot less, were it not for the public education, campaigning and lobbying of charities such as Friends of the Earth, WWF, Action Aid, Campaign for the Protection of Rural England and the National Federation of Women's Institutes. Add in non-registered, 'charity-like' organisations such as Greenpeace and Extinction Rebellion for a cocktail not being served in the early 1970s. An example at the heart of this history was winning disability rights legislation via a 500+ charity coalition using methods ranging from two-hour plus meetings with successive prime ministers through to red paint attacks on Downing Street.

RNIB has been part of that success story but this was not a foregone conclusion. While the sector has grown, several of the major actors have changed in these 40 years. Eight charities have dropped out of the top 20 (measured by total income), including Scope, Christian Aid and the Children's Society. Some are now virtually unknown, such as the British and Foreign Bible Society.

Between 1970 and 2010 RNIB grew threefold in real terms, that is, adjusted for inflation. It was an exciting time. From its core areas of coverage – accessible information, education, employment and rehabilitation, it added eye health, including low vision optometric services. From working through almost exclusively direct services to blind people, we recognised this could never meet all the needs and wishes of people with sight loss. So RNIB expanded significantly into indirect service provision – influencing other commercial, government and voluntary organisations, through advice and campaigning, to serve blind and partially sighted people better. Many examples are cited in this history ranging from disability legislation, putting £80 million a year into blind people's pockets through successful lobbying for social security gains, through to something apparently small but very important, getting braille onto all medicine labels. RNIB formally expanded its beneficiary group to include partially sighted people, as well as blind. Finally, we returned its governance from sighted to blind and partially sighted people.

Nevertheless, RNIB exists to improve the position of blind and partially sighted people and so the key questions are: has the position of blind and partially sighted people improved? – 'Yes'; has their position improved enough? – 'No'.

It is beyond the remit or capacity of this history to attempt to show what proportion of improvements can be attributed to RNIB. There are many agents for change in public services and other voluntary organisations. However, over this history RNIB remained one of the largest charities in the UK, the largest one in the visual impairment field, and the only one addressing comprehensively the needs and aspirations of all blind and partially sighted people. Moreover, very importantly, it changed from an organisation 'for' to 'of' blind and partially sighted people. It can claim some credit for improvements and must accept responsibility for failures.

Areas of improvement for blind and partially sighted people over the 40 years include: their financial position (increased social security benefits); accessible information (braille, large print and, especially, digital information access via computers phones and television); rights (the Disability Discrimination Act); eye health; leisure (e.g. audio description of television shows and films, and access to e-books).

Areas where advances are questionable, even doubtful, are employment (there have been real advances in choice of jobs but still massively high unemployment) and rehabilitation (we have improved knowledge of when and how to intervene, but there is probably less, or little more, service provision than there was). Even our successes in eye health can learn from eye clinic rehabilitation in Sweden (Reid and Simkiss 2013). While there has been massive improvement, there is still no chance of universal access to information. Also, there are still far too many people who could benefit from improvements achieved but who do not know about them or cannot access them easily.

In all these areas RNIB was in the forefront of change, but even the biggest optimist would acknowledge that there is a still a great deal more which has to be done across all areas of life, even those where improvements have been made. The social, economic and environmental challenges facing the world and the UK within it, look particularly daunting. So, it is abundantly clear that blind and partially sighted people need a strong RNIB, led by their blind and partially sighted representatives and friends – an RNIB continuing to provide useful help and services, as well as fighting for rights to be fulfilled and responsibilities taken up – an RNIB which continually assesses the efficacy of its impact and adapts accordingly.

That optimist would, I hope, also accept that our society needs more care, commitment, and social and environmental justice, as does the wider world and our planet. In the future charities can, should and, it is to be hoped, will play a much greater role in achieving these.

Postscript

I suspect there will be later editions of this attempt at the history of an important organisation, not least in electronic formats. So, I ask anyone who feels I have omitted something important or a person who should be mentioned to write to me: either by email: i.bruce1@btinternet.com or by post:

Ian Bruce CBE
Vice President
RNIB Headquarters

References

Access Economics. 2009. *Future Sight Loss (1): Economic Impact of Partial Sight and Blindness in the UK Adult Population.* London, RNIB.

Allen-King, J. 2010. *Just Jill: The Autobiography of Jill Allen-King OBE.* Clacton, Apex Publishing.

Bell, D., and Heitmueller, A. 2009. The Disability Discrimination Act in the UK: Helping or Hindering Employment among the Disabled? *Journal of Health Economics* 28: 2, 465-80.

Berry, L.L., and Parasuraman, A. 1991. *Marketing Services: Competing through Quality.* New York, Free Press.

Beveridge, W. 1948. *Voluntary Action: A Report on Methods of Social Advance* London, George Allen & Unwin Ltd.

Brown, S.D., and Reavey, P. 2013. Experience and Memory. In *Research Methods for Memory Studies*, ed. E. Keightley and M. Pickering. Edinburgh, Edinburgh University Press.

Bruce, I. 1985. Policy Guidelines for a Development Programme. *New Beacon*, January 1985.

Bruce, I. 1991. Employment of Disabled People. In *Disability and Social Policy*, ed. G. Dalley. London, Policy Studies Institute.

Bruce, I. 1997. RNIB Growth Patterns in Comparison with the 10 Largest UK Social Welfare Charities. RNIB Policy and Resources Committee.

Bruce, I. 2003. Strategic Planning and Implementation Exemplified by RNIB Experience between 1983 and 2003. London, Strategic Planning Society Conference, 16 June 2003.

Bruce, I. 2011. *Meeting Need: Successful Charity Marketing*, 4th edn. London, ICSA. 1st edn 1994.

Bruce, I. 2018. Good Practice Now: What Have Been the Effective Changes to Running Charities over the Last 25 Years. Paper given in the 25th anniversary Charity Talks series at Cass Business School, London, 21 February 2018.

Bruce, I., and Baker, M. 2001. *Access to Written Information: The Views of 1000 People with Sight Problems.* London, RNIB.

Bruce, I., and Baker, M. 2003. *Employment and Unemployment among People with Sight Problems in the UK: A Survey of 1000 People.* London, RNIB.

Bruce, I., and Baker, M. 2005. *Transport and Mobility for People with Sight Problems: The Views of 1000 People.* London, RNIB.

Bruce, I., and Chew, C. 2011. The Marketisation of the Voluntary Sector: Implications for Charities' Distinctiveness and Values, *Public Money and Management* 31: 3, 155-56.

Bruce, I., Harrow, J., and Obolenskaya, P. 2007. Blind and Partially Sighted People's Perceptions of Their Inclusion by Family and Friends. *British Journal of Visual Impairment* 25:1, 85-.

Bruce, I., McKennell, A., and Walker, E. 1991. *Blind and Partially Sighted Adults in Britain: The RNIB Needs Survey: Volume 1.* London, HMSO.

Bruce, I., and Milligan, M. 2001. How RNIB Development Compares to Other Charities as Measured by Income Growth, Total and by Source. In *Learning from the Past: A Review of RNIB Strategy 1994-2000.* London, RNIB, pp. 218-29.

Butler, R.J., and Wilson, D.C. 1990. *Managing Voluntary and Non-Profit Organizations: Strategy and Structure.* London, Routledge.

Caritas Data. 2001. *Top 3,000 Charities.* London, Caritas Data.

Caritas Data. 2011. *Top 3,000 Charities.* London, Caritas Data.

Charities Aid Foundation. 1983. *Charity Statistics 1982/83.* Tonbridge, CAF.

Charity Financials. 2020. *Top 3000 Charities.* London, Wilmington Charities.

Clark, J., Kane, D., Wilding, K., and Bass, P. 2012. *The UK Civil Society Almanac 2012.* London, NCVO.

Cleave Calculator. This was produced by Cleave Books and enabled the enquirer to calculate RPI-based equivalence of a financial sum for any year between 1930 and 2010. http://www.cleavebooks.co.uk/scol/calcoluk.htm.

Close, M. 2011. Disabled People's Movement: History Timeline. Disability Equality North West. http://disability-equality.org.uk/history/ (accessed 31 May 2022).

Clunies-Ross, L., Franklin, A., and Keil, S. 1999. *Blind and Partially Sighted Children in Britain: Their Incidence and Special Needs at a Time of Change*. London, RNIB, for the Nuffield Foundation.

Colligan, J.C. 1968. *Foresight: The Saga of 100 Years*, Centenary Exhibition Catalogue. London, RNIB.

Compass Partnership. 1993. RNIB Stakeholder Survey. Report to RNIB Policy and Resources Committee.

Cook, S., and Mason, T. 2021. *What Have Charities Ever Done for Us?* Bristol, Policy Press.

Davis Smith. J. 2019. *100 Years of NCVO and Voluntary Action: Idealists and Realists*. Cham, Palgrave Macmillan.

Deakin Commission. 1996. *Meeting the Challenge of Change: Voluntary Action into the 21st Century*. London: NCVO.

Eikenberry, A.M., and Kluver, J.D. 2004. The Marketization of the Nonprofit Sector: Civil Society at Risk? *Public Administration Review*, 64:2, 132-40.

European Disability Forum. 1998. *European Disability Forum Guide to the Amsterdam Treaty*. Brussels, EDF, Section 3, D2.

Fivush, R. 2013. Autobiographical Memory. In *Research Methods for Memory Studies*, ed. E. Keightley and M. Pickering. Edinburgh, Edinburgh University Press.

Foxhall, K. 2020. *Data Protection and Historians in the UK*. London, Royal History Society.

Garsten, N., and Bruce, I., eds. 2018. *Communicating Causes: Strategic Public Relations for the Non-Profit Sector*. Abingdon, Routledge.

Gladstone, F. 1979. *Voluntary Action in a Changing World*. London, Bedford Square Press.

Hall, L. 1982. *Who Are Britain's Blind People?* London, RNIB.

Hatch, M.J. 1997. *Organization Theory: Modern, Symbolic, and Postmodern Perspectives*. Oxford, Oxford University Press.

Hamlin, D., and Rubin, G. 2006. *Vision 2005 London: Proceedings of the Vision 2005 Conference, 4-7 April 2005*. London, Elsevier.

Harrow, J., and Palmer, P. 2003. *The Financial Role of Charity Boards*. Abingdon, Routledge.

Hems, L., and Passey, A. 1996. *The UK Voluntary Sector Statistical Almanac 1996*. London, NCVO.

Henderson. 1993. *The Henderson Top 1,000 Charities*. London, Hemmington Scott.

Hudson, B. 1972. Quoted in 'Knock It Down and Start Again'. Community Care, October 2005. https://www.communitycare.co.uk/2005/10/20/knock-it-down-and-start-again/ (accessed 31 May 2022).

Jas, P., Wilding, K., Wainwright, S., Passey, A., and Hems, L. 2002. *United Kindom Voluntary Sector Almanac*. London, NCVO.

Jennings, J. 2002. Including Children with Impaired Vision: Play It My Way. *Nursery World*, 8 January 2002. https://www.nurseryworld.co.uk/news/article/including-children-with-impaired-vision-play-it-my-way.

Jung, T., and Harrow, J. 2016. Philanthropy, the State and Public Goods. In *Doing Public Good? Private Actors, Evaluation, and Public Value*, ed. P. Guerrero and O. Wilkins, pp. 29-46. Abingdon, Routledge.

Keightley, E., and Pickering, M. 2013. *Research Methods for Memory Studies*. Edinburgh Edinburgh University Press.

Kendall, J., Mohan, J., Brookes, N., and Yoon, Y. 2018. The English Voluntary Sector: How Volunteering and Policy Climate Perceptions Matter. *Journal of Social Policy* 47:4, 759-82.

King, S., Cuthbert, S., Harvey, J., Sismore H. and Siggery, J. 2003. *Talking Books Report*. Peterborough, RNIB.

Leat, D. 2016. *Philanthropic Foundations, Public Good and Public Policy*. London, Cass (now Bayes) Business School.

Local Authority Social Services Act 1970, c. 42. London, HMSO.

Martin, J., Meltzer, H., and Elliot, D. 1988. *OPCS Surveys of Disability in Great Britain: Report 1: The Prevalence of Disability among Adults*. London, HMSO.

Medley, G.J. 1988. Strategic Planning for the World Wildlife Fund. *Long Range Planning* 21:1, 46-54.

Minassian, D., and Reidy, A. 2009. *Future Sight Loss (2): An Epidemiological and Economic Model for Sight Loss in the Decade 2010-20*. London, EpiVision and RNIB.

Monk, P. 1945. *Though Land Be Out of Sight: The Early Years of Chorleywood College*. London, National Institute for the Blind.

Myers, S.O. 1975. *Where Are They Now? A Follow-up Study of 314 Multi-handicapped Blind People, Former Pupils of Condover Hall School*. London, RNIB.

National Federation of the Blind. 1971. *An Equal Say in Our Own Affairs*. London, NFB.

National Federation of the Blind magazine, *Viewpoint*.

National League of the Blind and Disabled magazine, *Blind Advocate*.

NCVO Almanac, London, NCVO annual. First published in 1996, initially called *The UK Voluntary Sector Statistical Almanac 1996* and later renamed as the *UK Civil Society Almanac*, London, NCVO. Quoted in the text 1998, 2000, 2010 and 2012.

New Beacon. The semi-independent magazine of RNIB began in 1917 as *The Beacon: A Magazine Devoted to the Interests of the Blind*. It was renamed *New Beacon*, and is now *NB Online*.

Nightingale, B. 1973. *Charities*. London, Allen Lane.

Ockelford, A. 1994. *Objects of Reference*. London, RNIB.

Oliver, M., 2013. The social model of disability: Thirty years on. *Disability & society*, 28(7), pp.1024-1026.

Pharoah, C., Walker, C., Goodey, L., and Clegg, S. 2004. *Charity Trends 2004* (25th Anniversary edn). London, CAF.

Pharoah, C. 2011. *Charity Market Monitor 2011: Tracking the Funding of UK Charities*. London, Caritas Data/Cass Business School.

Purkis, A. 2020. The Inside Track or the Outside Track for Charities Seeking Change. Civil Society, 21 August 2020. https://www.civilsociety.co.uk/voices/andrew-purkis-the-inside-track-or-the-outside-track-for-charities-seeking-change.html (accessed 31 May 2022).

Reid, F., and Simkiss, P. 2013. *The Hidden Majority Summary Report: A Study of Economic Activity among Blind and Visually Impaired People in the UK, Sweden, Germany, Romania, Netherlands, Poland, France and Austria*. A report to the board of the European Blind Union.

RNIB. Annual Reports and Accounts of RNIB for the years 1968/69 to 2011/12.

RNIB. Minutes of RNIB committees and Executive Council.

RNIB. 1987. *Meeting the Needs of Visually Handicapped People: The RNIB Strategy*. London, RNIB.

RNIB. 1988. *RNIB Growth and Development: Corporate Strategy Review 1988*. London, RNIB.

RNIB. 1993. *Review of RNIB Strategy 1993*. London, RNIB.

RNIB. 1994. *Challenging Blindness: A Summary of RNIB's Strategy 1994-2000*. London. RNIB.

RNIB. 1995. *Play It My Way: Learning through Play with Your Visually Impaired Child*. London. RNIB.

RNIB. 1997. *RNIB Strategy 2000: Mid-term Review*. London, RNIB.

RNIB. 2001. *Learning from the Past: A Review of RNIB Strategy 1994-2000*. London, RNIB.

RNIB. 2000. *Strategic Direction 2000-2006: Inclusion, Support and Independence*. London, RNIB.

RNIB. 2003. *Human Resources Report*. London, RNIB.

RNIB. 2005. *The Future @ RNIB 2005-2009 Independent living: Campaigning for Lasting Change for People with Sight Problems*. London, RNIB.

RNIB. 2008. *Strategy 2009-2014: Ending the Isolation of Sight Loss*. London, RNIB.

RNIB. 2011. *Our Volunteers: The Difference They Make*. London, RNIB.

Rose, J. 1970. *Changing Focus: The Development of Blind Welfare in Britain*. London, Hutchinson.

Seebohm, F. 1968. *Report of the Inter-departmental Committee on Local Authority and Allied Personal Social Services, Cmnd 3703*. London, HMSO.

Shankland Cox. 1985. *Initial Demographic Study: A Review of Available Data on the Visually Disabled Population*. London, RNIB.

Shore, P. 1985. *Local Authority Social Rehabilitation Services to Visually Handicapped People*. London, RNIB.

Thomas, M.G. 1957. *The Royal National Institute for the Blind 1868-1956*. London, RNIB.

Top 3000 Charities. For 1993, see Henderson; 2001, see Caritas; 2010/12, see Caritas; 2020, see Charity Financials.

Union of the Physically Impaired Against Segregation and Disability Alliance (1976). *Fundamental Principles of Disability: A Summary of the Discussion Held on 22 November 1975*. London, UPIAS and DA.

United Nations. 1993. Standard Rules on the Equalisation of Opportunities for Persons with Disabilities. New York, UN.

Vanhala, L. 2011. *Making Rights a Reality? Disability Rights Activists and Legal Mobilization*. Cambridge, Cambridge University Press.

Wagg, H.J., and Thomas, M.G. 1932. *A Chronological Survey of Work for the Blind*. London, National Institute for the Blind.

Walker, E., Tobin, M., and McKennell, A. 1992. *Blind and Partially Sighted Children in Britain*: The RNIB Survey, Volume 2. London, HMSO.

Walsh, L., 1984. Report to Policy and Resources Committee. RNIB.

Wells. L.G. 1971. *Fifty Largest Fundraising Charities in the UK*. London, Wells International Donor Advisory Services.

Winyard, S. 2006. *Taken for a Ride*. London, RNIB.

World Intellectual Copyright Organisation, Marrakesh Treaty 2013, www.wipo.int/treaties/en/ip/marrakesh/ (accessed 30 May 2022).

Appendices

List of Organisational Initials and Acronyms

ABA	Association of Blind Asians
ABAPSTAS	Association of Blind and Partially Sighted Teachers and Students
ABCP	Association of Blind Chartered Physiotherapists
ABPT	Association of Blind Piano Tuners
AOP	Association of Optical Practitioners
BCAB	British Computer Association of the Blind
BCODP	British Council of Disabled People
BDA	British Deaf Association
BIP	Benefits Integrity Project
COGDO	Circle of Guide Dog Owners
CRUK	Cancer Research UK
DA	Disability Alliance
DAISY	Digital Audio Information System – home of tools, standards, advice and best practices for accessible publishing
DAN	Disability Action Network

DBC	Disability Benefits Consortium
DCC	Disability Charities Consortium
DDA	Disability Discrimination Act 1995
DIR	RNIB Directorate
DLA	Disability Living Allowance
EBU	European Blind Union
ECLO	Eye Clinic Liaison Officer
EDF	European Disability Forum
ER	RNIB External Relations Division
ESSN	RNIB Education Support Network
E&L	RNIB Education and Leisure Division
F&A	RNIB Finance and Administration Division
GDBA	Guide Dogs for the Blind Association
HMSO	Her Majesty's Stationery Office
JMU	RNIB Joint Mobility Unit which advised on all aspects of the DDA
LGBTQ+	Lesbian, Gay, Bi, Trans, Queer/Questioning plus
Mob A	Mobility Allowance
MHVI	Multi-handicapped Visually Impaired
MIND	National Association of Mental Health
OBAC	Organisation of Blind Africans and Caribbeans
NCVO	National Council for Voluntary Organisations
NLBD	National League of the Blind and Disabled
NFB	National Federation of the Blind of the UK
NLB	National Library for the Blind
NLSP	North London School of Physiotherapy

PDSA	People's Dispensary for Sick Animals
RADAR	Royal Association for Disability and Rehabilitation
RNC	Royal National College for the Blind
RNLI	Royal National Lifeboat Institution
RNIB	Royal National Institute of Blind People
RNID	Royal National Institute for Deaf People
RSPB	Royal Society for the Protection of Birds
SCOPE	Disability charity, originally focussed on cerebral palsy
TBs	RNIB Talking Books
TCS	RNIB Technical and Consumer Services Division
UPIAS	Union of Physically Impaired Against Segregation
VI	Visually impaired
VIPs	Visually impaired people
VSS	RNIB Vocational and Social Services Division
WBU	World Blind Union

Organisation Chart 1990

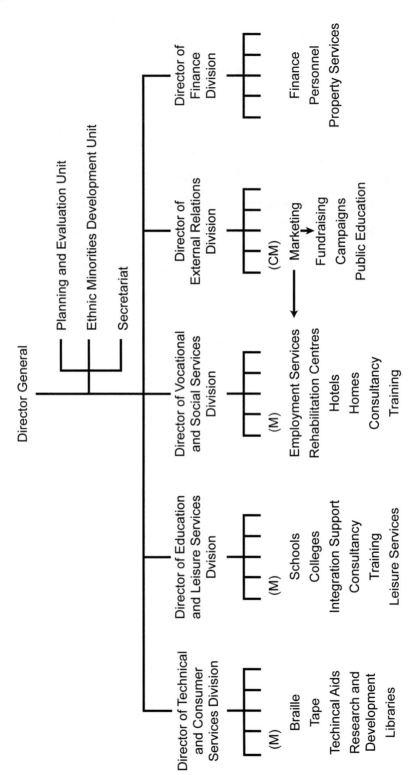

Director General

- Planning and Evaluation Unit
- Ethnic Minorities Development Unit
- Secretariat

Director of Technical and Consumer Services Division
(M)
- Braille
- Tape
- Techincal Aids
- Research and Development
- Libraries

Director of Education and Leisure Services Dvision
(M)
- Schools
- Colleges
- Integration Support
- Consultancy
- Training
- Leisure Services

Director of Vocational and Social Services Division
(M)
- Employment Services
- Rehabilitation Centres
- Hotels
- Homes
- Consultancy
- Training

Director of External Relations Division
(CM)
- Marketing
- Fundraising
- Campaigns
- Public Education

Director of Finance Division
- Finance
- Personnel
- Property Services

RNIB Management Conference
Attendance – 1985, 1991, 1997 and 2003

Commentary

Crucial to the successful development of RNIB for over the period 1983-2003 was the role of staff involvement in strategic planning, particularly via the biennial residential management conferences where strategic developments were debated. Thank you to all colleagues who contributed in this way. Below I list attendances at four of the nine conferences, separated by six-yearly intervals, showing the development of job titles, roles and organisational structures which I suggest would not be untypical of English social welfare charities. Some title developments are unsurprising, such as from headmaster/headmistress (1985) to principal/head (2003). However, not all title developments are aggrandising, for example, from eight geographic directors of regional fundraising (1985) to mainly heads of fundraising functions (2003). The 1985 list gives remaining evidence of a previous flatter managerial structure, while the 1997 conference section shows the major, real terms growth in RNIB size, functions, units and specialisms. Conference numbers steadily increased over the 20-year period: 80 in 1985; 130 in 1991; 170 in 1997; dropping to 112 in 2003. The 2003 figure is untypical. First, it was the only non-residential conference of the total of nine and, second, the number of invitees was cut to save money. Why did numbers rise over the 20 years? Two main reasons: first, I and my management committee (the senior staff group) wanted to maximise manager involvement in strategic development and review; second, there was considerable demand to attend from managers. Directors would come with numerous proposals for attendance and too many to accommodate, and I remember the anguish they expressed anticipating having to tell people that there was no room for them, such was the popularity of the conferences. Also below, the 1991 and 1997 lists report apologies, which were minimal.

In my judgement the values, camaraderie, hard work and occasional playfulness of participants at these conferences

did much to engender resolve to implement the strategies. As strategic planners know, plans are the easy part,
implementation is a greater critical success factor but is
more challenging. The lists below give the opportunity to
acknowledge and thank the individuals named, for their
contribution – powerful evidence of leading edge but typical,
growing managerial involvement and engagement in planning
and implementation exhibited by English charities. I apologise
to attendees of the intermediate conferences for not being
able to acknowledge and thank them personally but space
prevents including all nine conferences. The information which
follows records the historical documents faithfully except in
two respects. For the first conference I have removed the
marital status appellations for women (Mrs and Miss). Their
presence in the original documents is a stark reminder of
organisational culture as late as the middle 1980s. As the years
passed name descriptors became increasingly informal: from
'Smith, Dr John' to 'Smith John' to 'John Smith'. Second, in
the first conference I have removed the * against the names
of blind and partially sighted staff. While arcane, that indicator
at least had a functional purpose, indicating that people communicating in print should provide starred attendees with
alternative media. A point to note is that the roles recorded for
attendees were accurate for the specific date but appreciable
numbers of staff went on to assume other roles subsequently,
often more senior. What follows is a transcription from the
printed delegate lists for each conference.

I am grateful to the Royal Historical Society for its information
and advice (Foxhall 2020) which has helped me follow the
EU General Data Protection Regulation with its special
exemptions for academic and journalistic publications.

First Management Conference 1985

RNIB Palm Court Hotel, Eastbourne, 13-15 February 1985:

> Alexander, Margaret—Head, Committee Secretariat
> Aston, Tony—Head, Vocational and Social Services
> Attrill, Chris—Sports and Recreation Officer

Bell, Donald—Director of Publications
Bell, Stan—Principal, Commercial Training College
Bird, Robin—Manager, Palm Court Hotel
Brooks, Alan—Production Controller
Brown, Tom—Manager, Moon Branch
Bruce, Ian—Director General
Butcher, Pauline—Braille Transcription Manager

Clark, Paul—Management Accountant
Clarke, Sally—Deputy Head, VSS
Clayton, Fred—Manager, Century Hotel
Clunies-Ross, Louise—Deputy Education Officer
Croft, Chris—Employment Services Officer, VSS

Davies, Wendy—Administrator, Express Reading
    Services
Dodd, Alison—Vocational Research Officer, VSS
Dunford, Kay—Headmistress, Sunshine House,
    East Grinstead

Fisher, Virginia—Deputy Head, Appeals
Forest, Ken—Senior Bibliographer

Garland, Cedric—Technical Officer
Gifford, Barry—Finance Secretary
Gilbert, Alan—Director, South-Western Branch
Godber, John—Customer Liaison Manager

Hagger, Ron—Braille Production Manager
Hall, Lucille—Head, Press and Publicity
Hearn, Bob—Estates Surveyor
Heilbronn, Bill—Officer-in-Charge, Kathleen
    Chambers Home
Hoare, Bob—Head, Music Department
Howse, Gwen—Headmistress, Sunshine House,
    Leamington

Jackson, Don—Rehabilitation Services Manager
Jarvis, Anthony—Headmaster, Condover Hall

Kaplin, John—Computer Services Manager
Kingsley, Mary—Representing Education Advisers

Late, Gwen—Officer-in-Charge, Wavertree
Lavey, Ken—Personnel Officer
Lawrence, Hugh—Parliamentary Officer
Lawson, Neville—Education Officer
Long, Christine—Education Adviser

Maley, Tom—Braille Editor
Manthorp, Bob—Headmaster, Worcester College
Markes, Peggy—Headmistress, Chorleywood College
Moodie, Sue—Training Adviser
Murphy, Maggie—Director, Northern Ireland Branch
Murray, Allan—Director, Scottish Branch

Oldfield, Allan—Warden, Sir Nicholas Garrow House
Orr, Robert—Headmaster, Rushton Hall

Parsons, Malcolm—Regional Director, Northern Counties
Plant, Gail—Press Officer
Priest, Bill—Manager, Home Industries Department

Roskilly, Don—Technical Director, Sound Recording
Rowe, Dr Mike—Principal, Hethersett College
Ryan, Peter—Principal, National Mobility Centre

Sheldrake, Ron—Officer-in-Charge, Westcliff House
Shepherd, George—Director, Special Projects
Sheilds, Joan—Deaf-Blind Services Officer
Shore, Dr Penelope—Development Officer, VSS
Smith, Dr Christopher—Tape Services Manager
Smith, Cecil—Print Manager

Tatchell, Trevor—Director, Wales Branch
Teager, David—Principal, North London College of
    Physiotherapy
Tidmarsh, Ken—Director, Eastern Branch

Tierney, Beryl—Education Adviser
Townend, Helen—Headmistress, Sunshine House,
  Southport
Tulley, David—Manager, Alma Court Hotel
Twining, Elizabeth—Development Programme
  Co-ordinator

Walker, Maureen—Headmistress, Sunshine House,
  Northwood
Walsh, Liam—Management Consultant
Walsh, Peter—Director, South Eastern Branch
Walton, Harry—Sound Recording Manager
Wilkinson, Betty—Officer-in-Charge, Tate House
Willson, George—Deputy Director-General
Wright, Maurice—Production Director

Yates, Edward—Manager, Howard Hotel

In Attendance:
Bird, Carol—Personal Assistant to DG
Oliver, Rita—Assistant Committee Secretary

Attending for Thursday afternoon sessions:
Gill, Dr John—Consultant on Braille and Moon study
Lomas, Dr Graham—Consultant, (1) Tape Study
  (2) Employment Study
Mckennell, Professor Aubrey—Consultant on Needs
  Survey
Pegram, Nigel—Research Assistant on Welfare Right

Total 80

Fourth Inter-Divisional Conference 1991

Surrey University, Guildford, 20-21 March 1991:

(DIR = Directorate General; E&L = Education and Leisure;
ER = External Relations; F&A = Finance and Administration;

TCS = Technical and Consumer Relations; VSS = Vocational and Social Services)

Alexander, Margaret—Head, Committee Secretariat (DIR)
Andersen, Neil—LEA Development Officer (E&L)
Andrew, Ian—Internal Auditor (F&A)
Ashbee, Rose—Manager, Westcliff House (VSS)
Aston, Tony—Director, VSS
Attrill, Chris—Manger, Leisure Service (E&L)
Ayers, Brian—Regional Corporate Fundraising
    Manager (ER)

Barret, Corri—Employment Development Technology
    Manager (VSS)
Barrick, Andrew—Benefit Rights Officer (VSS)
Barrick, Jon—Housing Service Manager (VSS)
Bastiaan, Bas—Senior Hotels Manager (VSS)
Belfitt, Rosalind—Manager, Wavertree House (VSS)
Bird, Carol—PA to Chairman/International Secretary
    (DIR)
Boguslawski, Anita—Finance and Administration
    Manager (VSS)
Botheras, Richard—Assistant Education Officer
    (Administration) (E&L)
Bruce, Ian—Director General (DIR)
Buckton, Carole—Corporate Employee Relations
    Adviser (F&A)

Cartwright, Julian—Regional Corporate Fundraising
    Manager (ER)
Chatterton, Joyce—Education Field Officer Wales (E&L)
Clark, Paul—Chief Accountant (F&A)
Clunies-Ross, Louise—Assistant Director (E&L)
Coles, David—Manager, Multi-handicapped Visually
    Impaired (VSS)
Collis, Jenny—Personnel Officer, Welfare (F&A)
Connell, Kevin—Principal, RNIB Vocational College
    (VSS)

Cooper, Steve—Corporate Planning and Evaluation Manager (DIR)

Cotton, Carol—Sales and Export Manager (TCS)

Courtley, Peter—Print Floor Manager (TCS)

Crayford, John—Corporate Purchasing Manager (TCS)

Croft, Chris—Manager, Voluntary Agencies Link Unit (VSS)

Davies, Jillian—Branch Director/Corporate Manager, Wales (ER)

Davies, Wendy—Manager, Regional Recording (TCS)

Davis, Denis—Senior Pre-Vocational Officer, Torquay (VSS)

Davis, Joseph—Purchasing Officer, Furniture and Fittings (TCS)

Diston, Mary—Information Officer (E&L)

Docherty, Alan—Assistant Marketing Manager (TCS)

Dorr, Arthur—Technical Information Officer (TCS)

Ennals, Paul—Director, Education and Leisure (E&L)

Fazakerley, Tony—Management Accountant (F&A)

Fetton, Eamonn—Assistant Director, Education Support Services (E&L)

Firman, Roger—Executive Assistant to Director General (DIR)

Fisk, Alison—Fundraising Training Officer (ER)

Fleming, Bernard—Community Education officer (ER)

Garsten, Nicky—Senior Press Officer (ER)

Ghelani, Nutan—Finance and Administration Manager (ER)

Gifford, Barry—Director, Finance and Administration (F&A)

Gilbert, Judith—Planning Manager, Fundraising (ER)

Gill, John—Technical Development Manager (TCS)

Gladstone, Keith—Systems Development Manager (TCS)

Godber, John—TCS Marketing Manager (TCS)

Griffiths, John—Audio Production Manager (TCS)
Griffiths, Trevor—Head of Fundraising (ER)

Hamlin, Deborah—Managing Consultant (VSS)
Heesom, Sanchi—Corporate Marketing Manager (ER)
Hewitt, Brian—Centre Manager, Manor House (VSS)
Hibberd, Val—Head of Education Courses Service (E&L)
Hinds, Roger—Manager, Specialist Employment Unit
   (VSS)
Hockley, Lois—Education Field Officer (E&L)
Hunt, Paul—Property Services Manager (F&A)

Jackman, Geoff—Vice Principal, RNIB Vocational
   College(VSS)
Jarvis, Anthony—Headmaster, Condover Hall School
   (E&L)
Jennings, Gordon—Vice Principal, Hethersett College
   (E&L)

Kennedy, Elizabeth—Liaison Officer, Scotland (VSS)
Kent, David—Manager, Howard Hotel (VSS)
King, Stephen—Director, Technical and Consumer
   Services (TCS)
Kirkwood, Rita—Vice Principal, New College
   Worcester (E&L)
Knott, Ed—Finance and Administration Manager (TCS)

Lancaster, Mike—Director, External Relations (ER)
Lavey, Ken—Personnel Manager (F&A)
Lawrie, George—Manager, Alwyn House (VSS)
Lawson, Neville—Assistant Director (E&L)
Lee, Ann—Editor, *New Beacon* (E&R)
Locke, Gerald—Branch Fundraising Director, Leeds (ER)

MacDonald, Patrick—Administration Manager (F&A)
Macrae, Fraser—Trading Manager (ER)
Maley, Tom—Regional Employment Manager,
   Birmingham (VSS)

Mann, David—Wembley Manager (TCS)

Mann, Robin—Assistant Property Services Manager (F&A)

Manthorp, Bob—Principal, New College Worcester (E&L)

Marrino, Donna—Manager, Century Hotel (VSS)

McIlwrath, Mike—Liaison Manager, Northern Ireland (VSS)

McKelvie, David—Tactual Production Manager (TCS)

Mehta, Suzanne—Family Support Officer (EL)

Moran, Jim—Fundraising Director, North West Branch (ER)

Morton, Beryl—Manager, Small Business Unit (VSS)

Murphy, Maggie—Branch Fundraising Director, Northern Ireland (ER)

Murray, Allan—Branch Fundraising Director, Scotland (ER)

O'Keefe, Sharon—Magazines Editor (TCS)

Oakley, Ros—Parliamentary Officer (ER)

Orr, Patricia—Public Relations Manager (ER)

Oxley, Vivienne—Personnel Officer, Peterborough (F&A)

Parsons, Malcolm—National Fundraising Manager (ER)

Paschkes-Bell, Gill—Employment Rehabilitation Development Co-ordinator (VSS)

Patel, Kishor—Development Officer, Ethnic Minorities (DIR)

Patton, Brian—Assistant Education Officer (Higher and Further) (EL)

Priest, Bill—Financial Accountant (F&A)

Raffle Fred—Principal, National Mobility Centre (VSS)

Riley, Lorraine—Librarian Marketing (TCS)

Robinson, John—Assistant Director, VSS (VSS)

Rosenheim, Jill—Human Resources Adviser (F&A)

Rowe, Mike—Principal, Hethersett College (E&L)

Rowland, Peter—Regional Corporate Fundraising Manager (ER)

Roy, Archie—Student Adviser, Scotland and Northern Ireland (E&L)

Serle, Jeff—Director, London Branch (ER)
Shaw, Michael—Headteacher, East Grinstead (E&L)
Stephens, Peter—Deputy Head, Condover Hall School (E&L)
Sutter, Mavis—Assistant Director, Social Services (VSS)
Swaine, Barrie—Staff Development Officer VSS (VSS)

Teager, David—Principal, North London School of Physiotherapy (EL)
Thomas, Donna—Office Services Manager (TCS)
Thompson, Sean—Manager, Employment Services (VSS)
Tillet, Peter—Regional Corporate Fundraising Manager (ER)
Tishler, Gillian—Head of Public Affairs (ER)
Todd, Hilary—Publications Manger (ER)
Townend, Helen—Head, Southport Sunshine House School (E&L)
Treseder, Judy—Projects Manager (VSS)
Troon, Nigel—Senior Student Adviser (E&L)
Tulley, David—Manager, Alma Court Hotel (VSS)
Turner, Ian—Studio Manager (TCS)

Vost, Helen—Corporate Fundraising Manager (ER)

Walker, Errol—Corporate Research Officer (ER)
Walker, Maureen—Head, Northwood Sunshine House School (EL)
Wardrop-White, Carolyn—Manager, Health Services Unit (VSS)
Wheeler, Stan—Devices Development Manager (TCS)
Wilkinson, Betty—Manager, Tate House (VSS)
Williams, Lisa—Human Resources Project Assistant (F&A)
Wilson, Margaret—Customer Care Manager (TCS)

Wilson, Rod—Low Vision Development Officer (VSS)
Wood, David—Deputy Head, Rushton Hall (E&L)
Wyndham, Jerry—Transcription Manager (TCS)

Yates, Christopher—Reference Librarian (ER)

Total 130

Seventh Inter-Divisional Conference, 1997

Robinson College, Cambridge, 2-3 July 1997:

Community Services Division (CSD)

Community and Health Services

Chris Croft—Manager, Voluntary Agencies Link Unit
Sue Grindey—Manager, Eye Health Programmes
Deborah Hamlin—Assistant Director, CSD
Julie Joyce—Manager, Hampshire VI Services
Wendy Kane—Eye Health Promotions Manager
Pete Lucas—Manager, Social Services Consultancy
Mike McIlwrath—Service Manager, Northern Ireland
Frances Miller—Manager, Springfield Service, Scotland
Anne Veart—Manager, Social Services Development
  Unit

Apologies:
Caroline Brown—Deputy Manager, Springfield Service

CSD Directorate

Jon Barrick—Director, CSD
Anita Boguslawski—Finance and Administration Manager

Holiday and Leisure Services

Alison Harding—Manager, Holiday and Leisure
  Services
Lorraine Waddington—Manager, Century Hotel
Lisa Wilson—Acting Manager, Palm Court Hotel

Housing and Environmental Services

Rose Ashbee—Manager, Westcliff house
Nigel Caleb—Manager, Garrow House
Sandra Cronin—Development Officer
Fiona Derbyshire—Housing Liaison Officer
Shelly Devonshire—Care Support Services Manager
Andrew Gatenby—Local Authority Consultant
Barbara Scott—Manager, Kathleen Chambers House
Graham Smith—Manager, Tate House
Sally Wadsworth—Manager, Wavertree House

Apologies:
Peter Barker—Manager, Joint Mobility Unit

Information and Advocacy Services

Andy Barrick—Assistant Director, CSD
Stuart Davies—Information and Advocacy Officer,
  Wales
Laura Jacobs—Manager, Benefits Rights and
  Information Team

Apologies:
Val Slade—Co-ordinator, Garrow House

Directorate

Ian Bruce—Director General
Martin Milligan—Executive Assistant to Director
  General
John Wall—Chairman, RNIB

Apologies:
Carol Bird

RNIB Scotland

Liz Kennedy—Liaison Officer
Allan Murray—Director, Scotland

Education and Employment Division (E&E)

E&E Directorate

Richard Botheras—Finance and Administration
  Manager
Louise Clunies-Ross—Assistant Director, Education,
  Pre-16 Policy, Information and Research
Issy Cole-Hamilton—Children's Policy Officer
Paul Ennals—Director, E&E
Maria O'Donnell—Financial Administrator

Education Information Service

Nancy Chambers—Manager, Education and
  Employment Information Service
Colin Cribb—Local Government Development Officer
Ken Bore—Regional Education Officer, North
Joyce Chatterton—Education Officer, Wales
Rory Cobb—Regional Education Officer, Midlands
Katherine El Dahshan—Administration Manager
Eamonn Fetton—Assistant Director, E&E
Adam Ockelford—Head, National Education Service
Neil Todd—Education Officer, Scotland

Apologies:
Olga Miller—Development Officer, Multiple Disabilities

Post-16 Services

David Allan—Regional Manager, North (Employment
  and Student Support Network [ESSN])
Anne Boylan—Self Employment Development
  Manager
Emily Brothers—ESSN Manager
Kevin Connell—Principal, Vocational College
Joyce Deere—Principal, Redhill College
Susanna Hancock—Regional Manager (London & SE),
  ESSN

Brian Hewitt—Centre Manager, Manor House
Sue Hitchcock—Manager, Employment Development
   Technology Network
Stewart Long—Regional Manager (Central), ESSN
Robert Meadowcroft—Assistant Director, E&E
John Milligan—Senior Adviser, ESSN
Jane Owen-Hutchinson—Manager, Physiotherapy
   Support Service
Craig Stockton—Centre Manager, Alwyn House,
   Scotland
Kate Storrow—Regional Manager (Scotland), ESSN
Richard Stowell—Regional Manager (South West), ESSN
Christie Taylor——Development Manager

Post-16 Policy Unit

Gordon Dryden—Assistant Director, E&E, Post-16 Policy
Philippa Simkiss—Employment Research Officer

Schools and Colleges

Judy Bell—Headteacher, Southport Sunshine House
   School
Tony Best—Headteacher, Condover Hall
David Hussey—Headteacher, Rushton Hall
Rita Kirkwood—Northwood Sunshine House School
Neville Lawson—Assistant Director, E&E
Helen Williams—Principal, New College Worcester

External Relations Division (ER)

Communications

Olivia Belle—Senior Communications Officer
Joe Korner—Senior Communications Officer
Fiona McCarthy—Communications Officer, Advertising
Lynne Stockbridge—Head of Communications

Development and Marketing

Howard Lewis—Disability Legislation Co-ordinator
Jaqueline McMullen—Support Services Manager

Ros Oakley—Assistant Director (ER)
Jim Richardson—ER Training Officer

ER Directorate

Mike Lancaster—Director of External Relations
Bernard Fleming—Manager, Library and Public
    Information Service
Ann Lee—Editor, *New Beacon*
Margaret Meyer—Publications Manager
Hilary Todd—Information Services Manager

National Fundraising

Martin McEwan—Donor Development Manager
Mike Palfreman—Capital Appeal Director
Hilary Partridge—Head of National Fundraising
Sue Sharp—Marketing Manager, Trading

Apologies:
Paul Tranter—Trust Fundraising Manager

Regional Fundraising

Jane Desborough—Head of Regional Fundraising
Debora Jack—Deputy Head of Regional Fundraising

Apologies:
Peri O'Connor Volunteer Development Co-ordinator

(London and South East = LSE; Midlands and Anglia = MA;
North = N; Scotland and Northern Ireland = S&NI; Wales and
West = WW)

Douglas Thomson—Capital Appeal Fundraising
    Manager, LSE
Alison Allington—Corporate Fundraising Manager, LSE
Paul Marvell—Regional Fundraising Manager, LSE
Pauline Lutman—Regional Fundraising Manager, MA
David Miller—Corporate Fundraising, MA
Kath Howard—Regional Fundraising Manager, N

Phil Robertshaw—Corporate Fundraising Manager, N
Gwen McCreath—Regional Fundraising Manager, S&NI

Apologies:
Tish Bergman—Community Fundraising Manager
Lisa Dickinson—Community Fundraising Manager, WW
Patrick Holmes—Regional Fundraising Manager, WW

Finance and Administration Division (DFA)

Administration

Barry Goold—Senior Applications Development Manager
Jean Harding—Enquiry Services Co-ordinator
Patrick MacDonald—Head of Administration
David Mould—Operations and Network Manager
Tim Stone—Legacy Manager

Directorate

Barry Gifford—Director, DFA
Es Parker—Administration Manager

Finance

Ian Andrew—Chief Accountant
Tony Fazakerley—Management Accountant
David Pacey—Deputy Chief Accountant
Stephen Martin—Internal Auditor

Apologies:
Lis Goodwin—Financial Accountant Operations

Personnel

Alison Beesley—Human Resources Manager
Jenny Collis—Personnel Officer Welfare/Health and Safety
Trudy Hindmarsh—Senior Corporate Employee Relations Adviser
Ken Lavey—Head of Personnel

Maureen McMahon—Senior Personnel Officer
Recruitment
Howard Platt—Corporate Training Officer

Apologies:
Viv Oxley—Personnel Manager, Peterborough

Property Services

Paul Hunt—Property Services Manager
Robin Mann—Assistant Property Services Manager

Policy Division

Committee Services

Margaret Alexander—Manager of Committee Services

Corporate Planning and Evaluation

Joshua Archer—Corporate Planner
Nicholas Johnson—Corporate Marketing Co-ordinator
Linda Mears—Planning and Review Associate
Ruth Mountstephen—Strategy Implementation
Co-ordinator
Jane Peters—Head, Corporate Planning and
Evaluation
Egon Walesch—European Services Planning and
Development Co-ordinator

Apologies:
Christine Tillsley Principal Researcher

Policy Directorate

Fazilet Hadi—Director of Policy
Kishor Patel—Development Officer, Ethnic Minorities

Public Policy

Jan Nesbitt—Campaigns Officer
Alun Thomas—Parliamentary Officer
Steve Winyard—Head of Public Policy

Technical Consumer Services Division

Independent Living Support (ILS)

Silvana Berrill—Export Development Manager
Joyce Bis—Customer Services Manager
Martin Pugh—Distribution Services Manager
Bernard Quinn—Leisure Reading Services Manager
Janice Richards—ILS Focus Group Manager
John Siggery—Volunteer Development Officer
Ian Turner—Studio Manager

Apologies:
Carol Cotton ILS Product Manager

Learning and Employment Support (LES)

Wendy Davies—Group Manager, LES
Steve Tyler—Products and Direct Services Manager
Mandy White—Project Manager

Apologies:
John Crampton—LES Library Services Manager
Peter Osborne—LES Indirect Services and Transcription

Operations and Infrastructure

Pete Cleary—Office Services Manager
Chris Day—Assistant Director, TCS
Andrew Douse—Manager Print and Duplication
Angela Fuggle—Customer Care and Information
  Manager
Tony Gibbs—Customer Liaison and Publishing
  Services Manager
Rob Longstaff—LES Product Cordinator
David McKelvie—Technical Training Manager
Martin O'Keefe-Liddard—Origination Manager
Malcolm Staniland—Customer Response and
  Information Manager
Jerry Wyndham—Production Control Manager

Apologies:
Linda Brady—Customer Information Support Team
    Leader

TCS Directorate

John Crayford—Corporate Purchasing Manager
Keith Gladstone—Information Technical Systems and
    Services Development Manager
Dave Pawson—Business Process Improvement
    Facilitator
John Gill—Chief Scientist
John Godber—Divisional Service Development Manager
Stephen King—Director, TCS
Ian Vickers—TCS Management Accountant

RNIB Scotland

Liz Kennedy—Liaison Officer
Allan Murray—Director, Scotland

Total 163

Tenth RNIB Conference 2003

RNIB HQ, 105 Judd St, London, 18-19 June 2003:

(JS = Judd ST; L/bor = Loughborough, Fal Park = Falcon Park,
Wembley, PB = Peterborough, Tarp = Tarporley)

Directorate X3
Colin Low—Chairman, JS
Ian Bruce—Director General JS
Steve Torricelli—To be confirmed JS

Community Services Division (CSD) X17
Alison Harding—Assistant Director, Recreation and
    Life, JS
Andy Barrick—Assistant Director, Information and
    Advocacy, JS

Anita Boguslawski—Finance and Administration Manager, JS

Anita Lightstone—Head of Low Vision and Prevention, JS

Clive Philips—Practical Support Team Contracts Development Manager, Bristol

Deborah Hamlin—Assistant Director, Professional Support, JS

Denise Evans—Head of Broadcasting and Talking Images, JS

Fran McSweeney—Head of Advocacy Development, JS

Jon Barrick—Director, CSD, JS

Julia Polzerova—Talk and Support Project Manager, Garrow

Linda Seru—Assistant Director, Social Inclusion, JS

Lisa Carter—Hotel Manager, Eastbourne

Malcolm Wood—Assistant Director, Supportive Environments, JS

Maxine Miles—Homes Manager, Hove

Pete Lucas—Head, Practice Support Team, Birmingham

Simon Jones—Partnership Project Manager, Birmingham

Stuart Hornsby—Low Vision Officer, JS

Education and Employment Division (E&E) X23

Adam Ockelford—Deputy Director

Dave Allen Regional—Manager, North West, Liverpool

Eamonn Fetton—Director, E&E, JS

Elizabeth Clery—Children's Services Co-ordinator, JS

Geoff Jackman—Vice Principal, Vocational College, L/bor

Gillian Eldridge—Regional Manager, London and South East, JS

Harry Dicks—Principal, Condover Hall

Ian Bland—Regional Manager, Leeds

Jill Read—Centre Manager, Torquay

Judy Bell—Schools Partnership Officer, Birmingham

Kevin Connell—Post Compulsory Education Training, Nottinghamshire

Loraine Stewart—Head of Northwood

Madeleine Spears—Regional Manager, Birmingham
Martin Coleman—Business Development Manager, JS
Neville Lawson—Assistant Director, E&E, JS
Nick Ratcliffe—Principal, New College Worcester
Pat Howarth—Divisional Finance Manager, JS
Philippa Simkiss—Employment Services Co-ordinator, JS
Richard Orme—Assistant Director, Information
    Communications Technology, Birmingham
Rita Kirkwood—Head of Rushton Hall, Coventry
Rob Dyke—Regional Manager, South West, Bristol
Sue Wright—Acting Regional Manager, East Midlands,
    Nottinghamshire
Tracy de Berndhardt Dunkin—Principal, Redhill College

External Relations Division (ERD) X16
Ann Paul—Major Donor Development Manager, JS
Ciara Smyth—Communications Manager, JS
Demis De Sousa—Information and Communications
    Technology Manager, Fal Park
Fiona Blakemore—Head of Corporate Information and
    Publishing, JS
Gwenn McCreath—Head of Fundraising – Individuals,
    Fal Park
Karen Sutter—Donor Development Manager, Fal Park
Kath Howard—Head of Telephone
    Fundraising – Home-based
Katherine Eckstrom—Corporate Publishing Manager, JS
Lynne Stockbridge—Head of Communications, JS
Margaret O'Donnell—Website Manager, JS
Maria Pemberton—Corporate Partnerships Manager, JS
Mike Lancaster—Director, ERD
Nancy Maguire—Fundraising Development Manager, JS
Peter Story—Head of Fundraising – Strategy – Home
    based
Sharon Wilding—Senior Telelephone Fundraising
    Manager – Home based
Sioned Clutton—Head of Finance and Operations
    Support Fal Park

Finance & Administration (F&A) X15

Barry Branigan—Staff Communication – Home based
Barry Goold—Corporate IT Manager, PB
Caroline Dalton—Conference Organiser, JS
Es Parker—Administration Manager, JS
Giselle Low—Property Services Manager, Fal Park
Ian Vickers—Chief Accountant, PB
Jackie Weston—Davies Employee Relations
  Manager, JS
Jim Richardson—Corporate Training Manager, JS
Kate Stephens—Corporate Recruitment Manager, JS
Ken Lavey—Head of Personnel, JS
Kevin Geeson—Director, F&A
Maureen McMahon—HR Manager, JS
Patrick MacDonald—Assistant Director, F&R
Peri O'Connor—Volunteer Development Manager, Leeds
Tim Stone—Head of Legal Services, PB

Policy Division X11

Dan Vale—UK Campaigns Manager, JS
Evelyn Russell—Development Officer, JS
Fazilet Hadi—Director of Policy, JS
Fiona McKenzie—Head of Internal Audit, Stirling
James Rogers—Head, Governance Support, JS
Leen Petre—European Campaign Officer, JS
Nicholas Johnston—Head, Corporate Planning and
  Evaluation, JS
Nigel Charles—Research and Development Manager, JS
Stef Abrar—Corporate Equalities Manager, JS
Stella Smith—Manager, Strategic and Services
  Review, JS
Steve Winyard—Head, Public Policy, JS

Technical and Consumer Services (TCS) X11

Janice Richards—Assistant Director, Library Services,
  Fal Park
Jillian Harvey—Divisional Support Services Manager, PB
John Godber—Assistant Director, TCS, PB

Index of Names

Index of Subjects

Barnardos 214, 224, 270
Bayes Business School 110,
    172, 232, 258
benefits rights 54, 67, 85,
    220, 259, 260, 273, 277,
    304, 310
Best in Britain 82
blind – most deserving 34,
    37, 39
blind and partially sighted
    people, numbers
    reached 207
blind or partially sighted staff
    101, 112-3
Blind Veterans UK 265
Blindness Allowance 26,
    35, 37, 71, 91, 201-2, 247,
    252, 254
Braille Chess Association
    39, 41
braille xix, 25, 54, 61, 66,
    104, 169, 206, 225, 276
brand 75, 115-8, 125,137,
    140, 147, 150, 186, 235,
    238-44
British and Foreign Bible
    Society 281
British Computer
    Association of the Blind
    (BCAB) 8, 17, 196, 290
British Council of
    Organisations of Disabled
    People (BCODP) 71, 197,
    247, 250
British Deaf Association
    (BDA) 196, 295
British Gas 80-1
British Heart Foundation
    214, 240, 270

British Red Cross 270
broadcasting 87, 89, 141,
    255, 318

Campaign for the Protection
    of Rural England 239, 280
Campaign Supporters
    Network 151, 154, 163
campaigning 26, 69-72,
    88-95, 150-56, 185-8,
    220, 245-256, 265, 280-1
    1970s 26
    1980s 69-72
    1990s 141-9
    1970-2010: 245-56
Cancer Research UK 214,
    244, 270
Caritas data 163, 192, 265-
    6, 288, 291-2
Carmen Butler Charteris 167
Cass *see* Bayes
causes xxi, 37, 188-90, 246
Centre for Charity
    Effectiveness 110
Certificate in Management
    Studies (CMS) 53
change in RNIB (triggers of)
    societal influences xvii,
    19, 178-205, 280
    internal 19-20, 206-26
    able blind leaders 20-21,
    229, 246
    blind customer pressure
    21-22
    external pressures for
    34-35, 217-8
    international competition 22
Charity Commission 126,
    129, 218, 229, 239, 255-6

BV - #0011 - 240123 - C0 - 234/156/21 - PB - 9780718896409 - Gloss Lamination